MONTGOMERY COLLEGE LIBRARY
GERMANTOWN CAMPUS

THE ELEMENTS
OF
ENGLISH GRAMMAR

THE ELEMENTS
OF
ENGLISH GRAMMAR

BY

GEORGE PHILIP KRAPP
ADJUNCT PROFESSOR OF ENGLISH IN COLUMBIA UNIVERSITY, AND LECTURER IN ENGLISH, TEACHERS COLLEGE, COLUMBIA UNIVERSITY

GREENWOOD PRESS, PUBLISHERS
WESTPORT, CONNECTICUT

Originally published in 1908
by Charles Scribner's Sons, New York

Reprinted from an original copy in the collections
of the Yale University Library

First Greenwood Reprinting 1970

Library of Congress Catalogue Card Number 72-110830

SBN 8371-2669-X

Printed in the United States of America

PREFACE

THIS book is designed to serve as an introduction to the systematic study of grammar. It is intended for pupils who are making, for the first time or in review, a connected study of the elements of grammar. The author has assumed the privilege of defining his subject according to this purpose. It seems more sensible to define grammar as the study of the structure of the sentence, since in its elements it is that and nothing more, than to give it any of the vague and broad definitions, such as the science of language, or a systematic description of language, so commonly found in elementary grammars. Grammar as the science of language is an impossible subject for elementary study, and to define it so is either meaningless or positively misleading. On the other hand the structure and analysis of the sentence is a clearly limited and realizable subject, one also which offers a sufficiently large field of study.

From the nature of the case pupils who take up the study of formal grammar are already able, in speech and also in writing, to use sentences of considerable length and complexity. They should not be allowed, therefore, to labor under the misapprehension that grammar means something new and strange, a different kind of English from that which they have been using. On the contrary, they should be encouraged to see in grammar merely the definite statement of their own natural practice. By bringing into clear consciousness mental activities which the pupil performs in obscure consciousness, the study of grammar should increase the pupil's effectiveness and certainty in the use of language. It can never create, but merely strengthen, the ability to use language.

A few words may be said concerning the extent to which the analytical study of language should be carried. If it is granted that the main purpose in the study of grammar should be increased effectiveness in the practical use of language, it follows that there are limits beyond which the study of grammatical analysis ceases to be profitable. The purpose of elementary grammar should not be to provide the student with a complete scientific system whereby he can parse every word that may occur in any piece of English writing. There are many words in certain constructions which even the ripest and sanest scientific linguist finds difficulty in disposing of to his complete satisfaction; and it is the easiest thing in the world for a grammarian to entangle himself in a net of finely woven distinctions, logical, subtle, and perhaps true, yet without any bearing on the practical use of the language. This danger of oversubtilizing the present volume has endeavored to avoid. The aim has been to look at the language as it exists in the use of good speakers and writers to-day, and then to describe it in such a way as to bring out the main structural principles of it, trusting that when these main principles are clearly realized, that native sense of idiom without which any real command over language is impossible, will be strong enough and certain enough to lead the student safely where an attempt at exhaustive logical analysis might merely land him in confusion and doubt.

The author wishes to enter a plea for a certain amount of liberty in the interpretations which students may make of various grammatical constructions. The instances in which legitimate difference of opinion may exist are, it is true, relatively infrequent; yet such instances actually do occur. The student, for example, who analyzes the sentence *We asked for bread* as consisting of the subject *We*, the verb *asked for*, and the object *bread*, should not be utterly condemned, since his logic after all is perfectly sound. The preposition *for*, which is a relational or link word, indicating the relation between *asked* and *bread*, is certainly as closely united to one word as to the other, and therefore may as appropriately be grouped with one as with the other. The student who is capable of such a logical analysis should be given due credit and encouragement for it. The question as to how much independence of judgment pupils in general should be allowed and to what extent uniformity of terminology in class-room work is necessary must be left for every teacher to decide according to the special circumstances of each case. Complete uniformity, however, at the expense of an inquiring and independent attitude of mind on the part of the students, is certainly too dearly bought to justify itself. The author is personally of the opinion that nothing is lost and a good deal is gained by a frank confession that our system of grammatical classification and terminology is to a considerable extent arbitrary and conventional, and that in many instances other classification and terminology would be just as reasonable as those which we follow.

The exercises of the book are designed to furnish material for the three kinds of work, written, oral, and memory. At least the definitions given in the summaries of definitions should be committed to memory. A set form and order in parsing should also be insisted on, and systematic drill in parsing should be kept up until the pupils can go through the forms with facility. There is no better way of fixing in their minds the number and the nature of the details which they are to observe with respect to the various functions of words in context than parsing. It is the multiplication table of grammar, and it may profitably be carried to the verge of a routine exercise. Attention should also be given to the pronouncing of sentences with the proper pauses and intonations of the voice. Mere oral delivery, the mere cadence of it, will often convey the structural principle of a sentence when logical analysis fails. Don't be afraid, therefore, to put a good deal of dependence at first on the feeling for language. Afterward reason may be called in to draw out what the pupil has already felt, thus giving him the certainty which comes through the ability to examine his own constructive processes. It is perhaps not necessary to urge that the work in grammar be applied as much as possible to the pupils' own work, both oral and written. Examples of bad grammar, both in the written work and the conversation of the class-room, may be held up for general criticism; and as such examples will always be found in sufficient abundance, none have been inserted in this volume.

A system of sentence diagraming has been included in the volume because the author believes that it may be made a helpful way of studying the structure of sentences.

Undoubtedly the diagram may be abused, but discreetly used it undoubtedly also may serve a good end. It brings before the eye in a clear and simple way those principles of analysis which have been worked out in the mind. Mental analysis must always precede diagraming, but the diagram is an excellent short-hand device for holding together in a rapid survey a variety of complicated details which otherwise could be presented only by means of a lengthy description. Any system of diagraming which does this is a good one, and pupils should be encouraged to try their own ingenuity in working out devices which answer the purpose.

In conclusion the author wishes to say that he has not undertaken to write a new elementary grammar without some sense of the gravity of the undertaking. It is easy to write a poor elementary book, but nothing is more difficult than to write a good one. To strike the happy mean between scholarship and simplicity, between originality and conservatism, to hold fast to the old — but not too fast, to love the new only when it is good and necessary, not because it flatters the author's pride in his ingenuity, these are some of the difficulties which the writer of an elementary grammar has to face. The author of the present one is not so rash as to believe that he has always met and satisfactorily overcome these difficulties. He will be satisfied if his work prove to be practically helpful, and if it add ever so little toward the realization of that ideal method in the study of English grammar for which we must still look ahead to the future.

After his own experience in the teaching of elementary grammar, the author is chiefly indebted for help in the preparation of this volume to those Saturday morning classes in English grammar which he has had the pleasure of conducting in the Teachers College of Columbia University for the past four or five years. The free interchange of opinion at these sessions, among teachers who were not only interested but professionally informed in the subject, has been of the greatest assistance to the author; and he sincerely hopes that this formal presentation of the matter of many of these Saturday discussions may at least in part repay the debt which he owes to the participants in them.

NEW YORK, *January*, 1908.

TABLE OF CONTENTS

CHAPTER		PAGE
I.	WHAT GRAMMAR IS	1
II.	THE SENTENCE	
	The Complete Sentence	8
	Kinds of Sentences	10
	The Simple Sentence	24
	The Complex Sentence	26
	The Compound Sentence	27
	The Complex-Compound Sentence	28
III.	THE PARTS OF SPEECH	
	The Noun	40
	The Pronoun	68
	The Adjective	100
	The Verb	112
	The Adverb	194
	The Preposition	205
	The Conjunction	213
	The Interjection	221
	Numerals	222
IV.	INDEPENDENT AND ELLIPTICAL ELEMENTS .	225
V.	ANALYSIS AND DIAGRAM	231
	APPENDIX I. HISTORICAL SKETCH OF THE ENGLISH LANGUAGE	253
	APPENDIX II. PUNCTUATION AND CAPITALIZATION	264
	INDEX	273

THE ELEMENTS OF ENGLISH GRAMMAR.

CHAPTER I.—WHAT GRAMMAR IS.

1. Words and Sentences.—In order to express ideas, whether by speech, writing, or printing, we make use of words. These words are united into groups, and the groups of words which one properly forms for the expression of thought make **Sentences.** All speech and all writing is made up of a succession of sentences. In speaking we indicate the grouping of words into sentences by the tone of the voice and by pauses; but in printing and in writing, the sentences are marked by ending each sentence with a period, or a question mark, or an exclamation point, according to the nature of the sentence, and also by beginning every sentence with a capital letter.[1]

2. The Parts of Speech.—When a group of words forms a sentence, each word in the group has a definite part or function to perform. In the two sentences, *The horse gallops,* and *The dog barks,* the words *horse* and *dog* perform the same function. Their part is to name objects about which we wish to say something. So also *gallops* and *barks* perform the same function by showing what the horse and dog are doing. In order to make it easy to talk about these different functions of words in

[1] For further account of the rules of capitalization and punctuation, see Appendix.

the sentence, we give each function a name, that is, we call it a certain **Part of Speech.** Words like *horse* and *dog*, which name objects, are called nouns; words like *gallops* and *barks*, which state actions, are called verbs. There are, besides, six other functions of words in the sentence, giving altogether **eight parts of speech** in the English language. These eight are as follows:

(a) **The Noun,** the chief function of which is to name persons or things. The italicized words in the following sentences are nouns:

> (1) I have neither *paper, pen,* nor *ink.*
> (2) The *man* was sitting in his *wagon.*
> (3) We did not notice the *heat* in the *house.*
> (4) *Wealth* does not always bring *happiness.*
> (5) We saw *Mr. Lewis* at the *postoffice.*

(b) **The Pronoun,** which is used in place of the name of a person or thing. The italicized words are pronouns:

> (1) My brother intended to go away to-day, but *he* missed the train.
> (2) *They* threw the book into the corner, where *it* lay neglected.
> (3) *She* did not think *he* could come.
> (4) Have *you* seen *him?*
> (5) These houses are not old, but *they* have long been uninhabited.

(c) **The Adjective,** the chief function of which is to point out and describe persons or things. The italicized words are adjectives:

> (1) He picked up a *smooth, round* stone.
> (2) The *burnt* child dreads the fire.
> (3) We bought a *half* dozen of *sweet* apples.
> (4) The way is *long* and *difficult.*
> (5) *Many agreeable* and *nutritious* fruits grow there.

(d) **The Verb,** the chief function of which is to make some statement with respect to a person or thing. The italicized words are verbs:

- (1) The earth *trembled*.
- (2) He *laughed* and *said* nothing further.
- (3) The nightingale *sings* early in June.
- (4) Time *is* money.
- (5) Uneasy *lies* the head that *wears* a crown.

(e) **The Adverb,** the chief function of which is to modify the meaning of a verb, an adjective, or another adverb. Examples:

- (1) The Indians advanced *quickly* and *silently*.
- (2) *Silently* we laid him down.
- (3) We have considered the plan *very carefully*.
- (4) He kept *continually* changing his seat.
- (5) We *soon* found that we were *completely* lost.

(f) **The Preposition,** the chief function of which is to connect a noun or a pronoun with another word in the sentence, usually a noun or a verb, by showing the relation between them. The preposition *of*, for example, in the sentence, *We had a loaf of stale bread,* connects the two nouns *loaf* and *bread,* and the group of words consisting of the preposition and the words that follow it is called a **Prepositional Phrase.** The italicized words in the following sentences are prepositional phrases, the first word in each phrase being a preposition:

- (1) The shingles *on the roof* are new.
- (2) The boat slipped *into the water without a noise*.
- (3) I went *to Taffy's house* but Taffy was *in bed*.
- (4) They ate *from long trenchers with wooden spoons*.
- (5) The hope *of a nation* is its youth.

(g) **The Conjunction,** the function of which also is to

connect words, though it does so without making phrases like the preposition. The italicized words are conjunctions:

(1) An apple *or* a pear was his usual lunch.
(2) We walked *and* ran alternately.
(3) We usually sit in the garden *or* in the orchard.
(4) They are going for a walk *and* then they are going home.
(5) You may go *if* you have finished your lessons.
(6) I asked him *because* I thought he would know.
(7) He will come to-morrow *or* he will telegraph.

(h) **The Interjection,** the function of which is exclamatory, expressing emotions of surprise, joy, grief, and so forth. Examples:

(1) *Oh,* what a pity!
(2) *Hm!* I thought it would turn out that way.
(3) *Alas!* we never saw him again.
(4) *Why,* where did you come from?

3. Inflection.—The words of the sentence must be examined from still another point of view. If the two sentences given above (2) are changed so as to read *The horses galloped* and *The dogs barked,* it will be seen that the words still perform the same function and are consequently the same parts of speech, but that **they have been changed somewhat in form to indicate a corresponding change in meaning.** The noun *horse* has been changed to *horses* to show that more than one horse is meant, and the verb *gallop* has been changed to *galloped* to indicate that the action stated by the verb is not now taking place, but that it has taken place in past time. This change in the form of a word to correspond to a change in its meaning is called **Inflection.** The study of inflections is important, because the inflection of a particular word in the sentence

WHAT GRAMMAR IS. 5

is sometimes dependent upon the meaning of the other words of the sentence, as in *Your sheep are (is) here.*

EXAMPLES:

(1) This boy has no book.
(2) These boys have no books.
(3) A bee is a very industrious insect.
(4) Bees are very industrious insects.
(5) He has planted a new tree in front of his house.
(6) They have planted new trees in front of their houses.

4. Construction of Words.—Finally it is necessary to consider words not only by themselves, but also in their relations to each other in the sentence. Thus the words *horses* and *dogs* in the sentences given in (3) are in the same relation respectively to *galloped* and *barked*. And if we change the word *horses* to the word *they*, which is a pronoun and a different part of speech from the noun *horses*, the word *they* would still be in the same relation to *galloped* as *horses* is. The relation of a word to other words in the sentence is called its **Construction**.

5. What Grammar is.—We are now prepared to give a definition of the study of Grammar. **Grammar is the study of the Functions or Parts of Speech, the Inflections, and the Constructions of Words in the Sentence.**

EXERCISES.

1.—Read the following passage aloud and observe how the tones of the voice indicate the divisions into sentences:

RIP'S AWAKENING.

"Here, then, poor Rip was brought to a stand. He again called and whistled after his dog. He was only answered by the cawing of a flock of idle crows, sporting high in air about a dry tree that overhung a precipice, and who, secure in their elevation, seemed to look down and scoff at the poor man's perplexities. What was to be done? The morning was passing away, and Rip felt famished for want of his breakfast. He grieved to give up his dog and gun; he dreaded to meet his wife; but it would not do to starve among the mountains. He shook his head, shouldered the rusty firelock, and, with a heart full of trouble and anxiety, turned his steps homeward."

—IRVING, from *Rip Van Winkle.*

2.—Form sentences in which
   (1) The following words are used as nouns: boat, cap, basket, stone, match, light, speed, paper, fish, sail, box.
   (2) The following words are used as adjectives: hard, old, ruinous, smooth, oily, swift, dark, light, gentle, agreeable.
   (3) The following words are used as verbs: throw, fall, hung, talk, race, sail, bite, took, followed, saw, light.
   (4) The following words are used as adverbs: skilfully, soon, swiftly, eagerly, very, hastily, pleasantly, necessarily.
   (5) The following words are used as prepositions forming prepositional phrases: with, to, from, by, at, in, through, on, without.
   (6) The following words are used as conjunctions: and, or, if, because.

SUMMARY OF DEFINITIONS.

2. The Parts of Speech is the classification of words according to the functions which they perform in the sentence. In the English language there are eight parts of speech: the Noun, the Pronoun, the Adjective, the Verb, the Adverb, the Preposition, the Conjunction, and the Interjection.

3. Inflection is the variation in the form of a word to indicate a corresponding variation in its use and meaning.

4. The relation of a word to other words in the sentence is called its **Construction**.

5. Grammar is the study of the functions, or parts of speech, the inflections, and the constructions of words in the sentence.

QUESTIONS AND SUGGESTIONS FOR REVIEW.

1. With the help of the dictionary, write out the definition of *word*, of *junction*, of *punctuation*, of *capitalization*. 2. Show how in talking we indicate the division of our words into sentences. 3. How is the division of words into sentences indicated in writing and in printing? 4. What is meant by the term Parts of Speech? 5. Name the various parts of speech in the English language, and give a sentence illustrating each. 6. What is meant by Inflection? 7. Give two sentences containing the same word in different inflectional forms. 8. What is meant by the Construction of a word? 9. Define Grammar. 10. Choose some topic and write not less than five sentences on it. After you have written the sentences, pick out all the nouns, pronouns, adjectives, and verbs which you have used.

CHAPTER II.—THE SENTENCE.

6. The Complete Sentence.—Not every group of related words forms a sentence. The words, *in that tree*, for example, standing by themselves, do not form a sentence, but are merely a phrase. In order to form a sentence they must be united to other words so as to express some thought about the tree completely. Thus if we say, *I see a squirrel in that tree*, or *The nest is in that tree*, then we use complete sentences, because each group of words expresses a complete thought about the tree. In good writing and speaking it is necessary to use complete sentences, and the difference between the incomplete and the complete group of words should be carefully observed.

Definition: A **Sentence** is a word or a group of words expressing a thought completely.

Exercise.

Tell which of the following groups of words are complete and which are incomplete, and fill out the incomplete ones so as to make them complete sentences.

(1) The longest day of the year.
(2) It is high tide at eleven o'clock.
(3) His first attempt.
(4) He came to invite us to play tennis.
(5) On account of the rain.
(6) After a hurried dinner under the shelter of a rock.
(7) If you had come ten minutes earlier.

THE SENTENCE.

(8) While we were waiting, the sun began to shine.
(9) Never had I seen such a display of fruits and flowers.
(10) Because we had not time to do full justice to the exhibition.
(11) Down the street to the postoffice.
(12) It is time to go.
(13) Procrastination is the thief of opportunity.
(14) My oldest brother and my sister.
(15) He having finished his lessons.
(16) Walking down the street this afternoon.
(17) The horse, newly shod, walked without slipping.
(18) Skating is good exercise.
(19) Running about the field.
(20) Having spent two hours in the dark trying to find the little wharf at which we usually landed.
(21) How to sail a boat.
(22) The dark shadows, gathering in from all sides, soon shut out the view.
(23) At sunrise the army of the Nabob, pouring through many openings of the camp.
(24) The dexterity with which he managed his steed, and something of youthful grace which he displayed in his manner.
(25) As far as could be judged of a man sheathed in armor, the new adventurer did not greatly exceed the middle size, and seemed to be rather slender than strongly made.
(26) If I had come to see you day before yesterday as I had intended.

7. Sentences of One Word.—In the definition of the sentence, it was stated that a sentence may consist of a word or of a group of words expressing a thought completely, and a number of sentences which consist of a group of words have been cited. But how may we have sentences of a single word? It is in this way. If the commander of a regiment of soldiers who are drawn up for the battle should shout to them the word *Fire*, the men would have no uncertainty as to his meaning. The single word would convey as complete a meaning to them as the longer and less emphatic expression, *I command you to fire.* The word *Fire* would, therefore, in those circumstances, be a sentence, because it expresses a thought completely. Such sentences are called **Imperative Sentences** because they give commands.

Words, however, like *Oh!* and *Ah!*, which sometimes stand alone, are not sentences. For, if someone, in a moment of surprise, should exclaim *Oh!*, another person merely hearing the exclamation would not know exactly what it meant. It might mean *Oh, I didn't know you were here,* or *Oh, I didn't recognize you,* or one of many things. The word *Oh,* and similar words, are not capable by themselves of expressing a thought completely, and therefore they cannot be sentences. They are called interjections (see **2,** (h).

8. Kinds of Sentences.—Sentences are of different kinds. The sentence, *I see a squirrel in that tree,* merely states a fact. The sentence, *Fire,* expresses a command. Closely related to this second kind of sentence is that which expresses a wish or entreaty, as, for example, *Show me the squirrel.* A sentence like *Where is the squirrel?* asks a question, and a sentence like *How swift he is!* is an exclamation in the form of a sentence. We have, therefore, four different kinds of sentences:

(1.) **A Declarative Sentence states a fact or what is regarded as fact.**
(2.) **An Imperative Sentence expresses a command or entreaty.**
(3.) **An Interrogative Sentence asks a question.**
(4.) **An Exclamatory Sentence states a fact, or gives a command, or asks a question in a highly energetic or emotional manner.**

As to the exclamatory sentence, it should be observed that a declarative sentence may become an exclamatory sentence when it expresses a statement very emphatically, as, for example, *That is nonsense!*, or a command, as, *Be off with you!*, or even a question, as, *How could you do it!* The exclamatory sentence is thus seen to be dependent more upon the strength of the emotion with which it is uttered than upon the thought of it.

Declarative and imperative sentences end with a period.

Interrogative sentences end with a question mark.

Exclamatory sentences end with an exclamation point.

9. The Length of the Sentence.—The classification of sentences as declarative, imperative, interrogative, and exclamatory is not at all dependent on the length of the sentences. *I see a squirrel* is a declarative sentence, but so also is *I see a squirrel every morning in that chestnut tree on the other side of the road.* So also *Fire when you see the whites of their eyes* is as much an imperative sentence as the single word *Fire*. Always, therefore, in determining the kind of sentence, observe the nature of the thought, not the number of words it takes to express the thought.

Note also that a declarative sentence may contain a question or command.

(1) He said, "Who is your father?"
(2) The officer shouted "Let go the anchor!"

An imperative sentence may contain a declarative statement or a question.

(1) Think always "I have a duty to perform."
(2) Ask yourself "Who is my master?"

An interrogative sentence may contain a declarative statement or a command.

(1) Did the officer shout "Let go the anchor"?
(2) Did you say "I have lost my pen"?

When a declarative or imperative sentence ends with an inserted interrogative or exclamatory sentence, the usual period is omitted, and the sentence ends with the mark of punctuation appropriate to the inserted sentence.

Exercises.

1. Increase the following sentences in length as fully as you can without changing their kind:

(1) He arrived this morning.
(2) Who is that man?
(3) How high that tree is!
(4) There is not a cloud to be seen.
(5) Not a sound was heard.
(6) Come over to our house.
(7) Judge not.
(8) What a day that was!
(9) Listen!
(10) The earth is round.
(11) Let us go and see.
(12) Where is the city?
(13) "Fear not," he said.
(14) We asked the way to the city.

2. State the kind of sentence to which each of the following sentences belongs:

(1) We are going to the country to-morrow.
(2) Which do you like the better, the seashore or the mountains?
(3) I have never been to the seashore.
(4) How interesting it must be to keep continually visiting new places!
(5) England expects every man to do his duty.

THE SENTENCE. 13

(6) Can't you come to see us soon?
(7) Go down to the barn and see why Carlo is barking.
(8) Let no man speak evil of his neighbor.
(9) Where is my hat?
(10) Lend me yours until I can find mine.
(11) What a terrible thing deceit is!
(12) Thou, too, sail on, O Ship of State!
(13) There was a thunder of applause when I came to that part where Richard cries for "a horse, a horse!"
(14) So much the better! So much the better!
(15) Well, it looks more like a ruin than an inn.
(16) The chilliness of the apartment crept to their bones, and they were glad to return to a common chamber, or kind of hall, where was a fire burning in a huge cavern, miscalled a chimney.
(17) What should I do if my family should be ruined and brought upon the parish?
(18) Don't think that what is agreeable to you must for that reason be agreeable to everybody else.

3. State the kind of each of the sentences in the following paragraph:

A LONG VOYAGE.

"Six months at sea! Yes, reader, as I live, six months out of sight of land, cruising after the sperm-whale beneath the scorching sun of the Line, and tossed on the billows of the wide-rolling Pacific—the sky above, the sea around, and nothing else! Weeks and weeks ago our fresh provisions were all exhausted. There is not a sweet-potato left, not a single yam. Those glorious bunches of bananas which once decorated our stern and quarter-deck have, alas, disappeared. And the delicious oranges which hung suspended from our tops and stays, they, too, are gone. Yes, they are all departed, and there is nothing left us but salt-horse and sea-biscuit. Oh, ye state-room sailors, who make so much ado about a fourteen-days' passage across the Atlantic; who so pathetically relate the privations and hardships of the sea, where, after a day of breakfasting, lunching, dining off five courses, chatting, playing whist, and drinking champagne-punch, it was your hard lot to be shut up in little cabinets of mahogany and maple and sleep for ten hours, with nothing to disturb you but 'those good-for-nothing tars, shouting and tramping over-head,'—what would you say to our six months out of sight of land?"—MELVILLE, *Typee*, Chapter I.

10. The Constructions of Words.—Examine the following declarative sentences, and observe how easily they may be separated into their elements.

	Fishes	swim.	
	Dogs	hunt	rabbits.
(All the)	plants	flourished.	
(The)	fish	swam (rapidly).	
(The)	stroke (of noon)	ended (the tedious) ceremonies.	

In these sentences the words in the first column outside the parentheses all have the same relative position; that is, they are all in the same **Construction.** And so likewise the words of the second column are in the same construction, and those of the third column. Since these various parts are found regularly in sentences, it is convenient to give them names. In the sentence, *Fishes swim,* the word *Fishes* is called the **Subject,** and the word *swim* the **Predicate** of the sentence. In the sentence, *Dogs hunt rabbits,* the word *Dogs* is the **Subject,** *hunt* is the **Predicate,** and *rabbits* is the **Object.** The predicate of a sentence is always a verb, and the subject and object are usually nouns or pronouns. Every sentence must have a predicate, and, unless the sentence is an imperative sentence of a single word, also a subject; but all sentences do not require an object. The subject, predicate, and object are always the main words in the sentence, and, in order to find them, pick out from the rest of the sentence those words which are most necessary for making the statement of the sentence.

11. **Simple and Complete Subject.**—One must distinguish, however, between the **Simple Subject, Predicate,** and **Object,** and the **Complete Subject, Predicate,** and **Object.** In the sentence, *Fishes swim,* both subject and predicate are simple. In the second sentence subject, predicate, and object are all simple. But in the sentence, *All the plants flourished,* the word *plants* is the simple subject, the whole phrase *All the plants* being the complete subject. Likewise, in the fourth sentence, the simple subject is the word *fish,* the complete subject being the phrase *The fish;* the simple predicate is the word *swam,* the complete predicate is the phrase *swam rapidly.* In the fifth sentence, the complete subject is the phrase *The stroke of noon,* the predicate, which is simple, is the word *ended,* and the complete object is again a phrase, *the tedious ceremonies.*

The **Simple Subject** is the word which names the person, place, or thing, from which the assertion of the sentence proceeds.

The **Simple Predicate** is the word which makes the assertion of the sentence.

The **Simple Object** is the word which names the person, place, or thing which is directly affected by the assertion of the predicate.

The **Complete Subject, Predicate,** and **Object** consist respectively of the **Simple Subject, Predicate,** and **Object,** with the dependent words that go with them.

The **Simple Subject** is always a noun or a pronoun, or the equivalent of a noun.

The **Simple Predicate** is always a verb.

The **Simple Object** is always a noun or a pronoun, or the equivalent of a noun.

The other words which go to make up the complete subject, predicate, and object are of various parts of speech, and are called the **Modifiers** of the subject, predicate, and object.

12. Practical Test.—In a declarative sentence the subject is always the word or words which answer the question Who? or What? **before** the verb. Thus the sentence *Fishes swim*, when put into the form of the question *Who or What swim?*, demands the answer *Fishes*, which is the subject of the sentence. The object of a sentence is the word or words which answer the question Whom? or What? **after** the verb. The sentence, *Dogs hunt rabbits*, when put into the form of the question, *Dogs hunt whom or what?*, demands the answer *Rabbits*, which is the object of the sentence. Be careful not to mistake a prepositional phrase for the object of the sentence. The sentence, *The tree fell with a crash*, for example, has no object, since the verb does not require one; *with a crash* is merely a prepositional phrase, and as a whole it has the value of an adverb, modifying the verb *fell* by showing how the tree fell.

13. Order of Words.—The order of words is different in different kinds of sentences. In the declarative sentence the order is simplest, consisting usually of subject first, predicate next, and object, if there is one, following the predicate. But this is not always the order of words in the declarative sentence. Sometimes the subject comes last, as in the sentence, *There goes my hat.* Especially in poetry the order of words is likely to be involved and irregular. Thus the sentence, *Now glowed the firmament with living sapphires,* from Milton's *Paradise Lost,* would be in prose, *Now the firmament glowed with living sapphires;* and the sentence, *Twilight gray had in her sober livery all things clad,* would be in prose, *Gray twilight had clad all things in her sober livery.* When in doubt as to the construction of words, always change the sentence to its simplest prose order.

When the imperative sentence consists of a single word, as, for example, the verb *Halt!,* it is of course not capable of further analysis. Such a sentence contains only a predicate, the subject not being expressed at all. But in a sentence like *Perish the thought,* the word *Perish* is the predicate, and the complete subject is the phrase *the thought.* Sometimes, also, for the sake of emphasis, the pronominal subject of the imperative sentence is expressed, as in the sentence, *You go and shut the door;* this was more commonly done in earlier English than it is now, as in the sentence, *Look thou to my house,* from Shakespeare. Usually, however, the subject is not given at all, as in the following further examples:

Predicate.	*Object.*
(1) Close	the door.
(2) Shun	evil communications.
(3) Look!	
(4) Heed	your footsteps.
(5) Put out	the light.

EXERCISE.

In the following sentences point out the simple subject,

predicate, and, when there is one, the simple object of each:

(1) Distance lends enchantment.
(2) Water flows, wind blows.[1]
(3) The king lives.
(4) The sun warms the earth.
(5) The cold wind blows and the white snow falls.
(6) Light purses make heavy hearts.
(7) Time works wonders.
(8) Time and tide wait for no man.
(9) Oh, I see it!
(10) Great oaks from little acorns grow.
(11) Along the bridge Lord Marmion rode.
(12) Who goes there?
(13) The tide ran rapidly.
(14) Slowly and sadly we laid him down.
(15) At the door on summer evenings
Sat the little Hiawatha.
(16) Under a spreading chestnut tree
The village smithy stands.
(17) The dawn now lights the eastern hills.
(18) Charity begins at home.
(19) All bloodless lay the untrodden snow.
(20) Every cloud has a silver lining.
(21) Down fell the mast with a mighty crash.
(22) Haste makes waste.
(23) High over the gates the tall tower rose.
(24) Love me, love my dog.
(25) With my cross-bow I shot the albatross.
(26) The winds blew and the floods came.
(27) Roused by importunate knocks, I rose, I turned the key, and let them in.
(28) At the entrance to the castle sat a grim watchman.
(29) No man sees his own face.

[1] Some sentences, like this one, contain more than one subject, predicate, and, if objects are required, more than one object.

(30) Here the legion made its last stand.
(31) Who knows the secrets of the stars?
(32) Up hill and down dale rode the untiring messenger.
(33) Boldly they rode and well.
(34) Day after day the citizens awaited his return.
(35) With her hands full of flowers and a wreath around her head, the maiden welcomed us to her father's dwelling.
(36) A book with its leaves uncut reproaches its owner.
(37) He bought a house with a large garden back of it.
(38) The appearance of Rip, with his long, grizzled beard, his rusty fowling-piece, his uncouth dress, and an army of women and children at his heels, soon attracted the attention of the tavern politicians.
(39) The clouds in bars of rusty red
Along the hill-tops glow.
(40) The breaking waves dashed high
On a stern and rock-bound coast,
And the woods against a stormy sky
Their giant branches tossed.

14. The Verb-phrase.—The verb which forms the simple predicate of a sentence may consist of a single word, or it may consist of several words which together form a **Verb-phrase.** This verb-phrase has the same value and is to be treated exactly like the verb consisting of a single word. The words forming a verb-phrase are sometimes separated from each other by other words of the sentence. The verb-phrases in the following sentences are in italics.

(1) He *has bought* a house.
(2) They *have been building* a boat.
(3) *Have* you *seen* my brother?
(4) He *is coming* to-morrow.
(5) *Does* he *know* Mr. Thompson?
(6) They *must give* an answer or they *will be punished.*
(7) *Shall* I *see* you again before to-morrow?
(8) *Are* you *going* to the game?

(9) They *do* not *hear* you.
(10) *Will* the new president of the society *be elected* to-day?
(11) He *has* often *spoken* of you.
(12) Tom *will sing* a song.

15. Interrogative Sentences.—The order of subject, predicate, and object in the interrogative sentence varies. In the following examples it is the same as in the declarative sentence:

Subject.	Predicate.	Object.
(1) Who	sent	you?
(2) What rule	prevented	it?
(3) Whose house	was burnt?	
(4) Which team	won	the game?

But the object may come first, followed by the predicate and then the subject, as in the following examples:

Object.	Predicate.	Subject.
(1) What objections	have	you?
(2) What	said	they?

In sentences of this sort, however, the predicate usually consists of several words, that is, it is a verb-phrase, and the subject then comes between the parts of the predicate, as in the following sentences:

Object.	Predicate.	Subject.	
(1) Whom	did	you	see?
(2) Which candidate	did	they	elect?
(3) What	shall	we	say?

Sometimes also the predicate verb comes first, followed by the subject and then the object:

Predicate.	Subject.	Object.
Have	you	any **wool**?

But here also we usually have a verb-phrase as predicate, with the subject standing between the parts of the verb:

Predicate.	Subject.		Object.
(1) Have	you	seen	my brother?
(2) Do	you	believe	his story?
(3) Shall	I	cut	the string?

16. Exclamatory Sentences.—Since the exclamatory sentence may be either declarative, imperative, or interrogative in form, the order of subject, predicate, and object would be the same as in those kinds of sentences.

EXERCISES.

1. Give first the simple subject, then the complete subject, of the following sentences:
   (1) The curfew tolls the knell of parting day.
   (2) Over the hills and over the valleys the white horse sped.
   (3) He lifted the rock easily.
   (4) The newly elected chairman presided with dignity and authority.
   (5) Here comes your father.
   (6) Who killed cock-robin?
   (7) "I," said the sparrow.
   (8) After the game we rode home.
   (9) Leaning over the side, the boatman quickly seized him by the coat.
   (10) Tennis requires a quick eye.
   (11) Hunting develops all of one's resources.
   (12) In spite of their earnest efforts, the troops arrived too late.
   (13) Down he went on all fours.
   (14) Have you seen my new hat?
   (15) The great ship, after this exchange of courtesies, continued on its way.
   (16) Quick as a flash his fist shot out.

(17) That condition we could not fulfil.
(18) Rounding the point the little boat faced a head wind.
(19) A worse storm the captain had never experienced.
(20) Word of complaint spake he none.
(21) After all, books are very good friends.
(22) Five mortal hours the weary watch we kept.
(23) Lost in the forest the children almost perished from hunger.
(24) Again those soothing strains I hear.

2. In the following sentences the simple predicates are printed in italics. Give the complete subjects, predicates, and objects.

(1) The troops *entered* the city.
(2) The twenty pirates immediately *abandoned* the sinking ship.
(3) These large apples *grew* in our orchard.
(4) My younger brother *lost* his new hat.
(5) The new-fallen snow completely *covered* all the earth.
(6) Two troops of soldiers *came* to our rescue.
(7) The German Empire *contains* many small states.
(8) Who *brought* this beautiful flower?
(9) The big dog in our neighbor's yard *bit* two children.
(10) They *asked* many questions.
(11) Full many a gem of purest ray serene
The dark unfathomed caves of ocean *bear*.
(12) The castled crag of Drachenfels
Frowns o'er the wide and winding Rhine.
(13) The spacious firmament on high,
With all the blue ethereal sky,
And spangled heavens, a shining frame,
Their great Original *proclaim*.
(14) The imperial ensign, full high advanced,
Shone like a meteor streaming to the wind,
With gems and golden luster rich emblazed.
(15) Unto the multitude in the wilderness *came* the prophet Moses.

17. Compound Subject, Predicate, and Object.— Sometimes the simple subject consists of two or more words which have the same construction. The subject is then said to be a **Compound Subject.**

EXAMPLES:

(1) Pineapples and bananas are tropical fruits.
(2) Tom and Charles are first cousins.
(3) War, famine, and pestilence devastated the country.
(4) Time and tide wait for no man.
(5) Jack and Jill went up the hill.

Likewise we may have a **Compound Predicate** and a **Compound Object.**

EXAMPLES OF COMPOUND PREDICATE:

(1) The waves rose and fell.
(2) He sang and whistled all day long.
(3) My father designed and built this house.
(4) The horse whinnied and neighed.
(5) We stood and watched the procession.

EXAMPLES OF COMPOUND OBJECT:

(1) We built a house and a barn.
(2) I saw Charles and Mary yesterday.
(3) I enjoy a play or a novel.
(4) With the money he bought food and lodging.
(5) They raised wheat, corn, and potatoes.

The various parts of the same sentence may, of course, be compounded.

EXAMPLES:

(1) The farmer raised and sold   wheat, corn, and potatoes.

(2) The captain and the coach struggled and labored with the team.
(3) The soldiers and the firemen guarded and dispensed the food and the water.

18. The Simple Sentence.—Sentences are classified, according to their structure, as **Simple, Complex,** and **Compound.**

A **Simple Sentence** is one which contains only one subject, predicate, and object. The subject, predicate, and object of a simple sentence may be compound (**17**). Thus the sentence, *Thunder and lightning foretold the storm,* is a simple sentence, consisting of *Thunder and lightning* as the compound subject, and of *foretold,* the predicate, and of *storm,* the object. It contains only one subject, one predicate, and one object, and is therefore a simple sentence. But a sentence like *The thunder rolled and the lightning flashed* is not a simple sentence, because it contains two subjects, *thunder* and *lightning,* and two predicates, *rolled* and *flashed.* The following are examples of simple sentences. Point out the predicate of each.

(1) He wandered o'er the hills and valleys.
(2) Hope springs eternal in the human breast.
(3) Time works wonders.
(4) Life, like a dome of many colored glass,
    Stains the white radiance of eternity.

The simple sentence is often given an appearance of complexity by the presence in it of modifying word-groups, but when these groups are taken out, the simple structure becomes evident. Thus, in the last sentence above, if we remove the groups *like a dome of many colored glass* and *of eternity*, we have remaining only the simple subject, predicate, and the complete object, *Life stains the white radiance.*

19. The Phrase.—A group of words, like *of eternity*

and *like a dome of many colored glass,* which form parts of the sentence but do not themselves contain a verb, and therefore do not make an assertion, is called a **Phrase.** A phrase has the value of a single word modifying some other word; *like a dome of many colored glass,* for example, has the value of an adverb modifying *stains,* telling how life stains the radiance of eternity; *of eternity* has the value of an adjective modifying *radiance,* describing what kind of radiance is meant.

Definition: (A group of words which does not contain a verb and which is used with the modifying value of a single word, is called a **Phrase.**) A sentence may contain one, two, or more phrases, and still remain a simple sentence. The phrases in the following simple sentences are indicated by spacing and italics.

(1) I write   *with my left hand.*
(2) *To his father*   he always spoke   *in a very respectful way.*
(3) *At midnight*   the watchman kindled the fires   *on the tops   of the highest hills.*

EXERCISE.

Pick out eight phrases in Exercise 3, p. **13.**

20. The Clause.—When a group of words which forms part of a larger sentence itself contains a subject and predicate, we then have a **Clause.** Since the simple sentence is one which contains but one subject, predicate, and object, it is plain that a simple sentence cannot contain a clause. The clause, like the phrase, is always dependent upon some other word in the sentence (see **81, 122, 199**). The italicised words in the following sentences are clauses. Point out the predicates of each clause.

(1) We felt relieved *when we heard that.*
(2) Tom supposed *we would wait for him.*

(3) *Although we were compelled to give up our sail*, we did not pass an unpleasant day.
(4) I hope   *you will come   if you can.*
(5) No man knows *what Time has in store for him.*

21. The Complex Sentence.—The **Complex Sentence** is one which contains two or more subjects, predicates, and, when the predicates require them, objects. The complex sentence consists of two, or more, distinct parts, the **Principal Sentence,** which expresses a statement, command, or question like a simple sentence, and the **Subordinate Clause** or **Clauses,** which, as the name implies, are dependent on the principal sentence. The principal sentence of a complex sentence makes complete sense when standing alone, but the subordinate clause or clauses have meaning only as they are related to other parts of the sentence. It is for this reason that they are called subordinate. The complex sentence may contain two, three, or even more, subordinate clauses.

EXAMPLES:

(1) This is the man who found my watch.
(2) The questions which he asked were difficult to answer.
(3) John came, though he would have preferred to stay at home.
(4) If I find it, I shall send it to you.
(5) I asked him when he would meet me.
(6) His hat, which was a new one, was blown overboard while we were coming up the bay.
(7) After we had spent hours in looking for it, we reached the dock.
(8) The house in which we lived was surrounded by a dike that protected it from the floods to which the region was exposed.

In the above sentences, pick out first the predicates of the principal sentences and then the predicates of the subordinate clauses. Test the subordinate clauses by observing whether they make complete sense when standing alone.

22. The Compound Sentence.—When two or more simple sentences are joined to each other without subordination of one to the other, we have a **Compound Sentence.** The sentences of which a compound sentence is composed are called its **Members.** The members of a compound sentence may each stand alone and make complete sense. The simple sentences, or members, of a compound sentence are usually connected by conjunctions, but in a series of more than two sentences, the conjunction is generally omitted between all except the last two members. Occasionally all the conjunctions are omitted between the members of a compound sentence, the place of the conjunctions being taken merely by commas.

EXAMPLES:

(1) We visited the cave   and   then we ate lunch.
(2) I saw him   but   he did not see me.
(3) The sun came out   and   we soon dried off.
(4) He will come   or   he will send word.
(5) I will walk,   Tom will ride his bicycle,   and   the rest will come in the carriage.
(6) The witness arrived,   he gave his evidence,   and the decision of the jury was reversed.
(7) I came,   I saw,   I conquered.
(8) I pulled,   he pulled,   we all pulled together.

Sometimes the later members of a compound sentence omit some words which may be easily supplied from a preceding member of the sentence. Thus the fourth sentence given above may read, *He will come or send word*, and still remain a compound sentence. So also the sentence, *I have not written to him, but I have telephoned to him*, would be expressed more naturally by *I have not written, but have telephoned to him*, or *I have not written to him, but have telephoned*.

23. The Complex-Compound Sentence.—One member or both members of a compound sentence may be complex, but the two complex sentences being joined without subordination of one to the other, the sentence remains a compound sentence. Such a sentence is called a **Complex-Compound Sentence.** In the following sentence, for example, both members are complex: *He prospered because he was industrious, and he was happy because he was content.*

Examples:

(1) I said that I would come, and here I am.
(2) We hunted up the house which he mentioned, and the housekeeper obligingly showed us over it.
(3) The speaker spoke clearly, but the crowd complained that they could not hear him.
(4) The new inhabitants build houses, or they occupy those which are not inhabited.

Exercises.

In the following passages state which sentences are simple, which are complex, and which are compound. Separate the complex and the compound sentences into their elements.[1]

[1] Begin a new sentence after each period and each semi-colon.

THE SENTENCE.

1. A sullen pause of the storm, which now rose and sank in gusts, produced a momentary stillness. In this interval the report of a musket was heard, and a long shout, almost like a yell, resounded from the shores. Every one crowded to the window; another musket shot was heard, and another long shout, mingled wildly with a rising blast of wind. It seemed as if the cry came up from the bosom of the waters, for though incessant flashes of lightning spread a light about the shore, no one was to be seen.

Suddenly the window of the room overhead was opened, and a loud halloo uttered by the mysterious stranger. Several hailings passed from one party to the other, in a language which none of the company in the barroom could understand, and presently they heard the window closed, and a great noise overhead, as if all the furniture were pulled and hauled about the room. The negro servant was summoned, and shortly afterwards was seen assisting the veteran to lug the ponderous sea chest downstairs.

—WASHINGTON IRVING, *Adventure of the Black Fisherman,*
in *Tales of a Traveller.*

2. The lowing herd winds slowly o'er the lea,
The plowman homeward plods his weary way.
—GRAY'S *Elegy.*

3. THE BROOK.

I steal by lawns and grassy plots,
  I slide by hazel covers;
I move the sweet forget-me-nots
  That grow for happy lovers.

I slip, I slide, I gloom, I glance,
  Among my skimming swallows;
I make the netted sunbeams dance
  Against my sandy shallows.

I murmur under moon and stars
  In brambly wildernesses;
I linger by my shingly bars,
  I loiter round my cresses.

> And out again I curve and flow
> To join the brimming river;
> For men may come and men may go,
> But I go on forever.
> —TENNYSON.

24. Clauses as Subject and Object.—In the following complex sentences it will be observed that a whole clause is really used as the subject of the sentence:

(1) That he would yield immediately was not expected.
(2) Where he came from has remained a mystery.
(3) Why he should do this has puzzled me.
(4) That we had lost our way soon became evident.

Likewise a clause may be used as the object of the sentence, as in the following examples:

(1) I know that he will come.
(2) We believed that the worst was past.
(3) He inquired who lived there.

Clauses which are thus used as subject or object of the sentence are called **Noun Clauses** because they have essentially the same construction as nouns. It will be shown later (**83, 199**) that clauses may be used also as adjectives and adverbs, forming thus **Adjective** and **Adverb Clauses.**

When a sentence contains a direct quotation, as for example: *He asked, "What is your name?"* or *"Fudge!" said the half-pay officer*, the sentence is not really complex or compound, but simple, because the whole quotation is merely the object of the sentence, the simple subject in the first example being *He*, the simple predicate *asked*, and the simple object, *"What is your name?"*

THE SENTENCE.

Exercise.

Pick out the noun clauses in the following sentences and tell whether they are subject or object clauses.

(1) We believed that he was an honest man.
(2) That thou hast wronged me doth appear in this.
(3) We inquired what the price of the vessel was, and the captain said that she was not for sale.
(4) I don't know what to tell him when he comes.
(5) Whom do you think I saw yesterday?
(6) He could not remember when or where he had seen him.
(7) All hoped and prayed that he might come in time.
(8) We never supposed that he would be on time.
(9) Taking up his basket, he remarked that he still had a long way to go.
(10) That the light should go out just at that moment was most unfortunate.

Summary of Definitions: the Sentence.

6. The **Sentence** is a word or group of words expressing a thought completely.

8. A **Declarative Sentence** states a fact, or what is regarded as a fact.

An **Imperative Sentence** expresses a command or an entreaty.

An **Interrogative Sentence** asks a question.

An **Exclamatory Sentence** states a fact, or gives a command, or asks a question in a highly energetic or emotional manner.

11. The **Simple Subject** is the word which names the person, place, or thing from which the assertion of the sentence proceeds.

The **Simple Predicate** is the word which makes the assertion of the sentence.

The **Simple Object** is the word which names the person, place, or thing which is directly affected by the assertion of the predicate.

The **Complete Subject, Predicate,** and **Object** consist respectively of the simple subject, predicate, and object, with the dependent words that go with them.

The words dependent on the simple subject, predicate, and object are called the **Modifiers** of the subject, predicate, and object.

17. A **Compound Subject, Predicate,** or **Object** consists of two or more words in the same construction, connected by the conjunctions *and, or,* etc.

18. A **Simple Sentence** is one which contains but one subject, predicate, and object.

19. A **Phrase** is a group of words which does not contain a verb, and which has the value of a single word modifying some other word in the sentence.

20. A **Clause** is a group of words containing a subject, predicate, and if the predicate requires it, an object. The clause is always dependent upon some other word in the sentence.

21. A **Complex Sentence** is one which contains two or more subjects, predicates, and when their predicates require them, objects. A complex sentence consists of a **Principal Sentence** and a **Subordinate Clause** or **Clauses.**

22. A **Compound Sentence** is one which contains two or more simple sentences joined together without subordination of one to the other. The parts of a compound sentence are called its **Members**.

23. A **Complex-Compound Sentence** is a compound sentence, one or more of the members of which is a complex sentence.

QUESTIONS AND SUGGESTIONS FOR REVIEW.

1. Define the sentence. 2. Select from some book three sentences of twenty words or more each, and indicate the parts of which each is composed. 3. How can we have sentences of one word? 4. Why are interjections not sentences? 5. Define and illustrate by examples the Declarative, the Imperative, the Interrogative, and the Exclamatory sentence. 6. Under what conditions may a declarative, imperative, or interrogative sentence become exclamatory? 7. Illustrate the point that the kind of sentence is not dependent on the length of the sentence. 8. Define the Simple Subject, the Simple Predicate, and the Simple Object of the sentence. 9. Define the Complete Subject, Predicate, and Object of the sentence. 10. Choose five sentences from some book and give, first, the simple subjects, predicates, and objects of them (if all have objects), and second, the complete subjects, predicates, and objects. 11. What is meant by the Modifiers of the subject, predicate, and object? 12. Take any short poem, in some of the sentences of which the order of words is irregular, and change the words to the regular prose order. 13. Define the term verb-phrase and illustrate by examples. 14. What is meant by a Compound Subject, Predicate, or Object? Give illustrations. 15. Define Simple, Complex, and Compound sentences. 16. Is a

sentence with a compound subject necessarily a compound sentence? 17. Define the term Phrase. 18. Define the term Clause. 19. Choose a sentence, or sentences, from some book, and point out the phrases and clauses. 20. From a connected passage in some book, pick out five simple sentences, five complex sentences, and five compound sentences.

CHAPTER III.—THE PARTS OF SPEECH.

25. How to Tell the Parts of Speech.—In order to tell the part of speech to which a word belongs, observe first of all what function or duty it has to perform in the group of words of which it is a part. Its part of speech is then dependent absolutely upon this function. It often happens that the same word, at different times and in accordance with the different functions which it performs, may be of several different parts of speech. Thus the word *paint,* in the sentence, *This paint is too yellow,* is plainly a noun, since it names an object; but the same word in the sentence, *We paint our house every year,* is just as plainly a verb, since it states an action, what we do. The word *house* is a noun in *This house belongs to the mayor,* and a verb in *The city authorities house the poor during cold weather.* In the same way the word *city* is a noun in *The city was crowded with excursionists,* but in the sentence given above, *The city authorities,* etc., it is an adjective, because it modifies *authorities* by telling what kind of authorities they were. In the sentence, *This red apple is the best,* the word *red* is an adjective, modifying *apple;* but in the sentence, *Red is a cheerful color,* the word is a noun because it names an object, in this case the color, red. The word *under,* in the sentence, *The ball under the table is mine,* is a preposition, uniting the **prepositional** phrase *under the table* to the noun *ball;* but in the sentence, *We always pity the under dog, under* is an adjective, modifying the noun *dog.* Moreover, when words are quoted, as in the sentence, *He said " Halt,"* or are simply specified, as *Pronounce "moral" more distinctly,* they then have the grammatical value, that is, the part of speech which is demanded by their function or use in the context in which they occur. Thus *Halt* in the sentence given above is there a noun, object of the verb *said,* because it simply states what he said, although if the word *Halt* stood by itself it would be an imperative verb. So also the word *moral* in *Pronounce "moral" more distinctly,* is a noun, object of the verb *Pronounce;* in a sentence like *The moral law of the universe must be obeyed,* however, it is an adjective modifying *law.* Always, therefore, the part of speech of a word is determined by its function, the way in which it is used, and there is no method of determining its part of speech other than that of observing what duty it has to perform in the group of words in which it occurs.

Exercise.

1. Tell the part of speech of each of the italicized words in the following sentences, and give your reasons for each decision:

   (1) We *water* the flowers every day with the *water* from the hydrant.
   (2) In the night the soldiers *bridge* the stream and *cross* to the other side.
   (3) A large *cross* marked the spot where the *bridge* formerly stood.
   (4) *Paper* dishes will some day take the place of china.
   (5) A great deal of *paper* is made from wood-pulp.

(6) *Blot* his name from the book.
(7) We could not read the lines on account of a large *blot*.
(8) The printers *ink* the type with a large roller.
(9) Where there is *smoke*, there is always *fire*.
(10) Hunters often *fire* the grass and thus *smoke* the animals out of their hiding-places.

26. Review of the Parts of Speech. The eight parts of speech are the **Noun,** the **Pronoun,** the **Adjective,** the **Verb,** the **Adverb,** the **Preposition,** and the **Conjunction.** The full definitions of these are as follows:

(a) A **Noun** is a word which names a person, place, thing, or idea. Pick out the nouns in the following sentences and tell why they are nouns:

(1) The horse and wagon belong to his father.
(2) Charles sent a telegram, saying that Mr. Walker could not come.
(3) The ocean was very rough.
(4) Haste makes waste.
(5) We lived in Paris for two years.
(6) Charity begins at home.
(7) The quality of mercy is not strained.
(8) Contentment is a virtue.

(b) A **Pronoun** is a word which indicates a person, place, thing, or idea, without actually calling it by name. Point out the pronouns in the following sentences:

(1) Tom said he would come later.
(2) I saw Mrs. White yesterday, and she looked well.
(3) Her father gave me this book.
(4) Who is your friend?
(5) He not only preached honesty, but practised it.
(6) These poor people are industrious, but they are not provident.
(7) Mr. Wood gave us all his papers.
(8) Contentment is a virtue, but it is not a common one.

(c) An **Adjective** is a word which limits or modifies the meaning of a noun or pronoun. Pick out the adjectives in the following sentences:

(1) The new boat came to-day.
(2) What a fine, large apple!
(3) The daily papers have long accounts of the recent disaster.
(4) We missed the first train by two hours.
(5) The wind is cold but invigorating.

(d) A **Verb** is a word, or, in the case of the verb-phrase, a word-group, which asserts action or state of being with respect to some noun or pronoun.

EXAMPLES:

(1) The arrow hit the mark.
(2) We left as soon as it was day.
(3) I have seen your dog twice to-day.
(4) The president was elected without difficulty.
(5) He is sick.
(6) He looks worse than he did.

(e) An **Adverb** is a word which limits or modifies the meaning of a verb, an adjective, or another adverb.

EXAMPLES:

(1) He walked unhesitatingly to the gate.
(2) The flowers grew rapidly.
(3) It was a very dark night.
(4) He wore an unusually cheerful smile.
(5) They ran surprisingly swiftly.
(6) The boat arrived yesterday.

Adverbs generally answer the question *How, When, Where,* or *Why?*

(f) **Prepositions** are words which are used together with nouns and pronouns, and the modifiers of these nouns and pronouns, to form prepositional phrases, which have, as wholes, the value of adjectives or of adverbs. In the following sentences, pick out the prepositions, showing with what words they combine to form prepositional phrases, and how these phrases have the value of adjectives and adverbs:

EXAMPLES OF ADJECTIVE PREPOSITIONAL PHRASES:

(1) The man with the tall hat is my brother.
(2) The life of the city centres there.
(3) He occupies the house on the corner.
(4) A library of good books is a source of constant pleasure.
(5) The man in the yellow jacket is the master of the ship.

EXAMPLES OF ADVERBIAL PREPOSITIONAL PHRASES:

(1) He came after the appointed time.
(2) We were elected by a small majority.
(3) His hat blew into the river just as we turned around the bend.
(4) He crossed over the street and went into a store.
(5) We struggled with all our might, but it was all in vain.

(g) **Conjunctions** are words which are used to connect words, phrases, clauses, and even complete sentences. The most frequently used conjunctions are *and, or, but, if, yet, though, except, unless, since, because*. Point out what the conjunctions connect in the following sentences:

(1) Tom and Mary have gone home.
(2) Time and tide wait for no man.
(3) He cannot come, but he has sent a substitute.
(4) I asked him if he had heard the news.
(5) I will not go unless you go too.
(6) We changed our plans because the weather was too warm.
(7) Unless we hear from you, we sha'n't expect you to come.
(8) I had never seen him before, though I had often heard of him.

(h) **Interjections** are exclamatory words used to express emotions of surprise, joy, grief, and so forth.

EXAMPLES:

(1) *Alas,* poor Yorick! I knew him.
(2) *Ah,* that is another matter.
(3) *Pshaw,* I don't believe a word of it.

The Noun.

27. The Noun.—The number of words belonging to the class of nouns is greater than that belonging to any other part of speech. In general, a word which is used to name some object or person, or even an idea which does not have any outward visible or tangible form, concerning which we wish to make some statement, is a noun. Thus nouns may be the names

(1) Of objects: wood, sky, town, London, Maine.
(2) Of persons: man, boy, girl, Charles, Abraham Lincoln, Queen Victoria.
(3) Of actions: flight, laughter, delay.
(4) Of qualities of objects: bitterness, sweetness, fragrance, weight.
(5) Of states of being: sleep, death, health.
(6) Of pure ideas: love, mercy, thought, anxiety.

28. Kinds of Nouns.—It is convenient to make a classification of nouns on the basis of their meaning. They are thus classified as **Common** and **Proper,** and as **Masculine, Feminine,** and **Neuter Nouns.**

29. Common and Proper Nouns.—A **Common Noun,** as the name indicates, is one that may be applied to any one of a class of objects. Thus the word *chair* is a common noun, because it may be applied to any one of the large number of objects included under the term. Even when the word is more limited, as, for example, in the compound, *arm-chair*, it is still a common noun, because *arm-chair* is a word which is applicable to any single arm-chair.

A **Proper Noun,** on the other hand, is one which names a particular and individual person, place, or thing. Thus the word *city* is a common noun, because it is a name which applies to any one of the whole number of cities. But the names *Boston* and *Chicago* are proper nouns because these words are the names each of one particular city. Even when several places bear the same name, as, for example, the name *Springfield*, the word is still, according to its use, a proper noun, because whenever one uses the word *Springfield*, one uses it to designate a particular one of the various places of that name, the one intended being understood, or indicated by the addition of the name of the state in which it is situated. The same is true of the names of persons. There are many persons who bear the names *John, Edward, Mary*, etc., and the same family name is often borne by different people. But whenever these names of persons are used, they are always used to designate specific individuals, not all the various members of a class, and they are consequently proper nouns.

Proper nouns are also used as the names of individual objects, as, for example, *Monadnock*, of a mountain; *Mississippi*, of a river; *Kearsarge*, of a ship; and as the names of animals, as *Sport, Tray, Dobbin*, etc.

The names of peoples are also proper nouns, for example, *Yankee, Italian, Pole, Finn, German*, etc.

Proper nouns begin always with a capital letter, common nouns usually with a small letter. When common nouns are written with a capital letter they either stand at the beginning of sentences or are capitalized for the sake of emphasis.

Proper names sometimes consist of several words, as *New York, George Washington, King Charles, James Russell Lowell.*

30. Gender.—The classification of nouns as masculine, feminine, and neuter is based upon the sex of the objects which they name. The classification itself is called **Gender.**

Nouns which name male persons or animals, or objects thought of as male, as *man, boy, coachman, banker,* etc., are of the **Masculine Gender.**

Nouns which name female persons or animals, or objects thought of as female, as *woman, girl, maid-servant, priestess,* etc., are of the **Feminine Gender.**

Nouns which apply indifferently to either sex, as *child, parent, friend, teacher,* and nouns which name animals without indicating sex, as *bird, sheep, buffalo, chicken, cat, deer,* etc., are of the **Common Gender.**

Nouns which name objects or ideas which are without sex, as *house, street, tree, hour, haste,* are of the **Neuter Gender.**

31. There are three ways by which the different genders of nouns are indicated: (1) by the use of separate words; (2) by the use of prefixes denoting gender; (3) by the use of suffixes denoting gender.

(1) **Gender denoted by separate words.**—The number of word-pairs which have grown up for the purpose of distinguishing the masucline and feminine genders is large, and only a comparatively few examples can be given here. Such words have to be learned mainly by experience or by the aid of the dictionary.

Masculine.	*Feminine.*
bachelor	maid
boy	girl
bull	cow

THE PARTS OF SPEECH.

Masculine.	*Feminine.*
buck	doe
cock *or* rooster	hen
father	mother
husband	wife
gander	goose
drake	duck
king	queen
monk	nun
nephew	niece
ram	ewe
stallion	mare
uncle	aunt
wizard	witch

(2) **Gender indicated by prefixes.**—Compounds of this character are not very numerous.

Masculine.	*Feminine.*
man-servant	maid-servant
bull-moose	cow-moose
cock-sparrow	hen-sparrow
he-goat	she-goat
he-bear	she-bear

(3) **Gender indicated by suffixes.**—After the method of using different words, as described under (1), this is the most common way of indicating differences of gender. The most frequently used feminine-forming suffix is the syllable *-ess*, the corresponding masculine suffix being *-er*. The feminine suffix is added directly to the masculine form, or with some slight modification of it.

A few other feminine suffixes survive in single words, although they were formerly of much wider application. Such are the syllable *-ster* in *spinster*, originally the feminine of *spinner*, and the syllable *-en* in *vixen*, the feminine of *fox*. The syllable *-ine* of *heroine* is a feminine-forming suffix, but the whole word was merely borrowed from the French. Likewise, the syllable *-trix* in such word-pairs as *executor*, masculine, *executrix*, feminine; *testator*, masculine, *testatrix*, feminine; is used in only a few words derived from Latin. The following is a list of some of the words which form their feminines by adding *-ess* to the masculines.

(a) The syllable *-ess* is added to the masculine without other change:

Masculine.	*Feminine.*
poet	poetess
host	hostess
count	countess
priest	priestess
baron	baroness
heir	heiress
prophet	prophetess
lion	lioness
deacon	deaconess
patron	patroness

(b) The syllable *-ess* is added to the masculine in a slightly changed form:

Masculine.	*Feminine.*
abbot	abbess
songster, singer	songstress
adventurer	adventuress
emperor	empress
duke	duchess
actor	actress
master, Mr.	mistress, Mrs.
governor	governess
tiger	tigress
instructor	instructress
traitor	traitress
marquis	marchioness
benefactor	benefactress
[Masculine lacking]	seamstress
protector	protectress
defender	defendress

An interesting development in the modern use of gender permits words which were formerly only masculine to be used as common gender, that is, without any implication of sex. Thus the word *doctor* may now be used of either a male or female practitioner of medicine, the feminine form *doctoress* or *doctress* not being used at all. Likewise the words *author, teacher, artist, pianist,* and many more, may apply to either a man or a woman. Yet the limits of use are somewhat sharply defined. One may speak of a female writer as an *author*, but hardly of a female writer of verse as a *poet*.

32. Personification.—In our definition of gender (30) it was said that objects thought of as males were of the masculine gender, objects thought of as females, of the feminine gender. It thus happens that inanimate objects entirely without sex are given the characteristics of living persons or animals. Thus a ship is often spoken of as *she*, as is the moon, the sun being usually referred to as though it were a male being. In poetry, especially, it is common to treat inanimate objects, or even ideas, as though they were persons: thus hope, faith, peace, time, night, dawn, and many other words are referred to by *he* or *she*. This process of ascribing the characteristics of persons to inanimate objects or ideas is called **Personification.** The personified words are frequently capitalized like proper nouns, and are referred to by personal pronouns.

EXAMPLES:

1. *Thou* too sail on, O *Ship* of State!

2. When *Duty* whispers low, "Thou must,"
   The youth replies, "I can."

3. Yet *Hope* had never lost *her* youth;
   She did not look through dimmer eyes;
   Or *Love* but played with gracious lies,
   Because *he* felt so fixed in truth.
   —TENNYSON, *In Memoriam.*

4. But sometimes *Virtue* starves, while *Vice* is fed.
   What then? Is the reward of *Virtue* bread?
   That, *Vice* may merit, 'tis the price of toil;
   The knave deserves it when he tills the soil,
   The knave deserves it when he tempts the main,
   Where *Folly* fights for kings, or dives for gain.
   —POPE, *Essay on Man.*

NOTE.—A third classification of nouns according to their meaning as Concrete and Abstract is sometimes made by grammarians. According to this classification, names of objects which can be perceived by the senses of hearing, seeing, etc., like *ship, house, river, music,* etc., are called Concrete Nouns; names of ideas which have existence in thought only, like *hope, patience, mercy,* etc., and of qualities of objects thought of apart from the objects themselves, like *whiteness, warmth, splendor,* are called Abstract Nouns. This classification, however, has no grammatical significance, and the attempt to carry it out consistently on logical grounds results in many serious difficulties.

33. Inflection.—Inflection has already been defined (**3**) as the variations in the form of a word to indicate corresponding variations in meaning. Inflection may be shown in four different ways:

(a) By a change in the radical vowel of a word.
   EXAMPLES: one *man,* ten *men;* I *sing,* I *sang;* I *find,* I *found.*

(b) By the addition of a letter or a syllable.
   EXAMPLES: one *house,* ten *houses;* I *wish,* I *wished;* smooth, smoother, smoothest; poet, poetess.

(c) By the use of several words closely combined so as to form a phrase.
   EXAMPLES: I *go,* I *shall go,* I *shall have gone;* smooth, *more* smooth, *most* smooth.

(d) By the use of entirely different words.
   EXAMPLES: I *go,* I *went;* I *am,* I *was;* good, better, best.

THE PARTS OF SPEECH.

The parts of speech which are capable of undergoing inflection are nouns, pronouns, adjectives, verbs, and adverbs.

Nouns are inflected to show gender, number, and case. The inflection of a noun is called its **Declension**.

Pronouns are inflected to show gender, number, case, and person. The inflection of the pronoun is called its **Declension**.

Adjectives and adverbs are inflected to show differences in degree. This inflection is called **Comparison**.

Verbs are inflected to show person, number, tense, voice, and mood. The inflection of the verb is called its **Conjugation**.

The further discussion of the inflections of these various parts of speech will be taken up each in its proper place.

34. The Inflections of the Noun.—Inflection for gender in the noun has already been sufficiently discussed (see **30, 31,**) but it is necessary to say something further about **Number** and **Case**.

Number is the distinction in the use of words whereby they are made to name one person or thing or more than one person or thing.

A word which names a single person or thing is in the **Singular Number,** as *house, stone, tree, shoe, man.*

A word which names two or more persons or things is in the **Plural Number,** as *houses, stones, trees, shoes, men.*

35. Plurals in -s.—Most nouns form their plurals by adding the letter **-s** to the singular.

EXAMPLES: book, books; brick, bricks; hat, hats; elevator, elevators; color, colors; president, presidents.

36. Plurals in -es.—But nouns which already end in -s, or in a sound that does not readily combine with the sound of -s, form their plurals by adding -es.

EXAMPLES: class, classes; lash, lashes; tax, taxes; finch, finches; church, churches: perch, perches.

37. Nouns in -o.—Nouns ending in -o in the singular form their plurals by adding -s, as regularly, when the final -o is preceded by another vowel.

EXAMPLES: cameo, cameos; curio, curios; portfolio, portfolios; Hindoo, Hindoos; bamboo, bamboos.

But when final -o is preceded by a consonant, the plural is usually formed by adding -es.

EXAMPLES: buffalo, buffaloes; echo, echoes; hero, heroes; motto, mottoes; negro, negroes; potato, potatoes; tomato, tomatoes; volcano, volcanoes.

There are, however, a few exceptions to this rule, e. g., banjo, banjos; piano, pianos; solo, solos; octavo, octavos.

38. Nouns in -y.—Nouns ending in -y preceded by a consonant change this y- to -i and add -es to form their plurals. Nouns ending in -y preceded by a vowel form their plurals regularly by adding -s.

EXAMPLES: city, cities; remedy, remedies; fly, flies; duty, duties; ferry, ferries; army, armies; mercy, mercies. Valley, valleys; convoy, convoys; alley, alleys; alloy, alloys.

Nouns ending in -quy form their plurals in the same way as nouns ending in -y preceded by a consonant.

EXAMPLES: obloquy, obloquies; soliloquy, soliloquies; colloquy, colloquies.

39. Nouns in -f, -fe.—Many nouns ending in -f or -fe change f to v before adding the endings -es, or -s, respectively, to form their plurals.

EXAMPLES: calf, calves; loaf, loaves; leaf, leaves; wolf, wolves; thief, thieves; half, halves; knife, knives; wife, wives; life, lives.

But words which end with the sound -f written -ff or -gh do not make any change before adding the plural ending.

EXAMPLES: cliff, cliffs; skiff, skiffs; stuff, stuffs; cough, coughs; laugh, laughs; rough, roughs.

The word *staff* has an older plural, *staves*, but the usual form now is *staffs*.

40. Plurals in -n.—There are four nouns in English which make use of the inflectional element **-n (-en, -ren)** in forming their plurals. They are *ox, oxen; brother, brethren* (besides *brothers*); *child, children; cow, kine* (besides *cows*).

41. Mutation Plurals.—A few nouns form their plurals by changing the radical vowel of the word without the addition of an inflectional element. These are *man, men; woman, women; foot, feet; tooth, teeth; goose, geese; louse, lice; mouse, mice.*

The two words *brother, brethren;* and *cow, kine;* belong both to this class and the preceding, since they not only mutate the vowel of the word but also add the inflectional element **-n.**

42. Uninflected Plurals.—Another small group of nouns has the same form in both singular and plural. These are *deer, sheep, swine, neat* (meaning cattle), *fish, salmon, perch, shad, pike* (meaning the fish of that name), *trout, hundredweight, yoke* (of oxen), *head* (of cattle). In popular speech this use is frequently extended to words of weight and measure, as *foot, pound, gallon,* etc., used with plural numerals preceding. The feeling in all such cases is apparently for the quantity as a whole, rather than for the individual units of weight or measure of which it is composed. It is better usage, however, to use the plural form of the noun.

43. Double Plurals.—Some nouns have two forms for the plural. The two plurals in all such instances have separate meanings.

EXAMPLES:

Singular.	Plurals.
brother	brothers (of the same family). brethren (of the same society or organization).
penny	pennies (single coins). pence (in the names of English coins of the value of two or more pennies, *e. g.*, threepence, sixpence, etc.).
cloth	cloths (pieces of cloth). clothes (garments).
die	dies (used in stamping). dice (for gaming).
fish	fishes (kinds of fish). fish (thought of collectively).

44. Nouns without Plurals.—Many nouns are used only in the singular number. These are chiefly words which by the nature of their meaning do not permit the plural idea, like names of abstract ideas or qualities, *indifference, anger, wisdom, perseverance*, etc.; of sciences or arts, like *history, music, painting, sculpture, biology, botany*, etc.; of materials, like *gold, silver, iron, wheat, corn, rye*, etc. When names of materials like *iron, glass*, etc., are used in the plural, they either mean different kinds of the material named, or else have special significations, *e.g., irons=fetters*, or *smoothing irons; glasses= glasses for drinking, eye-glasses, telescopes*, etc.; *nickels= five-cent pieces*.

45. Nouns without Singulars.—On the other hand, some nouns are used only in the plural.

EXAMPLES: scissors, tongs, pincers, trousers, suspenders, lees, dregs, billiards, annals, proceeds, wages, oats, eaves.

46. Nouns Plural in Form.—Some nouns are plural in form, but are singular in use and meaning.

EXAMPLES: news, gallows, measles, summons, mathematics, physics, ethics, phonetics. A few nouns of plural form are used either as singular or as plural, *e. g.*, athletics, politics, acoustics, statistics, calisthenics, riches.

47. Collective Nouns.—Nouns which name objects that are made up of a number of individual elements, as, for example, the noun *army*, are called **Collective Nouns**. They may be regarded as singular or plural, according as one thinks of the collection of objects as a whole, or of the individual members which constitute the whole.

EXAMPLES: herd, troop, band, company, family, flock, covey, brood, pack, etc.

48. Plurals of Compound Nouns.—Compound nouns which are made up of a noun plus a suffix, as *handful, spoonful*, etc., add **-s** to the last syllable, *e. g., handfuls, spoonfuls*, to form the plural.

Most other compound nouns, made up of two separate words, also add **-s** to the final syllable.

EXAMPLES:

door-sill	door-sills
household	households
blackbird	blackbirds
school-house	school-houses
lamp-shade	lamp-shades
major-general	major-generals
overseer	overseers

But some compound nouns add the plural ending to the first element of the compound. The following is a list of the most important, which should be carefully learned:

father-in-law	fathers-in-law
mother-in-law	mothers-in-law
son-in-law	sons-in-law
attorney-at-law	attorneys-at-law
coat-of-mail	coats-of-mail
court-martial	courts-martial
commander-in-chief	commanders-in-chief
hanger-on	hangers-on
passer-by	passers-by
man-of-war	men-of-war

A few compound nouns pluralize both elements of the compound.

EXAMPLES:

man-servant	men-servants
woman-servant	women-servants
knight templar	knights templars

Nouns compounded with *foot, tooth, man,* etc. (see **41**) as the second element, form their plurals as the uncompounded word does, by mutation of the radical vowel:

EXAMPLES:

claw-foot	claw-feet
eye-tooth	eye-teeth
wash-woman	wash-women
fireman	firemen

THE PARTS OF SPEECH. 53

It should be noted that the syllable *-man* in *German, Mussulman, Ottoman, dragoman,* and *firman* is not the word *man* as contained in *watchman, Frenchman, Englishman,* etc., and that consequently these words form their plurals simply by adding *-s, e. g., Germans, Mussulmans, Ottomans, dragomans, firmans.*

49. Plurals of Foreign Nouns.—Nouns of foreign origin sometimes retain the plural inflection of the languages from which they were derived. Sometimes two plural forms are used, one with the foreign plural inflection, the other with the regular ending of English words. The following is a list of a few of the most common examples:

Singular.	*Plural.*
alumnus (masculine)	alumni
alumna (feminine)	alumnæ
appendix	appendices
axis	axes
bandit	banditti (but more commonly *bandits*)
calix	calices
cherub	cherubim (or cherubs)
crisis	crises
criterion	criteria (or criterions)
datum (rarely used in the singular)	data
dilettante	dilettanti
ellipsis	ellipses
erratum	errata
focus	foci (or focuses)
fungus	fungi
index	indices (in mathematics; as the index of a book, the form of the plural is usually *indexes*).

Singular.	Plural.
oasis	oases
parenthesis	parentheses
phenomenon	phenomena
radius	radii
stimulus	stimuli
thesis	theses

50. Letters of the alphabet, **figures, symbols,** and **words** regarded merely as words, form their plurals by adding apostrophe and **s**, *i.e.*, **'s**.

Examples

(1) Your *n*'s look like *u*'s.
(2) Mind your *p*'s and your *q*'s.
(3) Transpose the 6's and the 8's.
(4) Distinguish your +'s and ×'s more clearly.
(5) You have too many *and*'s and *if*'s and *so*'s in your writing.
(6) These little *if*'s and *and*'s are important words.

51. Plurals of Proper Nouns.—The plurals of proper nouns when united to titles are as follows:

(a) The plural of *Mr.* is *Messrs.*, the name itself remaining in the singular.
   EXAMPLE: *Mr. Smith, Messrs. Smith,* or *the Messrs. Smith.*

(b) The title *Mrs.* has no plural form. To indicate the plural the name itself adds *-s*.
   EXAMPLE: *Mrs. Smith, the Mrs. Smiths.*

(c) The title *Miss* is usually pluralized, the name remaining singular; but the singular form of the title and the plural of the name may also be used.
   EXAMPLE: *Miss Smith, the Misses Smith,* or *the Miss Smiths.*

(d) The title *Master* becomes *Masters* in the plural, the name remaining unchanged.
   EXAMPLE: *Master Smith, the Masters Smith.*

EXERCISES.

1. Write out sentences in which the plurals of the following words are correctly used: woman, child, sheep, cow, ox, die, city, tomato, deer, hero, bass, copper, penny, glass, leaf, capful, book-shelf, tooth, father-in-law, lighthouse, basis, alumnus, Mr. Chase, Miss Wallace, Mrs. Brown, Mussulman.

2. Give the rule for each of the plural formations which you have used.

3. Give the plurals of the singular nouns in the following sentences, and the singulars of the plural nouns, whenever it is possible to do so.

   (1) The chief of the clan was a MacGregor.
   (2) Virtue is its own reward.
   (3) The wretch deserves his fate.
   (4) The news was stale by the time it reached us.
   (5) Saturday is a holiday.
   (6) The phenomenon was not an unusual one.
   (7) He is a man of good sense, or at least has been always so considered.
   (8) Necessity is the mother of invention.
   (9) How all classes were being compacted into one people, the proceedings connected with Magna Charta may show.
   (10) The annals of the period were full of stories of crime and violence, of ancient rights disregarded, and of recent injustice.
   (11) The workmen filled their wheel-barrows with earth and trundled them along narrow gang-planks to the place where they emptied them.
   (12) Chairs, tables, plates, knives, forks, they had none. They sat, as I before said, on the earth or door-steps, and ate either out of their little cedar tubs or an iron pot, some few with broken iron spoons, more with pieces of wood, and all the children with their fingers. A more complete sample of savage feeding I never beheld.

4. Choose five of the examples given in each of the following sections (**44, 45, 46, 47, 48,** and **49**), and construct sentences in which they are properly used.

52. Case.—The second kind of inflection of which the noun is capable is that for **Case.** We distinguish three cases of the noun, the **Nominative,** the **Possessive,** and the **Objective** case. Of these the nominative and objective are always alike in form, and there are consequently only two inflectional forms to indicate the three cases. In early stages of the language there were not only separate forms for these three cases, but also for several other cases that have been completely lost.

53. Nominative Case.—The **Nominative Case** is the case of the word used as the subject of the sentence or clause.

EXAMPLES:

(1) The *audience* applauded.
(2) The *house* resembled a barn in appearance.
(3) The *streets* were crowded because the *weather* was fine.

When used after a form of the verb *to be*, for example, *am, is, are, was* or *were*, a noun or pronoun is in the **Predicate Nominative** case.

EXAMPLES:

(1) That man was my *father*.
(2) Their most profitable crop is *wheat*.
(3) The little animals were *field-mice*.

A noun used in direct address is said to be in the nominative case by direct address.

EXAMPLES:

(1) *John,* close the door.
(2) I told you, *Tom,* that I would meet you here.

THE PARTS OF SPEECH. 57

54. The Objective Case.—The **Objective Case** is the case of a word used as the object of a verb or after a preposition in a prepositional phrase.

EXAMPLES:

Nominative Case.	Predicate.	Preposition.	Objective Case.
The audience.	applauded		the *speaker*.
The audience	applauded	with	*enthusiasm*.
The boys	ate		the *apples*.
We	looked	for	the *captain*.

The object of a preposition, like the object of a verb, is the word, or words, which answers the question *Whom?* or *What?* after the preposition.

55. Verbs with Two Objects.—Some verbs take two objects.

EXAMPLES:

Nominative Case.		Objective Case.	Object Complement.
They	elected	him	president.
We	made	the owners	trustees.
He	named	the boat	"Sylph."
We	called	him	Tom.

In sentences of this kind the second of the two objects, since its purpose is to complete the meaning of the first object, is called the **Object Complement.**

Other examples of verbs with two objects are the following:

Nominative Case.		Dative Object.	Objective Case.
John	gave	Mary	a *book*.
He	lent	Tom	his *knife*.
The *stranger*	told	the *boys*	a *story*.
My *uncle*	has sent	me	a *present*.
They	gave	the *house*	a *coat* of paint.

In these examples it is the first of the two objects which have special characteristics and which require a special name. It will be observed that the objects *Mary, Tom, boys, me,* and *house* all express the person or object to whom or for whom something is done. These objects are all equivalent in meaning to prepositional phrases, consisting of the preposition *to* and the respective nouns, and in the earlier stages of the language the ideas would be so expressed, or would be expressed by the aid of a special case, the dative case, which has been lost in modern English. In order to distinguish the two objectives, however, we call the first one the **Dative Object.**

> NOTE.—Some grammars call the Dative Object the indirect object. The terminology is misleading, however, since the dative object is not less directly affected by the action of the verb than is the second object. Indeed, in sentences like *John gave James a ball*, or *John gave James a blow on the cheek*, the word *James*, which is the dative object, may fairly be said to be more immediately affected by the action of the verb than the words *ball* or *blow*.

56. The Possessive Case.—This case, as the name indicates, is the use of a noun as a possessive modifier of some other nouns. A noun in the possessive case is closely related in function to the adjective. It differs from the adjective, however, in that the noun is still felt to be merely an inflected form of the noun and not a pure adjective.

EXAMPLES:

(1) The *speaker's* audience was with him.
(2) The *dog's* collar was lost.
(3) *John's* ball struck *Mary's* doll.

Sometimes the possessive case is felt to express possession less than the general idea of *appertaining to* or *connected with.*

EXAMPLES:

(1) The *world's* work must be done.
(2) He would not permit a *moment's* delay.
(3) An *hour's* walk is long enough.

57. The **Possessive Case** can always be expanded into a phrase consisting of the preposition *of* and the noun in the objective case.

EXAMPLES:

(1) The *stranger's* determination to overcome the *landlord's* prejudice was evident.
(2) The determination *of the stranger* to overcome the prejudice *of the landlord* was evident.

The possessive case, when it has merely the idea of possession, is usually used only in nouns denoting persons, animals, and personified objects. Thus we speak of *a man's hat, a dog's tail,* and *the sun's rays;* but we hardly say *the store's windows* or *the shoe's sole,* in normal speech, but rather *the windows of the store* and *the sole of the shoe.*

58. Forms of the Possessive Case.—The **Possessive Case** always has a distinctive form. The **possessive case singular** is formed by adding the apostrophe and **s** (**'s**) to the nominative.

EXAMPLES: time, time's; man, man's; lady, lady's; John, John's; James, James's; Dickens, Dickens's; bricklayer, bricklayer's; commander-in-chief, commander-in-chief's.

The **possessive case plural** of words which do not end in **-s** is formed by adding **'s** to the nominative plural.

EXAMPLES: men, men's; children, children's; oxen, oxen's; mice, mice's; geese, geese's.

When the plural already ends in -*s*, as is usually the case, the possessive is formed by adding only the apostrophe.

EXAMPLES: boys, boys'; houses, houses'; cities, cities'; trees, trees'.

59. Double Possessives.—The possessive case is sometimes used after the preposition *of* in phrases which thus become **Double Possessives,** the idea of possession being once expressed by the preposition and a second time by the possessive inflection.

EXAMPLES.

(1) That house *of John's* will cost him dear.
(2) Do you remember that brother *of Tom's* who visited him at Christmas?

The double possessive is used only of persons.

60. The Group Possessive.—In groups of words, as, for example, *the King of England,* or when the names of two or more persons possessing the same thing are used, or when a title or descriptive noun is added to another noun, as *Mr. Smith, the minister,* only the last noun is given the mark of the possessive case.

EXAMPLES:

(1) *The King of England's* throne is hereditary.
(2) *The keeper of the seal's* duties are clearly defined.
(3) *The winner of the cup's* enthusiasm was not dampened.
(4) This is *Tom, Charles, and Harry's* room.
(5) *The earth and the sun's* motions are contrary.
(6) This is *Mr. Smith, the minister's* house.
(7) He followed out his *friend, the president's* commands.
(8) We called at *Mr. Clarke, the lawyer's house* last night.

61. The Absolute Possessive.—Sometimes the possessive case stands alone and is not followed by any noun which it limits or modifies. This is called the **Absolute Possessive.**

EXAMPLES:
(1) We called at *Mr. Clarke's* last night.
(2) *Thompson's* is a comfortable place to dine at.
(3) This place is called *St. Andrew's*.

It should be observed that this use of the *Absolute Possessive* is different from that in which a noun is easily supplied from the context, as, for example, *Judge Miller's is a large house,* equivalent to *Judge Miller's house is a large house.* In the absolute possessive no noun is implied in this way, and the possessive must be construed as standing alone.

EXERCISES.

1. Form sentences containing all the examples of the possessive case given in **58.**
2. Point out the nouns in the possessive case in the following sentences, and mention the particular characteristics of each.

(1) The squire's name was Wellington.
(2) Go over to the wheelwright's and tell him to finish my horse's collar right away.
(3) After a two week's vacation I found it hard to settle down to work.
(4) William the Conqueror, England's last foreign invader, was himself of Teutonic blood.
(5) Any advice of Mr. Ward's will be faithfully followed.
(6) He lived at Watson, the carpenter's for three years.
(7) The men's efforts were unavailing.

(8) I can come at a moment's notice.
(9) He smoothed and smoothed her hair away,
　　He kissed her forehead fair;
　　"It is my darling Mary's brow,
　　It is my darling's hair!"
　　　　　　　　　　　　　—Whittier.

(10) For who would bear the whips and scorns of time,
　　 The oppressor's wrong, the proud man's contumely,
　　 The pangs of despis'd love, the law's delay,
　　 The insolence of office, and the spurns
　　 That patient merit of the unworthy takes,
　　 When he himself might his quietus make
　　 With a bare bodkin?
　　　　　　　　　　　　—*Hamlet, Act III., Scene I.*

62. Apposition.—When one noun is placed beside another noun for the purpose of explaining it, the second noun is said to be in **Apposition** to the first one. Two nouns in apposition are in the same case, but when they are in the possessive case, only the second noun is given the inflection of the possessive (**60**).

Examples of Nominatives in Apposition:

(a) Subject:
　　My friend, the doctor, gave me some good advice.
　　The blacksmith, the first man to settle in these parts, was an influential citizen.

(b) Predicate nominatives:
　　It is Mr. Brown, the banker.
　　They were fishermen, inhabitants of a near-by village.

(c) Direct address:
　　O King, Ruler of Men, hear our petition.

THE PARTS OF SPEECH. 63

EXAMPLES OF OBJECTIVES IN APPOSITION:

(a) Object of a verb:
   I saw John, the gardener, at work in his garden.
   The teacher punished him, the chief offender, by giving him fifty strokes.
(b) Object of a preposition:
   It is built of granite, a very endurable material.
   He came with a crowd of followers, all the important inhabitants of the place.
(c) Object complement:
   They elected him president, the highest office in their gift.
   The master called him rascal, a not undeserved title.

EXAMPLES OF POSSESSIVES IN APPOSITION:

This is John, the carpenter's house.
He took Mr. Hall, the liveryman's horse.

63. Appositives Connected by "or."—Sometimes two appositive words are connected by the conjunction *or*. Two nouns thus connected stand for the same person or thing, the second noun being an alternative name for the person or thing.

EXAMPLES:

The bison, or buffalo, is an almost extinct animal.
Ferdinand, or Fred, was a promising lad.

Other words besides nouns may be in apposition, as, for example, the verbs in the following sentences:

He invited, or rather requested, all members to be present.
This material they desiccated, or dried, in the sun.

The word, whether a noun or verb, which is in apposition to a preceding word, together with its modifying words, is set off by commas. When the appositive words are in the possessive case, a comma is not placed after the noun which bears the possessive inflection. See the examples in this and the preceding sections.

64. Noun Equivalents.—Some words which are commonly used as other parts of speech are sometimes used with the functions of nouns, and thus become subjects and objects in the sentence.

EXAMPLES:

(a) Adjectives as nouns:
   (1) He did his *worst*.
   (2) The *good* die young.
   (3) The *best* is not too good.

(b) Adverbs as nouns:
   (1) *Now* is the accepted time.
   (2) *By-and-by* means *never*.

(c) Phrases and clauses as nouns (24):
   (1) "*Make haste slowly*" is a wise saying.
   (2) "*Be off with you*," he said.
   (3) "*Not till to-morrow*," she answered.
   (4) *That you have wronged me* doth appear in this.

65. Parsing.—Parsing consists in naming all the grammatical characteristics of a word. In parsing a noun, one should state its kind, whether common or proper, its gender, its number, and its case, and in giving the case one should also point out the construction of the noun with relation to the other words of the sentence. In the sentence, *After two days' rain, the sun shone brightly*, the nouns are parsed as follows:

   days' is a common noun, neuter gender, plural number, possessive case, limiting the noun *rain*.

THE PARTS OF SPEECH.

rain is a common noun, neuter gender, singular number, objective case, after the preposition *after*.
sun is a common noun, neuter gender, singular number, nominative case, subject of the verb *shone*.

In the sentence, *Thomas, the gardener, has twenty hens and two roosters*, the nouns are parsed as follows:

Thomas is a proper noun, masculine gender, singular number, nominative case, subject of the verb *has*.
gardener is a common noun, masculine gender, singular number, nominative case, in apposition to the subject *Thomas*.
hens is a common noun, feminine gender, plural number, objective case, object of the verb *has*.
roosters is a common noun, masculine gender, plural number, objective case, object of the verb *has*.

EXERCISE.

Parse the italicized nouns in the following passage:

1. This *warning* stopped all *speech*, and the hardy *mariners*, knowing that they had already done *all* in the *power* of *man* to insure their safety, stood in breathless anxiety, awaiting the result. At a short *distance* ahead of them, the whole *ocean* was white with foam, and the *waves*, instead of rolling on in regular succession, appeared to be tossing madly about. A single streak of dark *billows*, not half a *cable's* length in width, could be discerned running into this *chaos* of water, but it was soon lost to the eye amid the *confusion*. Along this narrow path the *vessel* moved more heavily than before, being brought so near the wind as to keep her sails touching. The pilot silently proceeded to the wheel, and with his own *hands* he undertook the *steering* of the ship. No noise proceeded from the frigate to interrupt the horrid tumult of the ocean; and she entered the *channel* among the breakers in dead *silence*.
—COOPER, *The Pilot*.

Point out the remaining nouns in the passage, and show what constructions they are in.

Summary of Definitions: The Noun.

26. A **Noun** is a word which names a person, a place, a thing, or an idea.

29. A **Common Noun** is one that may be applied to any one of a class of objects.

A **Proper Noun** is one which names a particular and individual person, place, or thing.

30. Nouns which name male persons or animals, or objects thought of as male, are of the **Masculine Gender**.

Nouns which name female persons or animals, or objects thought of as female, are of the **Feminine Gender**.

Nouns which apply indifferently to either sex, and nouns which name animals without indicating sex, are of the **Common Gender**.

Nouns which name objects or ideas which are without sex are of the **Neuter Gender**.

32. The process of ascribing the characteristics of persons (*e. g.*, gender) to inanimate objects or ideas is called **Personification**.

33. Inflection is the variation in the form of a word to indicate corresponding variation in meaning. The noun inflects for gender, number, and case. The inflection of the noun is called its **Declension**.

53. The **Nominative Case** is the case of the noun used as the subject of the sentence, or after a form of the verb *to be*, or in direct address. The nominative after a form of the verb *to be* is called the **Predicate Nominative**.

54. The **Objective Case** is the case of a noun used as the object of a verb, or after a preposition in a prepositional phrase.

56. The **Possessive Case** is the use of a noun as a possessive modifier of some other noun.

62. A noun is in **Apposition** to another noun when it is placed beside the first noun for the purpose of explaining it or of extending its meaning.

QUESTIONS AND SUGGESTIONS FOR REVIEW.

1. Name again the various parts of speech. 2. How does one determine the part of speech to which a particular word in a passage belongs? 3. Give sentences illustrating the point that the same word under different conditions may be different parts of speech. 4. Define Noun, giving illustrations. 5. Define Common Noun and Proper Noun. 6. What is meant by gender in nouns? 7. Define and illustrate (a) Masculine, (b) Feminine, (c) Common, (d) Neuter gender. 8. Name and give examples of three ways by which the gender of nouns is indicated. 9. What do you understand by Personification? 10. Do we ever use personification in ordinary conversation, *e. g.*, in speaking of a boat, engine, etc.? 11. Define Inflection, and name four different ways in which inflection can be shown. 12. What parts of speech are capable of being inflected in English? What is the inflection of each called? 13. Define Number in nouns. 14. Distinguish between singular and plural number. 15. How do most nouns form their plurals? 16. When do nouns add *-es* to form their plurals? 17. How do nouns ending in *-y* form their plurals? 18. How do nouns ending in *-f* form their plurals? 19. Give some examples of

mutation plurals. Of uninflected plurals. Of double plurals. Of nouns without plurals. Of nouns without singulars. Of nouns plural in form but singular in meaning. Of collective nouns. 20. How do most compound nouns form their plurals? 21. Give some examples of compound nouns that add -*s* to the first element of the compound. 22. Why is the plural of *German, Germans,* not *Germen?* 23. What do you understand by Case in the noun? 24. Tell what (a) the Nominative, (b) the Predicate Nominative, (c) the Possessive, (d) the Objective Case, respectively, are. 25. Give three sentences which contain Object Complements. 26. Give three sentences which contain Dative Objects. 27. Tell how the possessive case singular and the possessive case plural are formed. 28. What is meant by the Double Possessive? The Group Possessive? Give illustrations. 29. What is meant by Apposition? Give three sentences illustrating apposition. 30. What are the characteristics of the noun which we name in parsing it?

The Pronoun.

66. The Pronoun.—Often it is convenient to indicate a person or an object without using the noun which names this person or object. For this purpose one uses certain words which stand in place of the noun, and these words are called **Pronouns.** For example, in the second of the following sentences, note how much more convenient it is to use the pronouns, which are italicized, than it would be to keep repeating the nouns:

(a) The boys had a rifle. The boys owned the rifle in partnership and often the boys went out hunting with the rifle.

(b) The boys had a rifle. *They* owned *it* in partnership, and often *they* went out hunting with *it;* or, The boys had a rifle *which they* owned in partnership, and often *they* went out hunting with *it*.

67. The Kinds of Pronouns.—We distinguish five different kinds of pronouns, the classification of them depending on the way in which they indicate the nouns for which they stand. The five kinds are as follows:

- (a) **The Personal Pronoun** indicates the person speaking, the person spoken to, or the person or object spoken of. The most important of the personal pronouns are *I, you, we, us, he, him, his, she, her, it, its, they, their,* and *them*.

- (b) **Relative Pronouns** are used to join the subordinate clauses of complex sentences to the words on which they depend. For example, the two sentences, *This is the boy*, and *This boy won the prize*, may be made into a single sentence by replacing the noun *boy* of the second sentence by the relative pronoun *who*, giving thus *This is the boy who won the prize*. The relative pronouns are *who, whose, whom, which, what,* and *that*.

- (c) **Interrogative Pronouns** are used to introduce questions. They are *who, whose, whom, which,* and *what*. Examples are as follows: (1) *Who* will be the first to try? (2) Here are two roads; *which* shall we take? (3) *What* are you going to do about it?

- (d) **Demonstrative Pronouns** indicate persons or things emphatically and definitely. The principal demonstrative pronouns are *this, that, these, those*.
  Examples: (1) *This* is the very book I want. (2) If you don't like *those*, you can choose others.

- (e) **Indefinite Pronouns** are somewhat like the demonstrative pronouns, but differ from them in that they indicate persons or things generally and indefinitely. The number of indefinite pronouns is large, a few of the more common ones being *each, few, many, anybody, somebody, everyone,* etc.

Examples: (1) *Each* was provided with a large stick. (2) *Many* are called, but *few* are chosen. (3) *Anybody* can say that.

68. The Antecedent of the Pronoun.—The noun which the pronoun takes the place of is called its **Antecedent.** The antecedent of the pronoun is not always expressed in the sentence in which the pronoun occurs, but may be carried over from a preceding sentence. Care should always be taken, however, to make sure that the antecedent of the pronoun is perfectly clear. From the nature of the thought the pronouns *I*, *we*, and *you*, do not usually have antecedents, the person in each case being referred to only by the pronoun and not by the noun. Likewise, the interrogative pronoun, since it asks a question about some person or thing which is unknown, does not usually have an antecedent. In the following sentences all the pronouns and their antecedents, when the latter are expressed, are printed in italics; tell which pronouns have antecedents, and what they are:

(1) *I* told *Tom*, but *he* wouldn't agree.
(2) When the *cat* had caught the *bird*, *she* proceeded to eat *it*.
(3) *We* found the *man who* was to be *our* guide.
(4) *Mary* told the *gardener* to water the *flowers*, but *he* forgot to attend to *them*, and now *she* is afraid *they* will die.
(5) The *engine, which* was making *its* first trip, was thrown from the track.

69. Phrase and Clause as Antecedent.—The antecedent of a pronoun may be a phrase or a clause. For example, in the fourth sentence in **68,** we might say *Mary told the gardener to water the flowers, but he forgot to do it*, in which sentence the antecedent of the pronoun *it* would be the phrase *to water the flowers*. In the sentence, *You have done me an injustice and you know it*, the antecedent of *it* is *You have done me an injustice*.

EXAMPLES:

(1) That he has finished all his work may be true, but I doubt it.
(2) We wanted to stop at that place, but we thought it would be dangerous.
(3) He promised to wait for us, but he forgot it.
(4) To reach the harbor would take work, but we determined to try it.

70. Personal Pronouns.—Personal pronouns are divided into three classes: pronouns of the **First Person,** like *I, we, us,* which indicate the person speaking; pronouns of the **Second Person,** which indicate the person spoken to, like *you;* and pronouns of the **Third Person,** like *he, she, it, they,* which indicate the person or object spoken of. Personal pronouns of all three persons indicate **Person, Number,** and **Case** by their inflections, but only pronouns of the third person singular have inflectional forms for the different **Genders.**

71. Forms of the Second Person.—The normal forms of the pronoun of the second person are *you* for the nominative and objective cases, singular and plural numbers, *your* and *yours* for the possessive case, singular and plural. But the forms *thou* for the nominative singular, *thee* for the objective singular, *thy* and *thine* for the possessive singular, and *ye* for the nominative plural, are often used in elevated discourse, as, for example, in prayers, in the Bible, and in poetry. They are never used in daily conversation.

EXAMPLES:

(1) What I tell you in darkness, that speak ye in light; and what ye hear in the ear, that preach ye upon the housetops. —*Matthew x, 27.*

(2) Build thee more stately mansions, O my soul,
As the swift seasons roll!
Leave thy low-vaulted past!
Let each new temple, nobler than the last,
Shut thee from heaven with a dome more vast,
Till thou at length art free,
Leaving thine outgrown shell by life's unresting sea!
—HOLMES, *The Chambered Nautilus.*

72. Inflections of the Personal Pronouns.

FIRST PERSON.

	SINGULAR.	PLURAL.
NOMINATIVE.	I	we
POSSESSIVE.	my, mine	our, ours
OBJECTIVE.	me	us

SECOND PERSON.

	SINGULAR.	PLURAL.
NOMINATIVE.	you, thou	you, ye
POSSESSIVE.	your, yours, thy, thine	your, yours
OBJECTIVE.	you, thee	you

THIRD PERSON.

	SINGULAR.			PLURAL.
	Masc.	*Fem.*	*Neut.*	
NOMINATIVE.	he	she	it	they
POSSESSIVE.	his	her, hers	its	their, theirs
OBJECTIVE.	him	her	it	them

73. The Forms of the Possessive.—The personal pronouns, with the exception of *he* and *it*, have two forms for the possessive. The forms *my, our, your, thy, her,* and

their are used when the pronoun is followed by the **noun** which names the object possessed.

EXAMPLES:
(1) This is my ball.
(2) The way to our little retreat was a difficult one.
(3) We gave them their own way.

The forms *mine, ours, yours, thine, hers,* and *theirs* are used when the pronoun stands without a noun following. In these instances the pronoun is said to be used **Absolutely.**

EXAMPLES:
(1) This ball is mine.
(2) As they had lost their caps, we gave them ours.
(3) No will but thine I know.
(4) This pile is yours and that pile is theirs.

74. We as Plural of I.—In strict logic **we** cannot be regarded as the plural of **I,** or **us** as the plural of **me,** since the first person is by its nature singular. What is meant by the first person plural is that the speaker associates with himself certain others for whom he acts as spokesman. Somewhat similar is the explanation of the **Editorial we,** in newspaper writing, in which the writer expresses not his own personal opinion, but the opinion or policy of the newspaper organization which he represents, and the **Royal we,** used in address from the throne, because the ruler then speaks not in his own person, but as the head and representative of the state.

75. Order of Pronouns.—When a personal pronoun is used with other personal pronouns or nouns in a series, the pronoun of the first person always comes **last.**

EXAMPLES:

(1) Tom, Harry, and I went in together.
(2) You, he, and I are to be invited, *or* He, you, and I are to be invited.

76. Impersonal Subject and Object.—The pronoun **it** is used in certain idiomatic constructions as subject or object, without definite antecedent and without specific meaning. Since the pronoun here stands for no definite person or thing, it is called an **Impersonal Pronoun.**

EXAMPLES OF IMPERSONAL SUBJECT:

(1) It is I.
(2) It is the coachman.
(3) It is my brother and sister.
(4) It is raining.
(5) It grows late.
(6) It is ten o'clock.

EXAMPLES OF IMPERSONAL OBJECT:

(1) We tramped it all over the country.
(2) She gave it to him good and heavy.
(3) What do you make of it?
(4) I will leave it to you.

77. Anticipatory Subject.—A somewhat similar construction is that in which the pronoun *it* is used as a preliminary subject in place of a clause which follows later in the sentence. For example, the sentence, *It is easy to tell the difference*, is equivalent to *To tell the difference is easy*. But since, in the first form of the sentence, *It* really has no antecedent and is used in vague anticipation of some thought which follows, it is called the **Anticipatory Subject.**

EXAMPLES:

(1) It is worth while being on your guard = Being on your guard is worth while.
(2) It is doubtful whether he will be here or not = Whether he will be here or not is doubtful.
(3) It is now certain that the moon is uninhabited = That the moon is uninhabited is now certain.

78. Compound Personal Pronouns.—Besides the simple personal pronouns, we have a certain number of **Compound Personal Pronouns,** consisting of the simple pronoun united to the word *self*. The forms are as follows:

FIRST PERSON.

	SINGULAR.	PLURAL.
NOM. and OBJ.	myself	ourselves

SECOND PERSON.

	SINGULAR.	PLURAL.
NOM. and OBJ.	yourself thyself	yourselves

THIRD PERSON.

	SINGULAR.			PLURAL.
	Mas.	*Fem.*	*Neut.*	
NOM. and OBJ.	himself	herself	itself	themselves

The compound personal pronouns have no forms for the possessive case and are not used in that case.

The form for the nominative and objective is in all instances the same.

79. Uses of the Compound Personal Pronouns.—The **Compound Personal Pronouns** are used as follows:
(a) In apposition to another pronoun or to a noun in

order to emphasize the meaning of the first pronoun or the noun.

EXAMPLES:

(1) The master *himself* could not have done better.
(2) I told Mary *herself* not to expect me.
(3) I *myself* did it.
(4) He gave it to the sailors *themselves*.

Sometimes the compound personal is separated from the word with which it is in apposition.

EXAMPLES:

(1) *I* will do it *myself*.
(2) *She* gave it to me *herself*.
(3) *We* who had done so much for him were *ourselves* the victims of his avarice.

Occasionally the compound personal is used when no appositional word is expressed.

EXAMPLES:

(1) Who did this? It was *myself*.
(2) Come *yourself* and bring your sister with you.

(b) As objects of verbs where the object indicates the same person or thing as the subject. When they are used in this way they are called **Reflexive Pronouns.**

EXAMPLES:

(1) He deceived *himself*.
(2) We called *ourselves* kings of the island.
(3) The dog recognized *itself* in the mirror.
(4) The endeavor justified *itself* by the result.

The reflexive pronoun also appears as the object of a preposition, this object standing for the same person or thing as the subject of the sentence.

EXAMPLES:

(1) *We* tried to do it by *ourselves*, but could not.
(2) *You* will see for *yourself* what it means.
(3) The *walls* might have stood by *themselves*, but were better supported.

80. Parsing the Personal Pronoun.—In parsing a personal pronoun state (1) its person, whether first, second, or third; (2) its gender, if the gender can be determined; (3) its number; (4) its case, pointing out also its construction; (5) its antecedent, or, if no antecedent is found, state the special characteristics of its use; (6) if the pronoun is compound, state whether its use is emphatic or reflexive. In the sentence, *I told John to go to your house by himself and we would follow him*, the pronouns are parsed as follows:

I is a personal pronoun, first person, singular number, gender indeterminate, nominative case, subject of the verb *told*. It does not have an antecedent, its antecedent being understood to be the person speaking.

your is a personal pronoun, second person, singular number, gender indeterminate, possessive case, limiting the noun *house*. It does not have an antecedent.

himself is a compound personal pronoun, third person, singular number, masculine gender, objective case, object of the preposition *by*. It is used reflexively and its antecedent is *John*.

we is a personal pronoun, first person, plural number, gender indeterminate, nominative case, subject of the verb *would follow*. It has no antecedent.

him is a personal pronoun, third person, singular number, masculine gender, objective case, object of the verb *would follow*. Its antecedent is *John*.

EXERCISE.

Parse all the personal pronouns in the following passage:

SIR WALTER AND THE QUEEN.

"It seems to me," said Blount, "as if our message were a sort of labor in vain; for see, the Queen's barge lies at the stairs, as if her Majesty were about to take the water."

It was even so. The royal barge, manned with the Queen's watermen, richly attired in the regal liveries, and having the banner of England displayed, did indeed lie at the great stairs which ascended from the river. As they approached the gate of the palace, one of the sergeants told them that they could not at present enter, as her Majesty was in the act of coming forth.

"Nay, I told you as much before," said Blount; "I pray you, my dear Walter, let us take boat and return."

"Not till I see the Queen come forth," returned the youth, composedly.

At this moment the gates opened, and ushers began to issue forth. After this, amid a crowd of lords and ladies, yet so disposed around her that she could see and be seen on all sides, came Elizabeth herself, then in the prime of womanhood, and in the full glow of what in a sovereign was called beauty.

—SCOTT, *Kenilworth.*

81. Relative Pronouns.—Relative pronouns are so called because their function is to join or relate one clause to another. The clause introduced by the relative pronoun is a **Relative Subordinate Clause,** the clause to which it is joined being the **Principal Clause.** The relative clause introduced by *who, whose, which,* and *that* has always the value of an adjective limiting some word in the principal clause. This word in the principal clause is the antecedent of the relative. The relative clause introduced by *what* has the value of a noun used as subject or predicate nominative, or as object after a verb or preposition. The relative *what* has no antecedent and combines in itself the subject of the subordinate clause and the object of the main clause. Since it has this two-fold construction it is called the **Double Relative.**

EXAMPLES:

Principal Clause.	*Subordinate Adjective Clause.*
(1) He gave me the *book*	*which* I wanted.
(2) This is the *boy*	*who* won the prize.
(3) This is the *house*	*that* Jack built.
(4) He showed me the *man*	*whose* house was burned.

Principal Clause.	*Object Clause.*
(1) They ate	*what* was set before them.
(2) He knew	*what* the trouble was.
(3) I believed	*what* was told me.

Subject Clause.	*Principal Clause.*
(1) *What* you ask	is impossible.
(2) *What* was done	seemed of no importance.

Principal Clause.	*Predicate Nominative.*
(1) This is	*what* we need.
(2) The men were	*what* you might expect.

82. When the double relative *what* is used after a preposition, it has the double construction of object of the preposition, and subject or object of the verb of the subordinate clause.

EXAMPLES:

(1) We were not confident *of what* had been told us.
(2) Be content *with what* you have.

In the first of these two sentences, *of what* is equivalent to *of that which, that* being the object of the preposition *of,* and *which* the subject of *had been told.* In the second sentence, *with what* is equivalent to *with that which, that* being the object of *with,* and *which* the object of the verb *have.*

The antecedent of the relative pronoun in the principal clause may be a personal pronoun in the absolute possessive case, as in the sentence, *Fame is not always theirs who most covet it,* in which the antecedent of *who* is *theirs.*

83. A single sentence may contain two, or even more, subordinate relative clauses, in which case one or more of the subordinate clauses *may* be dependent upon words in another subordinate clause.

EXAMPLES:

(1) The house *which we bought recently,* we sold again to the man *who called yesterday.*
(2) We sold him the house *which we had bought from the man who called yesterday.*

In the first of these sentences, *which we bought recently* is an adjective relative clause, modifying *house,* object of the verb *sold; who called yesterday* is also an adjective relative clause, modifying *man,* the object of the preposition *to.* The principal clause, therefore, consists of *we sold the house again to the man,* the rest of the sentence consisting of the two relative clauses dependent on the principal clause.

In the second sentence, the clause, *which we had bought from the man,* is an adjective clause modifying *house* in the principal sentence; the second relative clause, *who called yesterday,* is also an adjective clause modifying *man* in the first subordinate clause.

84. Restrictive and Non-Restrictive Relatives.—
Adjective relative clauses are of two kinds, illustrated by
the following sentences:

(a) The house which we live in is very old.
(b) The house, which was a low, rambling structure, was very old.

It will be observed that in sentence (a) the relative clause serves to limit or restrict the word *house* in such a way as to show just which house is meant. In sentence (b) the relative clause merely adds a descriptive detail concerning the word *house*, without further limiting or restricting it in its application. It has purely the value of a descriptive adjective. The relative clause in sentences like the first one is called a **Restrictive Relative Clause;** in sentences like the second one, the clause is a **Non-Restrictive Relative Clause.**

A restrictive relative clause is *not* set off from the rest of the sentence by punctuation. A non-restrictive relative clause *is* separated from the rest of the sentence by commas.

Tell which of the relative clauses in the following sentences are restrictive and which are non-restrictive, and give the reasons for the classification:

(1) A wagon which was standing by the roadside was our only shelter.
(2) We approached the mountain, which was completely covered with snow.
(3) We approached the mountain which was completely covered with snow.
(4) A man who has blood in his veins will not sit idly by.

(5) A man, who had not yet observed us, was seen coming over the ridge.
(6) I like a house which has a great many rooms in it.
(7) The old house, which we had lived in so many years, was torn down.
(8) I was protected from the annoyance of the insects which occasionally hovered in the air.
(9) The insects, which are very troublesome, are also very numerous.
(10) It was planted with trees, whose interlacing branches formed a leafy canopy.

85. Omission of the Relative.—In restrictive relative clauses the relative pronoun, when it is in the objective case and is not preceded by a preposition, may be omitted.

EXAMPLES:

(1) The house which we live in is very old, *or* The house we live in is very old.
(2) The man whom we wanted we couldn't get, *or* The man we wanted we couldn't get.
(3) This is the book that you were looking for, *or* This is the book you were looking for.

86. Inflections of the Relative.—The only one of the relatives which is capable of changing its form by inflection is *who*. The other relatives have the same form for all genders, persons, numbers, and cases. The relative *who* inflects for case only as follows:

Singular and Plural.
NOMINATIVE.   who.
POSSESSIVE.   whose.
OBJECTIVE.   whom.

87. Cases of the Relative.—Although the relative clause as a whole is either an adjective clause or a noun clause dependent on a principal clause, the relative pronoun itself always has a case and construction which is dependent upon its use in its own clause. Thus the relative may be:

(a) The subject of a verb in the nominative case:

EXAMPLES:

(1) I saw the man *who* found the book.
(2) This is the house *which* was on fire last night.
(3) We both admired the essay *that* won the prize.

(b) The object of a verb in the objective case. In this construction the relative always stands at the head of its clause, preceding both the verb and the subject of the relative clause.

EXAMPLES:

(1) This man, *whom* all the world now honors, was once a poor farmer boy.
(2) I have enjoyed the book *which* you gave me.
(3) He recognized it as the road *that* he had travelled before.

(c) The object of a preposition in the objective case:

EXAMPLES:

(1) I know the man of *whom* you speak.
(2) We tried the road by *which* you came.
(3) We have been thinking about *what* you said.

When the preposition which governs the pronoun does not stand immediately in front of it, it is placed at the end of the clause.

EXAMPLES:

(1) You are the very man *whom* we were speaking *about.*
(2) He won the prize *which* he was trying *for.*
(3) I don't know *what* you are thinking *of.*

(d) In the possessive case:

EXAMPLES:

(1) We know no man *whose* knowledge is greater.
(2) This is Charles, *whose* father you met yesterday.

In this construction the antecedent of *whose* is usually a person, but sometimes the antecedent is an inanimate object, as in the sentence, *We passed a house whose roof had blown off*. In most sentences of this sort, however, it will be found stylistically a little better to use the prepositional phrase *of which* than the possessive *whose*, although both are grammatically correct. A better form of the above sentence would be, therefore, *We passed a house the roof of which had blown off*.

88. Antecedents of Relatives.—(1) The antecedent of *who, whose,* or *whom* is always a person.

(2) The antecedent of *which* as a relative is never a person.

(3) The antecedent of *that* may be a person, an animal, or a thing.

There is no definite rule determining whether one shall use *that* or *who* when referring to a person, and each instance has to be determined largely by the speaker's or writer's feeling for the language.

89. The Relative As.—The word *as* is used as a relative pronoun when it is preceded by *such* or *same* in the main clause. It is equivalent in value to *that* or *which*.

EXAMPLES:

(1) I used such means *as* I thought would be effective.
(2) I used the same means *as* I had formerly employed.
(3) Such talent *as* I have shall be freely granted.

90. The Relative But.—The word *but* is occasionally used as a relative pronoun, equivalent to *who (that)* . . . *not*.

EXAMPLE:

There is no man *but* would give ten years of his life to write such a book.

91. That as Relative.—The relative pronoun *that* should be kept clearly distinguished from the same word used as a conjunction, a use which is discussed in **216, 218**.

EXAMPLES OF *THAT* AS RELATIVE:

(1) It is the very thing that I expected.
(2) This is the house that I had in mind.

EXAMPLES OF *THAT* AS CONJUNCTION:

(1) He said that he would come.
(2) We believed that he was speaking the truth.

92. Compound Indefinite Relative Pronouns.—The compound relative pronouns are *whoever, whichever, whatever; whosoever, whichsoever,* and *whatsoever*. The compounds in this second group are used only in elevated style. The first element of the compounds with *who-* is inflected for case as in the simple forms of the word. The other compounds are not inflected.

93. Constructions of the Compound Relatives.—The compound relatives differ from the simple relatives in that they are indefinite in meaning, and may stand both for the relative and its antecedent. The same word may have, therefore, two constructions, one in the principal clause and one in the subordinate clause. Thus the sentence, *Whoever breaks this law shall suffer for it*, is equivalent to *He who breaks this law shall suffer for it*. But in the first form of the sentence, the principal clause, *shall suffer for it*, has no subject other than that implied in *whoever*, the subject also of the subordinate clause. In the sentence, *Whatever you do will be acceptable to me*, *whatever* is subject of *will be acceptable* and also object of *do*.

Sometimes in poetry the simple relative *who* is used with the same double and indefinite value as the compound relative, as, for example, in the sentence, *Who steals my purse steals trash*, where *Who* is equivalent to *He who*, and is subject of both verbs of the sentence.

94. Relative Adjectives.—The relatives *which*, *what*, *whichever*, and *whatever* are frequently used with both relative and adjective function combined. They are used to join clauses, and at the same time they stand before and modify nouns. Such relatives are called **Relative Adjectives.**

EXAMPLES:

(1) He knows *which* house is the right one.
(2) I forget *what* day you said.
(3) Choose *whichever* book you wish.

In these sentences the relative clauses introduced by *which*, *what*, and *whichever* are noun clauses, and are objects of the verbs *knows*, *forget*, and *choose*. At the same time the relative pronouns modify as adjectives the nouns *house*, *day*, and *book*.

95. Relative Adverbs.—Somewhat in the same way as the relative adjectives, certain words combine in themselves the function of a relative pronoun and an adverb. For example, in the sentence, *This is the hour when he* *is expected,* the clause *when he is expected* is plainly an adjective clause limiting *hour* in the same way that the equivalent relative clause limits it in the following form of the sentence: *This is the hour at which he is expected.* Yet the word *when* has plainly also the value of an adverb of time, and such words are best designated as **Relative Adverbs.** Other examples are as follows:

> (1) This is the house where Hawthorne was born, *equivalent to* This is the house in which Hawthorne was born.
> (2) I know no source whence he could have derived it, *equivalent to* I know no source from which he could have derived it.

The relative adverb may also be used in connection with a preposition, forming a compound word equivalent to a preposition and its object, as in the sentence, *That is the only place wherein you have fallen short,* equivalent to *That is the only place in which you have fallen short.*

96. Parsing.—In parsing a relative pronoun, give (1) its kind, whether restrictive or non-restrictive, double or compound, (2) its number, (3) its case and construction, (4) its antecedent, and (5) tell what clauses it joins, and whether the relative clause is an adjective or a noun clause. The relatives in the sentence, *The man, who had come to examine it twice, decided to buy the house that faced the street,* are parsed as follows:

> *who* is a non-restrictive relative pronoun, singular number, nominative case, subject of the verb *had come;* its antecedent is *man,* and it joins the adjective clause, *who had come to examine it twice,* to the antecedent.
> *that* is a restrictive relative pronoun, singular number, nominative case, subject of the verb *faced;* its antecedent is *house,* and it joins the adjective clause *that faced the street,* to the antecedent.

In the sentence, *We gave what we had,* the relative is parsed as follows:

> *what* is a double relative pronoun, singular number; it is used both as the object of *gave* in the principal clause and *had* in the subordinate clause, the sentence being equivalent to *We gave that which we had;* its antecedent is contained within itself, and it joins the noun clause, *What we had,* as object to the principal clause, *We gave.*

Exercises.

Parse the relative pronouns in the following sentences:

(1) To him who has, much shall be given.
(2) Whosoever will may come.
(3) I enjoyed drawing, for which I seemed to have a special aptitude.
(4) They have rights who dare maintain them.
(5) Such of his poems as were original were uninteresting.
(6) The boat after which this one was built won the cup last year.
(7) No one of us, however busy we may think ourselves to be, but has time for a little quiet meditation each day.
(8) The prize shall be his who wins it.
(9)   Who asks does err,
Who answers, errs; say naught.
                         —E. Arnold.
(10) Who is the happy warrior? Who is he
That every man in arms should wish to be?
It is the generous Spirit, who, when brought
Among the tasks of real life, hath wrought
Upon the plan that pleased his boyish thought;
Whose high endeavors are an inward light
That makes the path before him always bright;
Who, with a natural instinct to discern
What knowledge can perform, is diligent to learn;
Who, doomed to go in company with Pain,

And Fear and Bloodshed, miserable train!
Turns his necessity to glorious gain;
In face of these doth exercise a power
Which is our human nature's highest dower;
Controls them and subdues, transmutes, bereaves
Of their bad influence and their good receives.
—WORDSWORTH, *Character of the Happy Warrior.*

97. Interrogative Pronouns. — The **Interrogative Pronouns** are three in number, *who, which,* and *what.* As with the relatives, the only one capable of inflection is *who,* the forms of which are the same as the relative. Since the interrogative pronoun is a word used to stand in place of a noun or pronoun concerning which information is sought, it naturally does not have an antecedent. The chief function of the interrogative pronoun, as its name indicates, is to ask questions.

EXAMPLES:

(1) *Who* told you?
(2) *Whom* do you mean?
(3) *What* will you do?
(4) *What* became of it?
(5) *Which* is the shorter way?
(6) *Which* of the boys is the fastest runner?

The interrogatives *who* and *which* are used of persons, *which* is used of persons and things, but *what* is used only of things.

98. Cases of Interrogatives.—The case of the interrogative pronoun is determined by its use in the sentence. The order of words, however, in the interrogative sentence sometimes differs from that in the declarative sentence, and it is therefore necessary at times to recast the sentence in order to indicate the construction of the words. Thus the sentence, *Whom do you mean?* would be made to read *You do mean whom?* in order to bring out the usual order of subject, predicate, and object.

99. Indirect Questions.—When a question is used as a clause in a declarative sentence, it is called an **Indirect Question.** It is necessary to distinguish clearly the indirect question from the relative clause. In the indirect question the interrogative pronoun is plainly felt as such, and is not a relative pronoun joining an adjective clause to a principal clause. It is easy also to separate the sentence containing an indirect question into its elements, making the indirect question direct. Thus the sentence, *I asked who told him that* is made up of the two elements, *Who told him that?*, an interrogative sentence, and *I asked*, a declarative sentence. The sentence, *I don't know who said it* is made up of the interrogative *Who said it?* and the declarative sentence *I don't know*.

The sentence containing an indirect question is, as a whole, a declarative sentence, and therefore ends with a period.

EXAMPLES:

(1) I wonder   who told him that.
(2) They asked   for whom I had bought it.
(3) He will see   who has it.
(4) I inquired   who it was.
(5) The judge inquired   which of the men had been the last to leave the building.

100. Interrogative Adjectives.—Like the relative adjectives, the interrogatives *which* and *what* are used in asking questions with the combined values of interrogative pronouns and of adjectives. In such constructions they are called **Interrogative Adjectives.**

EXAMPLES:

(1) *Which* way did you take?
(2) *Which* candidate was elected?
(3) *What* time is it?
(4) *What* flavor do you prefer?

101. Interrogative Adverbs.—Adverbs of time, place, and manner are used in introducing questions. They are then called interrogative adverbs, and should be distinguished from interrogative pronouns and adjectives. See **202.**

EXAMPLES:

(1) *When* will they come?
(2) *Where* have you been?

Interrogative adverbs may combine with prepositions forming compound words equivalent to a preposition and its object. See **95.**

EXAMPLES:

(1) Wherein have I failed? *Equivalent to* In what have I failed?
(2) Wherewith shall we be fed? *Equivalent to* With what shall we be fed?

102. Clauses introduced by interrogative adjectives and interrogative adverbs may also take the form of indirect questions.

EXAMPLES:

(1) I don't know *which way we ought to take.*
(2) He wanted to know *what horse to drive.*
(3) I wonder *where you have been.*
(4) He inquired *when they would come.*

103. Exclamatory What. In certain very emphatic questions, which thus become exclamatory sentences, the word *what* is used as a sort of introductory word.

EXAMPLES:

(1) *What* a fall was there!
(2) *What* a surprise to see you here!
(3) *What* majesty sat upon his brow!

EXERCISES.

1. Write seven interrogative sentences, using in each a different interrogative pronoun or interrogative adjective.

2. Turn each of these seven sentences into sentences containing an indirect question.

3. Point out the interrogative pronouns, adjectives, and adverbs in the following sentences. Give the case of each interrogative pronoun and show how it is governed.

(1) Who knows where Homer sleeps?
(2) What would you have?
(3) Which house shall we enter?
(4) Who was it that told you this?
(5) From whom or from what book have you received greatest help?
(6) I wonder which horse we had better drive.
(7) Whom did this come from?
(8) What shall we say to that?
(9) Wherefor have ye done this?
(10) I inquired whose authority he considered greater, his or mine.
(11) For what should we be grateful?
(12) In whose name do you speak?
(13) Nobody knows which has the better right to the property.
(14) We wanted to find out what we were expected to do.
(15) When shall we three meet again?

THE PARTS OF SPEECH. 93

(16) What man would have done this for me?
(17) Whom do men say that I am?
(18) After giving the matter careful deliberation, we feel unable to decide what would be the wisest plan to pursue.
(19) Whence comest thou and whither goest thou?
(20) Who would have supposed that he was there all the time?
(21) We felt great curiosity to know for whom the package was intended.
(22) We tried to discover at whose request the regulation had been made.

104. Demonstrative Pronouns.—The **Demonstrative Pronouns** are *this, that* in the singular, and *these, those* in the plural. They are called demonstratives (from Latin, *demonstro,* "I point out") because they indicate something specifically.

EXAMPLES:

(1) *This* is all we can expect.
(2) *That* was not to be expected.
(3) *These* are the first fruits of our labor.
(4) *Those* fit me better.

105. Uses of the Demonstrative.

(a) The demonstratives *this* and *these* are used to point out objects near at hand, as in the sentences, *This is my hat* and *These are your shoes, that* and *those* being used to indicate objects which are relatively more distant, as *That is my hat* and *Those are your shoes.*

(b) *This* and *that* are used in the sense of various things, one thing and another, in sentences like *Some said this and some said that, but no one mentioned the real point.*

(c) *That* and *those* are used in the sense of *the one, the ones,* to prevent repetition of a preceding noun, as in the sentence, *This fish is not as large as that we caught yes-*

terday, or *The cities of Europe are cleaner than those of America.*

(d) *This* and *that*, *these* and *those* are also used in summing up a preceding statement.

EXAMPLES:

(1) To live with due regard for the rights of your neighbors, *this* is the test of true civilization.
(2) To be or not to be, *that* is the question.
(3) How all this wealth was won, *that* is worth reflecting on.
(4) When we realize the danger of it and the little to be gained by success, *these* are thoughts to make one hesitate.

106. Demonstrative Adjectives.—The demonstrative pronoun, like the interrogative, may combine the demonstrative and the adjective function. It is then called the **Demonstrative Adjective.**

EXAMPLES:

(1) *This* house has been sold to *that* man.
(2) *These* houses have been sold to *those* men.

107. "So" as Demonstrative.—Sometimes the word *so*, primarily an adverb, is used with the combined value of adverb and demonstrative pronoun, the latter value predominating.

EXAMPLES:

(1) Is he here? I don't think *so*.
(2) He was poor, but honestly *so*.
(3) I told him *so*.

In these sentences *so* does not mean merely *in that way*, as it would if it were an adverb, as in the sentences, *It was lost so completely that there was no hope of recovering it,* or *I don't know how you do it, but I do it so,* but it is used as practically the equivalent of *that*, and may best be regarded as a demonstrative pronoun.

108. Indefinite Pronouns.—The indefinite pronouns somewhat resemble the demonstratives, but they differ from them in that they indicate objects not by pointing them out specifically, but in a more general and indefinite way. They are numerous, and the following is only an incomplete list of them: *each, neither, either, both, some, such, one, none, other, another, few, many, most, all.* Some of these are compounded, though often the compounds are written without hyphens: *anybody, everybody, nobody, somebody, everyone, each one, each other, one another, everybody else, nobody else, somebody else,* etc.

109. Inflections of the Indefinites.—Of the indefinites only four are capable of inflection: *one*, which takes a possessive *one's* and a plural *ones;* the compounds with *body*, which take a possessive *body's;* the compounds with *else*, which take a possessive *else's;* and *other*, which takes a possessive *other's* and a plural *others.*

EXAMPLES:

(1) It is *one's* duty to do so.
(2) These are not the *ones* I hoped you would bring.
(3) It isn't *anybody's* business.
(4) It isn't *anybody else's* business.
(5) They studied *each other's* lessons.
(6) They could wear *one another's* clothes.
(7) I like the *others* better.

The following sentences illustrate the uses of the indefinites:

SIMPLE INDEFINITES:

(1) *Each* took his seat without further disturbance.
(2) *Either* will do for me.
(3) *Some* were much better than *others*.
(4) *One* would be glad to think so if *one's* judgment were not likely to be called in question.
(5) *Another* will do as well.
(6) *Few*, if *any*, succeed in that way.
(7) *Most*, if not *all*, were satisfied.
(8) *Such* are the ways of the wicked.
(9) *None* was better pleased than he.
(10) *None* were permitted to enter.

COMPOUND INDEFINITES:

(1) *Anybody* could do that if he had time.
(2) *Somebody* gave me this book, but I forget who it was.
(3) *Everybody else* had gone to his seat.
(4) He had taken *somebody else's* hat.

The possessive of *else* may stand in the absolute position, as in the sentence, *Is this your hat? No, it must be somebody else's.*

110. Indefinite Adjectives.—All the indefinites, except *none*, may combine the function of the pronoun and the adjective, so as to form **Indefinite Adjectives**. The word *every* is used only as an indefinite adjective.

EXAMPLES:

(1) *Each* boy took his seat.
(2) *Another* clue has been discovered.
(3) *Such* apples can be found only here.
(4) *Neither* side would yield.
(5) *Some* men never recognize other's rights.
(6) We tried *every* plan we could think of.

111. Each other, one another.—The compound indefinites *each other* and *one another* are used interchangeably to express a mutual relation between two or more persons, as in the sentence, *They hated each other with a consuming hatred,* or *They hated one another with a consuming hatred.*

112. Repetition of one.—When the simple indefinite *one* is referred to again in the same sentence, the pronoun *one* itself is repeated.

EXAMPLE:

One does not know when *one* will have to pick up and leave.

But the compound indefinites *anyone, everyone, anybody, everybody, somebody,* etc., are always referred to by the forms of the third person singular masculine of the personal pronouns, *he, his, him.*

EXAMPLES:

(1) *Anyone* who is not satisfied with *his* share, will say so.
(2) *Everybody* was satisfied with *his* share.
(3) *Nobody* was satisfied with *his* share.
(4) *Everybody* must do as *he* thinks best for *himself*.

EXERCISES.

Pick out all the words in the following sentences which have pronominal function, tell the special class to which each belongs, and give its other grammatical characteristics.

(1) His career was memorable not so much for what he did as for what he caused others to do.
(2) Mistakes themselves are often the best teachers.
(3) When each man is true to himself, then must all things prosper.

(4) Our sweetest songs are those that tell of saddest thought.
(5) It is not desirable to go out of one's way to be original, but it is to be hoped that it may lie in one's way.
(6) Rip Van Winkle, however, was one of those happy mortals, of foolish, well-oiled dispositions, who take the world easy, eat white bread or brown, whichever can be got with least thought or trouble, and who would rather starve on a penny than work for a pound.
(7) How far away from us do you think the sun is? On a fine summer's day, when we can see him clearly, it looks as if we had only to get into a balloon and reach him as he sits in the sky, and yet we know roughly that he is more than ninety-one millions of miles distant from our earth.
(8) But yesterday the word of Cæsar might
Have stood against the world: now lies he there,
And none so poor to do him reverence.
O masters, if I were dispos'd to stir
Your hearts and minds to mutiny and rage,
I should do Brutus wrong and Cassius wrong,
Who, you all know, are honorable men.

SUMMARY OF DEFINITIONS: THE PRONOUN.

66. Pronouns are words which indicate persons or objects without using the nouns which name these persons or objects. Pronouns stand in place of nouns.

67. (a) A **Personal Pronoun** indicates the person speaking, the person spoken to, or the person or object spoken of.

(b) **Relative Pronouns** are used to join the subordinate clauses of complex sentences to the words on which they depend.

(c) **Interrogative Pronouns** are used to introduce questions.

(d) **Demonstrative Pronouns** indicate persons or things emphatically and definitely.

(e) **Indefinite Pronouns** indicate persons or things generally and indefinitely.

68. The noun which the pronoun takes the place of is called its **Antecedent.**

99. When a question is used as a clause in a declarative sentence it is called an **Indirect Question.**

QUESTIONS AND SUGGESTIONS FOR REVIEW.

1. Define the pronoun, and name the five different kinds of pronouns. 2. What is the Antecedent of a pronoun? 3. What grammatical characteristics do the personal pronouns show by inflection? 4. Give the inflections of the personal pronouns of the first, second, and third persons. 5. What is the order of the personal pronouns when two or more are used in a series? 6. Describe the use of *it* as an impersonal pronoun. 7. Describe the use of *it* as anticipatory subject. 8. Give some examples of compound personal pronouns. 9. Select three sentences from some book, each of which contains one or more relative subordinate clauses, and determine whether the subordinate clauses are noun or adjective clauses. 10. Find three sentences in which restrictive relative pronouns are used, and the same number in which non-restrictive relatives are used. 11. Find three sentences in which the relative pronoun is omitted. 12. Give the inflections of the relative *who*. 13. How do you determine the case of a relative pronoun in a sentence? Find a sentence in which the relative is in the nominative case, another in which it is in

the possessive case, another in which it is the object of a verb, and another in which it is the object of a preposition. 14. Give three sentences illustrating the use of the relative adjective. 15. Name the interrogative pronouns. 16. Which of these is capable of inflection? 17. How do you determine the case of an interrogative pronoun in a sentence? 18. What is an indirect question? 19. Give three sentences illustrating the use of the interrogative adjective. 20. Name the main uses of the demonstrative pronouns. 21. Give three sentences illustrating the use of the demonstrative adjective. 22. Name some of the most common indefinite pronouns. 23. Which of these are capable of inflection? 24. Give three sentences illustrating the use of the indefinite adjective.

The Adjective.

113. Adjectives.—It is often necessary not only to name objects but also to mention some accompanying characteristic or descriptive detail that will serve more nearly to indicate the object. Thus we may say *He bought an apple;* but we may wish also to say more about the apple, and so may add further details, as, for example, *He bought a large, yellow apple.* The words *large* and *yellow* are adjectives, and such adjectives as these are called **Descriptive** or **Qualifying Adjectives,** because they give some quality or descriptive feature of the nouns.

But we may want to add to the meaning of the noun not by giving some descriptive detail, such as color, size, or other characteristic, but (a) by some indication of number or quantity, as *All* men are born free and equal, *Twenty* sheep were lost, etc., or (b) by indicating the country, people, or person with which the object for which the noun stands is connected, as *the American* Constitution, *the Roman* baths, *Spartan* courage, etc. We have, accordingly, three kinds of adjectives, (1) Descriptive Adjectives, (2) Adjectives of Quantity, and (3) Proper Adjectives. These three kinds of adjectives are illustrated in the following sentences; tell to which class each adjective belongs.

(1) On our *second* trip to the woods, we found the *lost* child.
(2) The *Napoleonic* wars disturbed the peace of Europe for *twenty* years.
(3) This is the *last* time our *obliging* postman will call.
(4) A *furious* snowstorm was raging with *midwinter* violence.

114. Pronominal Adjectives.—We have already spoken in preceding paragraphs (see **94, 100, 106, 110**) of relative pronouns, interrogative, demonstrative, and indefinite pronouns which are used with adjective as well as pronominal function. Adjectives of these various kinds may all be grouped together as **Pronominal Adjectives.**

115. Possessive Adjectives.—At first glance it might seem that the possessive case of the noun and pronoun in the sentence, *John's cap is like his coat*, should be classed as adjectives, because they limit the nouns *cap* and *coat* very much as a demonstrative pronoun does by pointing out just which and whose cap and coat are meant. They thus resemble the adjective in function, and they might be classed as Possessive Adjectives. On the other hand, they are distinctively felt to be cases of a noun and a pronoun, and as this is their usual function, it seems best to classify them as such.

116. Nouns as Adjectives.—Words which usually are nouns become adjectives when they are used with adjective function. Thus *glass*, in a *glass house;* *tin*, in *a tin drinking-cup;* *coal*, in *a coal fire;* *water*, in *a water famine*, are all adjectives. Sometimes the noun thus used with adjective function is written together with another noun, thus forming a compound noun, as in *house-dog, window-sill, book-worm,* etc., in which case the whole is to be taken together as one word.

117. Adjectives as Nouns.—On the other hand, when used with noun function certain adjectives become nouns. Thus *good*, in *The good die young*, and *brave* and *fair*, in *None but the brave deserve the fair*, are nouns.

EXAMPLES:

Ah! Well-a-day! what evil looks
Had I from *old* and *young!*
Instead of the cross, the Albatross
About my neck was hung.

118. Comparison.—Adjectives may indicate different degrees of the quality which they name, as, for example:

This is a high tree.
This is a higher tree.
This is the highest tree.

This change in the adjective to indicate difference of degree is called its **Comparison**. The first form of the adjective, which denotes simple quality, is the **Positive Degree**. The second, which compares an object with another, is the **Comparative Degree,** and the third, which indicates that an object has the highest degree of the quality expressed by the adjective, is the **Superlative**

Degree. The adjective has two ways of expressing comparison: (1) by adding the syllable *-er* to the positive to form the comparative degree, and *-est* to the positive to form the superlative degree; (2) by prefixing the adverb *more* to the positive and *most* to the positive to form respectively the comparative and superlative degrees.

EXAMPLES:

POSITIVE. He is an able man.
COMPARATIVE. He is an abler man than his brother. He is a more able man than his brother.
SUPERLATIVE. He is the ablest of the brothers. He is the most able of the brothers.

119. Irregular Comparison.—The following adjectives have one or more irregular forms in their comparison:

Positive.	Comparative.	Superlative.
bad, evil, ill	worse	worst
far	farther	farthest
fore	former	foremost, first
[forth, *adverb*]	further	furthest
good, well	better	best
late	later, latter	latest, last
little	less	least
many, much	more	most
near	nearer	nearest, next
old	older, elder	oldest, eldest

120. Comparative with than.—When a comparative is used with *than*, the person or object which is compared must always be excluded from the general class with which it is compared. Thus the sentence, *My father is older than all the family put together*, must read *My father is older than all the rest of the family put together;* the sentence, *Texas is larger than any state in the Union* must be *Texas is larger than any other state in the Union;* the sentence, *The governor is more powerful than any officer in the state*, must be, *The governor is more powerful than any other officer in the state.*

121. Constructions of the Adjective.—The adjective may modify a noun in one of several ways:

(1) **Attributive Adjective.**—The usual position of the adjective is immediately before the noun which it modifies, as, for example, *white*, in *He drove a white horse.* The adjective is then called an **Attributive Adjective.**

(2) **Appositive Adjective.**—Instead of preceding its noun, sometimes the adjective immediately follows it, standing in somewhat the same relation to the noun that an appositive noun does to its appositional noun. Such an adjective is called an **Appositive Adjective.** The two adjectives *dark* and *heavy* in the sentence, *The cloud, dark and heavy, threatened to break every moment,* are examples of the appositive adjective.

(3) **Predicate Adjective.**—When the adjective is used after a form of the verb *to be* (see **53**), or some other copulative verb (see **134**), in the construction similar to the construction of the noun in the predicate nominative, it is called a **Predicate Adjective.**

EXAMPLES:

(1) This orange is *sour*.
(2) The new president was *eager* to take up his duties.
(3) He looks *angry*.
(4) This apple smells *sweet*, but it tastes *sour*.
(5) The night grew *darker*.
(6) You seem *well*.

(4) **Objective Complement.**—The object of a verb is sometimes limited by an adjective which is necessary to complete the meaning of the verb and object. This adjective is called the **Objective Complement.**

EXAMPLES:

(1) They laid the country *waste*.
(2) They licked the platter *clean*.
(3) His keepers drove him *mad* by their cruelty.
(4) The pot called the kettle *black*.

122. Phrases and Clauses as Adjectives.—Certain groups of words as wholes sometimes perform the functions of adjectives in that they modify some noun. These groups of words are called **Adjective Phrases** or **Clauses.** They are as follows:

(1) **Prepositional Adjective Phrases** consist of a preposition with its dependent words used with the value of an adjective. Thus, in *a man of wealth, of wealth* is a prepositional adjective phrase modifying *man*, and is equivalent to the adjective *wealthy*. In the sentence, *A man with a green flap over his eye was seen to enter the back door of the house*, the adjective prepositional phrase, *with a green flap*, modifies *man*, the phrase, *over his eye*, modifies *flap*, and the phrase, *of the house*, modifies *door*.

(2) **Relative Clauses** may be used with the function of adjectives (see **81**).

EXAMPLES:

(1) The house *which I have bought* is not a new one.
(2) We found the book *for which we had been searching.*
(3) This is the house *that Jack built.*

(3) **Verbal Phrases,** that is, phrases introduced by a participle or an infinitive, the nature of which is explained below (**164** and following) have sometimes the function of adjectives, and are to be classed as **Adjective Verbal Phrases.** In the sentence, *The train, rushing forward at full speed, was immediately derailed,* the participial phrase, *rushing forward at full speed,* has the value of an adjective limiting *train.* In the sentence, *They begged for bread to eat, to eat* is an infinitive phrase with adjective value, modifying *bread.*

EXAMPLES:

(1) *Sitting around the fire,* we began to tell stories.
(2) I found the poor old dog *sleeping in the sun.*
(3) Here is money *to pay for what you need.*
(4) His clothing, *draggled and torn from much hard use,* hardly clung to his body.

123. Articles.—The two words, *the,* and *a, an,* which are called **Articles,** require special treatment because of the peculiarities of their use. By their nature, and, historically, by their origin, they are closely related to the adjective, particularly to the demonstrative adjective. Yet in modern times their adjective function has become very much weakened, and at times they hardly seem to have any value at all. The following sentences illustrate the main differences in their use:

(1) *The* boat put off from shore. (2) *A* boat put off from shore.
(3) *The* owl was captured. (4) *An* owl was captured.

The first sentence might be paraphrased as follows: The boat, which we knew about, put off from shore. It supposes some definite boat. The second sentence might be paraphrased: Some boat or other put off from shore. In this sentence there is no indication that any definite boat was in the mind of the speaker.

The article *the* is called the **Definite Article** because it is used when definite or specific persons or things are mentioned.

The article *a, an* is called the **Indefinite Article** because it is used when persons or things are named in an indefinite and general way.

The article *the* is used with a singular noun to indicate the kind or species of objects indicated by the **noun**.

Examples:

(1) The alligator is an amphibious animal.
(2) High altitudes are sought out by the chamois.
(3) The steam engine is a comparatively recent invention.

124. A and **An.**—In the use of the indefinite article, the form *a* is used before words beginning with a consonant.

Examples:

(1) A stiff breeze was blowing.
(2) He tried to build a hut.
(3) There was a great waste of material in the process.

Before certain words which are spelled with an initial vowel, but are pronounced as though they began with a consonant, *a* is also used.

EXAMPLES:

(1) He wore a uniform of bright red.
(2) It was a eulogy to be proud of.
(3) They brought a utensil in which they prepared their food.
(4) He is not a European.
(5) We found not a one in all our search.

The form *an* is used before words beginning with a vowel.

EXAMPLES:

(1) Robin Hood was an outlaw.
(2) He took an interest in the matter.
(3) They made an apology.

Before words which are spelled with an initial *h*, the form *an* is sometimes used. In such instances, the initial *h*, usually in an unaccented syllable, has almost entirely disappeared from pronunciation, and the word thus practically begins with a vowel. Usage varies, however, in cases of this sort, and the form *a* may be used in both instances.

EXAMPLES:

a herald	an heraldic device
	or
	a heraldic device.
a history	an historical novel
	or
	a historical novel.

125. When two or more nouns refer to the same person or thing, the article is used only with the first of the group.

Thus the phrase, *The author and publisher*, in the sentence, *The author and publisher of this book deserves great praise*, means that the author and publisher are one and the same person. So, also, *a citizen and householder of the town*, in *They killed a citizen and householder of the town*, means but one person who was citizen and householder. When the two nouns refer to different persons or things, the article must be repeated with each, as in *The uncle and the guardian of the boy have come to visit him;* or, *The author and the publisher of this book deserve great praise.*

EXERCISE.

Give the reasons for using, or for omitting to use, the articles, as the case may be, before the nouns in the following sentences:

(1) Which do you like better, the picture or the frame?
(2) The bison, or buffalo, is almost extinct.
(3) The occupant and the owner of this house have a hard time to get along.
(4) Washington, the soldier and statesman, was the first great American.
(5) A white and a black cow were in the field.
(6) A white and black cow was in the field.
(7) Yesterday we visited my cousin, the captain and coach of the football team.
(8) We called on the manager, the captain, and the coach of the football team.

126. Parsing the Adjective.—In parsing the adjective tell (1) the kind of adjective it is, (2) the degree of its comparison, if it has comparison, (3) the noun or pronoun which it modifies, (4) the way in which it modifies a noun or pronoun, whether attributively, appositively, as predicate adjective, or as objective complement. In parsing the adjective phrase or clause, tell (1) what kind of phrase or clause it is, (2) what word the phrase or clause modifies. In the sentence, *This old house, ramshackle and deserted, is the one in which my grandfather was born,* the adjectives are parsed as follows:

> *This* is a pronominal, demonstrative adjective, and it is an attributive modifier of the noun *house.*
>
> *old* is a descriptive adjective, positive degree; it modifies *house* attributively.
>
> *ramshackle* and *deserted* are descriptive adjectives; they are in the positive degree and modify *house* as appositive adjectives.
>
> *the* is a definite article and it modifies the pronoun *one.*
>
> *in which my grandfather was born* is a relative adjective clause, modifying the pronoun *one.*

EXERCISE.

Parse all the adjectives in the following sentences, and point out the adjective phrases and clauses, indicating what words they modify.

BEFORE THE BLIZZARD.

The day was warm and sunny. The eaves dripped musically, and the icicles, dropping from the roof, fell occasionally with pleasant crash. The snow grew slushy, and the bells of wood-teams jingled merrily all the forenoon, as the farmers drove to their timber lands five or six miles away. The room was uncomfortably warm at times, and the master opened the outside door. It was the eighth day of January. During the afternoon recess, as the boys were playing in their shirt-sleeves, Lincoln called Milton's attention to a great cloud rising in the west and north—a vast, slaty-blue, seamless dome, silent, portentous, with edges of silvery, frosty light. . . . When Lincoln set out for home, the sun was still shining, but the edge of the cloud had crept, or more properly slid, across the sun's disk, and

its light was growing cold and pale. In fifteen minutes more the wind from the south ceased—there was a moment of breathless pause, and then, borne on the wings of the north wind, the streaming clouds of soft, large flakes of snow drove in a level line over the homeward-bound scholars, sticking to their clothing and faces and melting rapidly.
—GARLAND, *Boy Life on the Prairie.*

SUMMARY OF DEFINITIONS: THE ADJECTIVE.

113. An **Adjective** is a word which limits or modifies the meaning of a noun or pronoun.

118. The change in the adjective to indicate difference of degree is called its **Comparison.** The adjective has three degrees of comparison, the **Positive,** the **Comparative,** and the **Superlative.**

121. (3) When the adjective is used after a form of the verb *to be,* or some other copulative verb, it is called a **Predicate Adjective.**

123. The **Article** *the* is called the **Definite Article** because it is used when definite or specific persons or things are mentioned.

The **Article** *a, an,* is called the **Indefinite Article** because it is used when persons or things are named in an indefinite and general way.

QUESTIONS AND SUGGESTIONS FOR REVIEW.

1. Define the adjective, and tell what is meant by descriptive or qualifying adjectives, numeral adjectives, and proper adjectives. Give illustrations of each kind. 2. Why is not the possessive case of the noun and pronoun to be regarded as an adjective? 3. How may nouns be-

come adjectives? How may adjectives become nouns? Give illustrations. 4. What is meant by the comparison of the adjective? 5. Name the three degrees of comparison. 6. What two ways has the adjective of indicating comparison? 7. Give some illustrations of irregular comparison. 8. What is meant by the term predicate adjective? By objective complement? Give illustrations. 9. In some passage of literature find five examples of prepositional adjective phrases, and the same number of relative adjective clauses. 10. Name the definite and the indefinite articles. 11. State the conditions under which the two forms of the indefinite article are used. 12. State the rule for the use of the article with two or more nouns referring to the same person or thing and to different persons or things. Give sentences in illustration.

The Verb.

127. The Verb.—It is the function of the verb in the sentence to make a statement with respect to the person or object named by the noun or pronoun. The verb may express action with respect to the noun or pronoun, as in the sentence, *The citizens elected him mayor;* or it may express merely the state of being of the person or object named by the noun or pronoun, as in the sentence, *He is the mayor.* We therefore define the verb as follows: The **Verb** is a word, or, in the case of the verb-phrase, a word-group, which asserts action or state of being with respect to some noun or pronoun.

Exercise.

Review **10-16,** and pick out all the verbs in the exercises given under **23** and **96.**

128. Classification of the Verb.—Verbs are classified with respect to the way in which they make assertions as **Transitive, Intransitive,** and **Copulative Verbs.**

129. Transitive Verbs.—A transitive verb is one in which the assertion of the verb passes over from one person or thing, the grammatical subject, from which or whom the action proceeds, to another person or thing, the grammatical object, which is directly affected by the action of the verb. Every sentence which contains an object must contain a transitive verb.

EXAMPLES OF TRANSITIVE VERBS:

(1) John *struck* James.
(2) The hunter *shot* the squirrel.
(3) Charles *whistled* a tune.
(4) I *found* the book which you lost.
(5) I have *met* your brother.
(6) *Have* you *seen* my hat?
(7) I *heard* that you were ill.

130. Intransitive Verbs.—An intransitive verb is one in which the action of the verb does not pass over from the subject causing the action to an object immediately affected by the action, but in which the action is completely expressed by the subject and predicate. Intransitive verbs, therefore, do not have objects.

EXAMPLES:

(1) The wind *rose.*
(2) You *have come* in good season.
(3) The rain *fell* in torrents.
(4) The workmen *struck* for higher wages.
(5) Why *do* you *laugh?*
(6) We *lay* on the grass and *talked.*

131. Transitivity.—Some verbs which are transitive in one sentence may be intransitive in another. The verb *write*, in *This child can't write*, is intransitive, but in *He wrote an essay*, it is transitive. Whether a verb is transitive or intransitive can only be told from its use in the sentence. The following are only a few of the many verbs which may be used either transitively or intransitively:

Transitive.	*Intransitive.*
(1) She *plays* the piano.	She *plays* well.
(2) He *ran* a hotel.	He *ran* away.
(3) He *breathed* new life into the movement.	He *breathed* with difficulty.
(4) The rocks *broke* the ship into pieces.	The waves *broke* over the ship.
(5) Who *wrote* this book?	When *will* you *write*?
(6) I *sent* a message to you.	Your father *has sent* for you.
(7) He *is seeking* a position. Do you know where he *can find* one?	Those who *seek* shall *find*.
(8) *Can* you *sail* a boat?	Do you like *to sail*?

132. Cognate Object.—Some verbs which are usually intransitive become transitive when they are followed by an object of like meaning. This object is called the **Cognate Object.**

EXAMPLES:

Intransitive.	*Transitive.*
(1) The boys *ran*.	The boys *ran* a *race*.
(2) He *sleeps*.	He *sleeps* the *sleep* of the just.
(3) They *fought* fiercely all day.	We *have fought* a good *fight*.

It should be noted that *ran* in *He ran a mile, talk* in *He talked two hours*, etc., are not transitive verbs, and that *mile* and *hours* are not objects of *ran* and *talked*, but are adverbial modifiers of the verbs; see **206** (2).

133. Copulative Verbs.—Notice how the verbs in the following sentences make assertions with respect to their subjects:

(1) That man *is* the mayor of the city.
(2) The brothers *were* members of the same organization
(3) He *has been* president for two years.
(4) They *remained* trustees of the club.
(5) The captain *seemed* a well-meaning person.
(6) The privates soon *became* officers.

In these sentences the verbs do not express positive action, not what the subject does, but rather what it is. They assert, therefore, a state of being rather than an action which passes over from a subject to an object. What these verbs do is simply to join two nouns into a sort of equation; they assert that the object named by the noun or pronoun which precedes the verb is the same as that which follows it. Thus we might replace the verbs merely by the sign of equality and get the same meaning: *That man=the mayor of the city*, or *He=president for two years*, etc. Since the chief use of these verbs is to unite words into this sort of equation, they are called **Copulative Verbs,** a word which means to couple or link together. The principal copulative verbs are *am, is, are, was, were, been, seem, remain, become.*

The subjects of all verbs are in the nominative case; the object of a transitive verb is in the objective case; but the noun or pronoun which the copulative verb joins to the subject is in the **Predicate Nominative Case.** The forms of the personal pronoun which are used after the copula are therefore the nominative forms.

EXAMPLES:

(1) It is *I*.
(2) That man on the last seat was *he*.
(3) I thought it was *she*.
(4) I should not have guessed that it was *he*.

The copulative verb is not always followed by a predicate nominative, but it may assert state of being with respect only to a subject.

EXAMPLES:

(1) The apples *were* in the house.
(2) *Were* you here yesterday? I *was*.
(3) The saddest words of tongue or pen
Are these: It *might have been*.

NOTE.—In colloquial speech *It is me* is often used and must be regarded as permissible, though not the most careful, use. But *It is him* and *It is her* are heard only in the speech of the very careless and the uneducated.

134. Predicate Adjective.—When the copulative verb is followed by an adjective, as in *He is sick, They were glad to see him, Your father seems well*, the adjective is called a **Predicate Adjective.** The number of verbs which can be used thus as copulative verbs followed by predicate adjectives is much larger than the number of those which are followed by predicate nominatives. The following are a few of the more common:

(1) He *grew old* rapidly.
(2) This fruit *looks fresh*.
(3) The ground *feels warm*.
(4) The flowers *smell sweet*.

(5) This milk *tastes sour.*
(6) It *turned sour* last night.
(7) He *flushed red.*
(8) The violins *sound* a little *loud.*

NOTE.—In constructions of this nature the verb often has quite as much asserting value as most intransitive verbs. The only thing which prevents their being classed simply as intransitive verbs is the fact that they may be followed by a predicate adjective. They seem to combine, therefore, the functions of the copulative and the intransitive verbs, a sentence like *This fruit looks fresh* being equivalent to *This fruit is fresh in its looks.*

135. Inflections of the Verb : Tense.—The verb in its inflections has a large number of different forms and uses. The first of these to be considered is that of Tense. In the sentences, *My brother lives in California* and *My brother lived in California,* the first sentence indicates an action as still continuing in present time, the other indicates an action which took place in time which is past. We may add to these two sentences still another, in which the verb expresses action which is to take place in time to come, *My brother will live in California.* These distinctions of time expressed by the verb are distinctions of Tense. We have three main tenses in English: present, past, and future.

A verb which asserts action or being in present time is in the **Present Tense.**

A verb which asserts action or being in past time is in the **Past Tense.**

A verb which asserts action or being in time to come is in the **Future Tense.**

EXERCISE.

Give the tenses of the verbs in the following sentences, and change the verbs in the present tense to the corresponding forms of the past tense:

(1) We bought a dozen oranges.
(2) A little steamboat travels up and down the river.
(3) Tom knows the way to the village.
(4) This road leads in the opposite direction.
(5) Thursday will be the last day of June.
(6) You told me to bring you a book, but I think this paper is very interesting.
(7) My bird sings all the time.
(8) You will recognize him when you see him.
(9) He sympathized deeply at his friend's misfortune.
(10) I wonder who has my hat.
(11) We went the quickest way we knew.
(12) I come from haunts of coot and hern,
I make a sudden sally,
And sparkle out among the fern,
To bicker down a valley.

By thirty hills I hurry down,
Or slip between the ridges,
By twenty thorps, a little town,
And half a hundred bridges.
—TENNYSON, *The Brook.*

136. Person.—A second characteristic of the verb is that of **Person.** We say *I sing, You sing,* but *He sings.* We may distinguish here three persons in the verb, just as we distinguish three persons in the pronoun (see **70**). The only inflection of the verb, however, which is distinctive for its person is the third person when the subject of the verb is singular; this form regularly ends in *-s.* We may speak of the person of the other forms of the verb, even though they do not have a distinctive ending, since we may infer the person of the verb from the person of the subject.

137. Number.—Likewise we speak of the **Number** of verbs, meaning thereby that the subject is singular or plural as the case may be. Again, the only form of the verb which is distinctive for number is the third person singular of the present tense, where the ending *-s* serves to indicate both the person and number of the verb. We speak of the other forms of the verb as singular or plural when we see that the subject is singular or plural.

A verb agrees with its subject in **Person** and **Number.**

138. Conjugation.—The inflections of a verb are called its **Conjugation.** The following is the conjugation of the verb *drive* in the present and past tenses:

PRESENT.

PERSON.	*Singular.*	*Plural.*
1.	I drive.	We drive.
2.	You drive.	You drive.
3.	He drives.	They drive.

PAST.

PERSON.	*Singular.*	*Plural.*
1.	I drove.	We drove.
2.	You drove.	You drove.
3.	He drove.	They drove.

The following is the conjugation of the verb *walk* in the present and past tenses:

PRESENT.

PERSON.	*Singular.*	*Plural.*
1.	I walk.	We walk.
2.	You walk.	You walk.
3.	He walks.	They walk.

PAST.

PERSON.	Singular.	Plural.
1.	I walked.	We walked.
2.	You walked.	You walked.
3.	He walked.	They walked.

139. The Verb "to be."—The conjugation of the verb *to be* in the present and past tenses is as follows:

PRESENT.

PERSON.	Singular.	Plural.
1.	I am.	We are.
2.	You are.	You are.
3.	He is.	They are.

PAST.

PERSON.	Singular.	Plural.
1.	I was.	We were.
2.	You were.	You were.
3.	He was.	They were.

140. The Verb "to do."—The conjugation of the verb *to do* in the present and past tenses is as follows:

PRESENT.

PERSON.	Singular.	Plural.
1.	I do.	We do.
2.	You do.	You do.
3.	He does.	They do.

PAST.

PERSON.	Singular.	Plural.
1.	I did.	We did.
2.	You did.	You did.
3.	He did.	They did.

141. Verb-phrases: the Future Tense.—It has already been pointed out that the verb may consist of several words which together constitute a **verb-phrase.** Some of the tenses of the verb cannot be expressed by simple forms like *drive, drove,* but require several words together, that is, verb-phrases, to form the tenses. Thus *shall* and *will* are used in verb-phrases to form the future tense, which is conjugated for the verb *drive* as follows:

FUTURE.

PERSON. *Singular.* *Plural.*
1. I shall drive. We shall drive.
2. You will drive. You will drive.
3. He will drive. They will drive.

Words like *shall, will, have, do, am,* etc., when used to form verb-phrases are known as **Auxiliary Verbs.**

142. The Perfect Tenses.—The forms of the verb *have* are also used to form verb-phrases to express tense. The conjugation of this word, when standing alone, is as follows:

PRESENT.

PERSON. *Singular.* *Plural.*
1. I have. We have.
2. You have. You have.
3. He has. They have.

PAST.

PERSON. *Singular.* *Plural.*
1. I had. We had.
2. You had. You had.
3. He had. They had.

Observe now the times of the verb-phrases in the following sentences:

He has finished his task.
He had finished his task.

In both sentences the verb refers to past time. But they differ somewhat from the simple past, like *I finished*, and demand separate names. In the first of the two sentences, the verb indicates an action which is completed just at the time of speaking. It is called the **Present Perfect Tense**. In the second sentence the verb indicates an action completed at some past time before some other action took place. The verb here is in the **Past Perfect Tense**.

Likewise we may combine the forms of *shall* and *will* with *have* in order to express action that will be completed at some future time, as in the sentence, *You will come before I shall have finished my breakfast*. A verb like *shall have finished* is in the **Future Perfect Tense**.

143. The Perfect Tenses.—We may add, therefore, to the conjugation of the verb (see **138-142**) the following tenses:

PRESENT PERFECT.

PERSON. *Singular.* — *Plural.*
1. I have driven. — We have driven.
2. You have driven. — You have driven.
3. He has driven. — They have driven.

PAST PERFECT.

PERSON. *Singular.* — *Plural.*
1. I had driven. — We had driven.
2. You had driven. — You had driven.
3. He had driven. — They had driven.

FUTURE PERFECT.

PERSON. *Singular.* — *Plural.*
1. I shall have driven. — We shall have driven.
2. You will have driven. — You will have driven.
3. He will have driven. — They will have driven.

PRESENT PERFECT.

Singular.   *Plural.*

PERSON.
1. I have walked.   We have walked.
2. You have walked.   You have walked.
3. He has walked.   They have walked.

PAST PERFECT.

Singular.   *Plural.*

PERSON.
1. I had walked.   We had walked.
2. You had walked.   You had walked.
3. He had walked.   They had walked.

FUTURE PERFECT.

Singular.   *Plural.*

PERSON.
1. I shall have walked.   We shall have walked.
2. You will have walked.   You will have walked.
3. He will have walked.   They will have walked.

The form of the verb which follows *shall* or *will* in verb-phrases is called the **Infinitive.**

The form of the verb which follows *have, has,* or *had* is called the **Past Participle.**

> NOTE.—The future perfect tense is not frequently used. In most instances where the future perfect would be strictly appropriate, the present perfect answers as well. Thus we may say, *I shall come to see you after I shall have finished my visit here,* or *I shall come to see you after I have finished my visit here.*

EXERCISE.

1. Write sentences using each of the following verbs in the six tenses which have thus far been conjugated: *talk, write, find, think, ride, drink, bind.*

2. Insert in the blank spaces of the following sentences appropriate verbs in the right tenses, persons, and numbers:

(1) He ———— his lessons quickly when he tries.
(2) I ———— my new ball yesterday.
(3) Tom ———— to the rack and took his gun.
(4) I ———— known this since yesterday.
(5) Heavy black clouds ———— the sky.
(6) He says he ———— ———— on time.
(7) We ———— one more chance.
(8) After you ———— ———— your lessons, come over and see me.
(9) I ———— ———— by the two o'clock train.
(10) He ———— to New York after he ———— ———— his college course.

144. Shall and Will.—The use of **shall** and **will** in forming verb-phrases to express the future tense, and for other purposes, requires special consideration. The custom of different communities varies in the use of these auxiliaries, especially in every-day speech; and since the standard literary use of them is often made a test of education and cultivation, it behooves every one to know what the standard forms are. The fact seems to be that the feeling for the literary, or standard, use of *shall* and *will* is not firmly fixed in the language. This is partly due to the fact that in daily speech the full forms are seldom used, their place being taken by abbreviated forms like *I'll, you'll, he'll, we'll*, etc., in which the contraction may stand indifferently for *shall* or *will*. The distinction which is made in the careful use of *shall* and *will* often seems therefore artificial. After a little familiarity, however, with the standard forms the feeling of strangeness and artificiality wears off, and one acquires a sense for the correct and standard use of the words.

In expressing simple futurity the following are the standard forms in the various persons:

I shall go.　　　　We shall go.
You will go.　　　You will go.
He will go.　　　 They will go.

In the interrogative forms of the future tense, the proper form for the first person is always *shall*, as also for the second person. The third person uses *will*. The proper forms are as follows:

Shall I go?　　　Shall we go?
Shall you go?　　Shall you go?
Will he go?　　　Will they go?

Examples of Simple Futures:

(1) *I shall have* to come back to-morrow if I don't see him to-day.
(2) If you stay ten minutes longer, *you will still have* time to catch your train.
(3) *He will not pay* any attention to them.
(4) If you can come, *we shall be* glad to see you.
(5) If they can come, *they will be* welcome.
(6) *Shall I see* you at the game to-morrow?
(7) *Shall you go* to the game to-morrow?
(8) *Will he arrive* in time for the rehearsal?
(9) *Shall we go* down this road?
(10) If they wait, *will they have* time to change their clothes?

Exercises.

Insert the proper future forms of the verbs (*shall* or *will*) in the following sentences:

(1) If possible, I —— be there before ten o'clock.
(2) They —— reach here before you are ready.
(3) —— we come now, or —— we wait awhile?
(4) —— you be in town next week?
(5) I don't know if they —— think of it in time.
(6) We doubt if we —— be able to come.

(7) —— I have the pleasure of seeing you to-night?
(8) I wonder if they —— know where to look for us?
(9) Do you think he —— come on time?
(10) —— he have the courage to stick it out?
(11) —— I open the door?
(12) Nothing —— ever make me forget that.
(13) This boy —— be ten years old to-morrow.
(14) A house built on sand —— not endure.
(15) We think we —— come by train and not by boat.
(16) I don't know who —— take care of him.
(17) Of course we like to think that they —— be able to take care of themselves.
(18) He asks me if you —— speak to your father about it.
(19) Do you suppose they —— know where to stop?
(20) I hope we —— not be too early.
(21) They imagine that they —— have enough without it.
(22) You can never tell what —— happen.
(23) I believe I —— never see its like.
(24) We hope that you —— not feel disturbed if we come in here.
(25) We —— have plenty of time, if they —— only slow up at the corner.

145. The past tense of *shall* is *should* and of *will* is *would*, and in forming future verb-phrases with *should* and *would*, one uses *should* where one would use *shall* in the present, and *would* where one would use *will* in the present.

EXAMPLES:

{ He asks if I shall go.
{ He asked if I should go.

{ If you go, you will see him.
{ If you went, you would see him.

{ If they come, they will have a good time.
{ If they came, they would have a good time.

For further discussion of *should* and *would* in forming verb-phrases, see **193**.

EXERCISE.

In the sentences under **144** change *shall* to *should* and *will* to *would* in all the complex sentences, changing also the tenses of the other verbs to agree with *should* and *would*.

146. Other Uses of Shall and Will.—Besides forming simple future verb-phrases, *shall* and *will* form other verb-phrases in which their use differs from the future verb-phrases. Thus, when *will* is used in the first person, it expresses not merely simple futurity, but also a strong added idea of willingness, intention, or determination.

EXAMPLES:

(1) I will send you a copy right away (Willingness or Intention).
(2) We will meet you wherever you wish (Willingness).
(3) I will send it, whether he wants me to or not (Determination).
(4) We will not yield one inch (Determination).

When *shall* is used in the second and third persons, it does not express simple futurity, but threat, command, resolution, or promise.

EXAMPLES:

(1) You shall suffer for this (Threat).
(2) He shall be paid if it takes my last dollar (Resolution).
(3) You shall have a vacation if your lesson is perfect (Promise).
(4) Thou shalt not steal (Command).
(5) Somebody shall suffer for this (Threat).

In the interrogative forms, *shall* is always used in the first person, singular and plural, except occasionally when in the plural it immediately follows a declarative sentence with *will*, indicating willingness or intention, in which case *will* may be repeated in the interrogative sentence. Thus we may say, *We will grant his request, will we not?* (or, in the abbreviated form, *won't we?*); we cannot say, however, *Will we grant his request?*, but must say, *Shall we grant his request?*

In the second person of the interrogative, *will* always implies willingness or desire, as in *Will you be so good as to move your chair a little?* or, *Will you have some more of the chicken?*

In the third person of the interrogative, *shall* expresses command, intention, or resolution, as it does in the direct statement.

EXAMPLES:

(1) Shall he close the door now?
(2) Shall the wicked have any part in the final reward?
(3) Shall there be no more cakes and ale?

The forms of *shall* and *will*, therefore, which are used in verb-phrases expressing something more than simple futurity are as follows:

I will go (Willingness, etc.). We will go (Willingness, etc.).
You shall go (Command, etc.). You shall go (Command, etc.).
He shall go (Command, etc.). They shall go (Command, etc.).

Shall I go? (Command, etc.). Shall we go? (Command, etc.).
Will you go? (Willingness, etc.). Will you go? (Willingness, etc.).
Shall he go? (Command, etc.). Shall they go? (Command, etc.).

Exercise.

In the following sentences determine which of the verb-phrases are simple futures and which have some added meaning, stating just what the added meaning is:

(1) He shall have his share.
(2) I will not inconvenience myself.
(3) The soprano will not sing to-night.
(4) The stars shall obey thy will.
(5) Thou shalt not kill.
(6) What shall we say?
(7) How shall the signal be given?
(8) Will you have tea or coffee?
(9) I will fight it out on this line if it takes all summer.
(10) I will do all I can for him.
(11) Shall you go by boat or train?
(12) They wrote that they would be here at noon.
(13) The officers promised that we should not suffer.
(14) They shall pay dearly for this.
(15) Will you please call at my house?
(16) I hope they will not be in the way.
(17) Nobody knows, until he experiences it, what he will do under such circumstances.
(18) Shall you have time to see me to-morrow?
(19) What will your father say to that?
(20) What shall be done with this coat?
(21) Will you give me another chance?
(22) I will come, if you will promise not to change your plans.
(23) I will be master in my own house.
(24) Nobody will be the wiser or the better for it.
(25) A horse will not eat out of a dirty manger.
(26) Hear me, for I will speak.
(27) Whosoever will, may come.
(28) I shall not yield an inch.
(29) You will compel me then to read the will.

(30) If your critic will examine this matter closely, he will find—at least I hope he will find—that there is more in it than he supposes.

147. Progressive Verb-Phrases.—Certain verb-phrases formed by the aid of the inflected forms of the verb *to be* are used to indicate that the action of the verb is in progress at the time referred to by the tense of the verb. The following examples give the progressive forms of the present tense:

PROGRESSIVE PRESENT TENSE.

PERSON.
Singular.	*Plural.*
1. I am walking.	We are walking.
2. You are walking.	You are walking.
3. He is walking.	They are walking.

The form of the verb which follows *am, are, is*, etc., in progressive verb-phrases, is called the **Present Participle.** It always ends in *-ing.*

148. Past and Future Progressive Verb-Phrases.—The conjugation of the past tense and the future tense in their progressive forms, is as follows:

PAST TENSE.

PERSON.
Singular.	*Plural.*
1. I was walking.	We were walking.
2. You were walking.	You were walking.
3. He was walking.	They were walking.

FUTURE TENSE.

PERSON.
Singular.	*Plural.*
1. I shall be walking.	We shall be walking.
2. You will be walking.	You will be walking.
3. He will be walking.	They will be walking.

Exercise.

Change the verbs in the following sentences into the corresponding progressive forms:

(1) I walked beside the horse which he rode.
(2) A strange man showed the people to their seats.
(3) She stood on the shore and watched the breakers.
(4) He turned the leaves slowly and absent-mindedly.
(5) You follow very uneconomical methods.

149. Emphatic Verb-Phrases.—Verb-phrases formed by the aid of the verb *to do* in the present and past tenses express the action of the verb with emphasis. Compare the following sentences:

I know where it is.	I knew where it was.
I do know where it is.	I did know where it was.

It will be observed that *do know* and *did know* express the same ideas as *know* and *knew*, but express them much more strongly. Such verbs are called **Emphatic Verb-Phrases**.

150. Interrogative and Negative Verb-Phrases.—In questions and negative statements the verb-phrase with *do* is generally used, but in these instances the verb-phrase does not have emphatic value, but is used with the same value as the simple verb.

Examples:

Do you know where it is?	You do not know where it is.
Did you know where it was?	You did not know where it was.

Exercises.

Change the verb-phrases to simple verbs in the following sentences, and tell which are emphatic, which progressive, which interrogative, and which negative:

(1) I do hereby command you to appear before this court.
(2) How it did rain!
(3) I was walking beside the horse which he was riding.
(4) Where do you live now?
(5) I am thinking of a trip to the mountains this summer.
(6) We did not see the summit.
(7) A strange man was showing the people to their seats.
(8) They certainly do suffer from the cold in severe weather.
(9) Did you hear that noise?
(10) I did know his father before, but was glad to see him again.
(11) I did not think it would prove to be so easy.
(12) After much persuasion he finally did go.
(13) We were waiting in the anteroom.
(14) He does shoot with most extraordinary accuracy.
(15) I am waiting for you.

151. There are several special rules that require separate consideration:

(a) The **Future Tense** is regularly formed by the aid of the auxiliaries *shall* and *will* (see **141**), but sometimes we have a future which does not differ in form from the present. In this usage the future is made more vivid, and it is generally used only when the action is immediately impending.

EXAMPLES:

(1) He *arrives* to-morrow on the noon train.
(2) I *leave* to-night at six o'clock.
(3) My brother *comes* to-night, but the rest of the party will not come until to-morrow.

(b) **Habitual Action** is expressed by a verb in the present tense, but without specific reference to present or to future time. The verbs in the following examples express what one is accustomed to do, or what takes place regularly:

(1) I *study* in the afternoon but never at night.
(2) The sun *rises* and the sun *sets* and there *is* no one to heed.
(3) Time and tide *wait* for no man.

152. Contraction.—In colloquial language and informal written language, the verbs *shall, will, have, has, do, does, am, are, is*, etc., when combined with the negative particle *not*, are frequently contracted. The following are the correct forms:

Full Forms.	Contracted Forms.
I shall not.	I sha'n't.
You will not.	You won't.
He will not.	He won't.
We shall not.	We sha'n't.
You will not.	You won't.
They will not.	They won't.
I have not.	I haven't.
You have not.	You haven't.
He has not.	He hasn't.
We have not, etc.	We haven't, etc.
I had not, etc.	I hadn't, etc.
I do not.	I don't.
You do not.	You don't.
He does not.	He doesn't.
We do not, etc.	We don't, etc.
I am not.	I'm not.
You are not.	You're not, *or* You aren't.
He is not.	He's not, *or* He isn't.
We are not, etc.	We aren't, etc.
I was not.	I wasn't.
You were not.	You weren't.
He was not.	He wasn't.
We were not, etc.	We weren't, etc.

153. The Number of Verbs.—One or two special applications of the rule that a verb agrees with its subject in number must be noted.

(a) **A Compound Subject,** the parts of which are connected by *and*, is usually followed by a verb in the plural number.

EXAMPLES:

(1) Tom and his brother were in the yard.
(2) The horse and his keeper love each other.
(3) Time and tide wait for no man.

Rare exceptions to this rule occur when the subject is made up of two nouns so closely related in meaning that they may be regarded as constituting a single idea. In such instances the verb may be singular.

EXAMPLES:

(1) The *cause and origin* of all this *is* not hard to find.
(2) The *end and aim* of life *is* to succeed.
(3) A *truce and conference was agreed* upon.
(4) The *shouting and the tumult dies*,
 The captains and the Kings depart,
 Still stands thine ancient sacrifice,
 An humble and a contrite heart.
 —KIPLING, *The Recessional.*
(5) The *boast* of heraldry, the *pomp* of power,
 And *all* that beauty, all that wealth e'er gave,
 Awaits alike th' inevitable hour:—
 The paths of glory lead but to the grave.
 —GRAY, *Elegy.*

(b) **A Compound Subject,** the parts of which are connected by *or, either . . . or, neither . . . nor*, usually takes a verb in the singular.

EXAMPLES:

(1) The wagon or the carriage usually *stands* here.
(2) Either Tom or Jerry *makes* this distance in half an hour.
(3) Neither he nor I *was* to see that day.

(c) **Collective Nouns** take sometimes a singular and sometimes a plural verb, the number of the verb depending upon the way in which the subject is regarded. When the individual objects or persons which make up the collective noun are thought of as individuals, the verb is usually plural; when they are thought of as together constituting a single idea, a unit, the verb is singular.

EXAMPLES:

(1) The jury *was* unable to come to a decision.
[The jury is here thought of as a single thing, without stress upon the fact that it is composed of a number of individuals.]
(2) The jury were a long time in making up their minds.
[In this sentence the idea uppermost in the mind is the fact that the jury is made up of individuals.]
(3) The *family was cared for* by the local charity organization.
(4) The *family were* all very much disturbed about the matter.
(5) The audience *was* not a large one.
(6) The audience *were* of many minds with respect to the performance.

(d) Nouns which have a plural form, but which are singular in meaning, usually take a singular verb.

EXAMPLES:

(1) The *news was* not unexpected
(2) *Quadratics comes* next in the book.
(3) *Marbles is* a boy's game.
(4) *Mumps doesn't* make one very sick.

But here again the same rule applies as in the case of collective nouns. When the subject is thought of as plural, the verb is also plural.

EXAMPLES:

(1) *Ethics is* the study of morals. (Singular.)
(2) The *ethics* of a people *are* an index of their civilization. (Plural.)
(3) *Athletics is* a recognized part of modern education. (Singular.)
(4) *Athletics take up* too much of his time. (Plural.)

154. Regular and Irregular Verbs.—Verbs are classified as **Regular** or **Irregular** in accordance with the manner in which they form their past tenses and past participles. Observe the following forms:

Present.	*Past.*
I walk, etc.	I walked.
I love.	I loved.
I hate.	I hated.
I drive, etc.	I drove.
I sing.	I sang.
I drink.	I drank.
I bear.	I bore.

It will be seen that these verbs form their past tenses in two different ways, the verbs of the first class by adding -*d* or -*ed* to the uninflected form of the present, the verbs of the second class by changing the root-vowel of the present. Verbs which form their past in the first manner are called **Regular Verbs,** those which form their past in the second manner are called **Irregular Verbs.** The regular verbs are far the more numerous in the language.

NOTE.—Some grammars call the Irregular Verbs strong verbs and the Regular Verbs, weak verbs. The origin of the terminology strong and weak is as follows: Strong verbs were so called because they could form their past tenses by internal change without calling in outside help; weak verbs were so named because they had to call in the aid of the syllable -*d* or -*ed* to form their past tenses. The terminology strong and weak, though somewhat fanciful, is historically the better one, and if we were studying the English language historically, we should have to use it. The terms do not, however, describe the state of affairs of modern English, since many verbs which are historically **weak**, like *buy, bought, bought,* have now all the appearance of strong or **irregular** verbs. Since, therefore, the weak, or regular class, is the more numerous and the normal one in modern English, it seems best to class such **verbs** together and to place all others in the class of irregular verbs.

155. Past Participles and Principal Parts.—The past participles of the regular verbs are always the same as their past tenses, but the past participle of the irregular verbs are usually different both from the present and the past tense. The first person singular of the present tense, of the past tense, and the past participle of a verb are together called its **Principal Parts.**

156. Principal Parts of Regular Verbs.—As has already been stated, the past tense and the past participle of most regular verbs is formed by adding -*d* or -*ed* to the uninflected form of the present. When the present ends in *y*, however, this ending is sometimes changed to -*i* before the ending -*d* or -*ed* is added.

EXAMPLES:

Present Tense.	*Past Tense.*	*Past Participle.*
like	liked	liked
talk	talked	talked
work	worked	worked
shade	shaded	shaded
rely	relied	relied
ally	allied	allied
defy	defied	defied
reply	replied	replied
say	said	said
pay	paid	paid
lay	laid	laid
play	played	played
employ	employed	employed
decay	decayed	decayed
convey	conveyed	conveyed

157. Irregular Verbs.—The principal parts of the irregular verbs must be learned by heart, as there is no general rule governing the formation of them all. They are, however, among the most familiar words of the language, and there are not many occasions when one is likely to make a mistake. It should be observed that sometimes a verb has a regular form and also an irregular form, like *kneel, kneeled, kneeled,* besides *kneel, knelt, knelt,* or *light, lighted, lighted,* besides *light, lit, lit.* Occasionally, also, we have verbs of which the principal parts are all alike, such as the verbs *bet, hit, let, put,* etc. The following is a list of the most important of the irregular verbs:[1]

Present Tense.	*Past Tense.*	*Past Participle.*
abide	abode	abode
alight	{ alighted alit	{ alighted alit
arise	arose	arisen
awake	{ awoke awaked	awaked
bear (to bring forth)	bore	born
bear (to carry)	bore	borne
beat	beat	{ beaten beat
begin	began	begun
behold	beheld	beheld
bend	bent	{ bent bended (as adjective)
bereave	{ bereft bereaved	{ bereft bereaved
beseech	besought	besought
bet	bet	bet
bid (to command)	bade	bidden
bid (to offer money, etc.)	bid	bid

[1] When a verb has two forms, the commoner form is the one given first.

Present Tense.	Past Tense.	Past Participle.
bind	bound	bound
bite	bit	bitten / bit
bleed	bled	bled
blend	blended / blent	blended / blent
bless	blessed	blessed / blest (as adjective)
blow	blew	blown
break	broke	broken
breed	bred	bred
bring	brought	brought
build	built / builded	built / builded
burn	burned / burnt	burned / burnt
burst	burst	burst
buy	bought	bought
cast	cast	cast
catch	caught	caught
chide	chid / chided	chidden / chided
choose	chose	chosen
cleave (to split)	clove / cleft	cloven / cleft
cling	clung	clung
clothe	clothed / clad	clothed / clad
come	came	come
cost	cost	cost
creep	crept	crept
crow	crowed / crew	crowed
cut	cut	cut
dare	dared / durst	dared

Present Tense.	Past Tense.	Past Participle.
deal	dealt / dealed	dealt / dealed
dig	dug / digged	dug / digged
do	did,	done
draw	drew	drawn
dream	dreamed / dreamt	dreamed / dreamt
dress	drest / dressed	drest / dressed
drink	drank	drunk / drank
drive	drove	driven
dwell	dwelt	dwelt
eat	ate	eaten
fall	fell	fallen
feed	fed	fed
feel	felt	felt
fight	fought	fought
find	found	found
flee	fled	fled
fling	flung	flung
fly	flew	flown
forbear	forbore	forborne
forget	forgot	forgotten / forgot
forsake	forsook	forsaken
freeze	froze	frozen
get	got	got / gotten
gild	gilded / gilt	gilded / gilt (as adjective)
gird	girt / girded	girt / girded

Present Tense	Past Tense.	Past Participle.
give	gave	given
go	went	gone
grind	ground	ground
grow	grew	grown
hang	hung / hanged (only when execution by hanging is meant)	hung / hanged
have	had	had
hear	heard	heard
heave	heaved / hove	heaved / hove
hew	hewed	hewn
hide	hid	hidden / hid
hit	hit	hit
hold	held	held
hurt	hurt	hurt
keep	kept	kept
kneel	knelt / kneeled	knelt / kneeled
knit	knit / knitted	knit / knitted
know	knew	known
lade	laded	laden / laded
lead	led	led
lean	leaned / leant	leaned / leant
leap	leaped / leapt	leaped / leapt
leave	left.	left
lend	lent	lent
let	let	let
lie (to recline)	lay	lain
light	lighted / lit	lighted / lit

Present Tense	Past Tense	Past Participle
lose	lost	lost
make	made	made
mean	meant	meant
meet	met	met
mow	mowed	mowed / mown
pen (to enclose)	penned / pent	penned / pent
put	put	put
quit	quit / quitted	quit / quitted
rap	rapped / rapt	rapped / rapt
read	read	read
rend	rent	rent
rid	rid	rid
ride	rode	ridden
ring	rang	rung
rise	rose	risen
rive	rived	riven / rived
run	ran	run
see	saw	seen
seek	sought.	sought
seethe (to boil)	seethed	seethed / sodden
sell	sold	sold
send	sent.	sent
set	set	set
shake	shook	shaken
shear	sheared	sheared / shorn
shed	shed.]	shed
shine (intransitive)	shone	shone
shoe	shod	shod
shoot	shot	shot

Present Tense.	Past Tense.	Past Participle.
show	showed	shown / showed
shred	shredded / shred	shredded / shred
shrink	shrank	shrunk
shrive	shrived / shrove	shriven / shrived
shut	shut	shut
sing	sang	sung
sink	sank	sunk
sit	sat	sat
slay	slew	slain
sleep	slept	slept
slide	slid	slidden / slid
sling	slung	slung
slink	slunk	slunk
slit	slit	slit
smell	smelt / smelled	smelt / smelled
smite	smote	smitten
sow	sowed	sowed / sown
speak	spoke	spoken
speed	sped	sped
spell	spelt / spelled	spelt / spelled
spend	spent	spent
spill	spilt / spilled	spilt / spilled
spin	spun	spun
spit	spit	spit
split	split	split
spoil	spoiled / spoilt	spoiled / spoilt
spread	spread	spread

Present Tense.	Past Tense.	Past Participle.
spring	sprang	sprung
stand	stood	stood
stave	{ stove staved }	{ stove staved }
steal	stole	stolen
stick	stuck	stuck
sting	stung	stung
strew	strewed	strewn
stride	strode	stridden
strike	struck	{ struck stricken }
string	strung	strung
strive	strove	striven
strow	strowed	{ strowed strown }
swear	swore	sworn
sweep	swept	swept
swell	swelled	{ swelled swollen }
swim	swam	swum
swing	swung	swung
take	took	taken
teach	taught	taught
tear	tore	torn
tell	told	told
think	thought	thought
thrive	{ throve thrived }	{ thriven thrived }
throw	threw	thrown
thrust	thrust	thrust
tread	trod	trodden
wear	wore	worn
weave	wove	woven
weep	wept	wept
wet	wet	wet
win	won	won

Present Tense.	Past Tense.	Past Participle.
wind	wound	wound
work	{ worked / wrought	{ worked / wrought
wring	wrung	wrung
write	wrote	written

158. Voice.—Compare the verbs in the following sentences:

(1) Tom found a knife. — A knife was found by Tom.
(2) Lightning struck the house. — The house was struck by lightning.
(3) They saw him. — He was seen by them.
(4) The board elected him president. — He was elected president by the board.

The sentences in the first column, although they mean exactly the same as the corresponding sentences in the second column, are, nevertheless, entirely different in grammatical structure. The sentences of the first column represent the subject as doing something with respect to an object, the lightning, for example, as striking the house. A verb which thus asserts the action of a subject upon an object is in the **Active Voice.**

In the second group of sentences the action of the verb does not pass over from a subject as agent to an object which receives the action. In these sentences the subject does not act at all, but is acted upon, as, for example, in the statement that the house was struck by lightning. Verbs which express the subject as receiving the action of the verb are in the **Passive Voice.**

159. Formation of the Passive Voice.—The passive voice is formed by combining the various forms of the copulative verb *to be*, that is, *am, is, was, were*, etc., with the past participle of the verb. The passive voice has thus all the six tenses of the active voice. The following is the conjugation in the active and passive voice of the verb *love*.

ACTIVE VOICE.

PRESENT TENSE.

	Singular.	*Plural.*
PERSON.		
1.	I love.	We love.
2.	You love.	You love.
3.	He loves.	They love.

PAST TENSE.

	Singular.	*Plural.*
PERSON.		
1.	I loved.	We loved.
2.	You loved.	You loved.
3.	He loved.	They loved.

FUTURE TENSE.

	Singular.	*Plural.*
PERSON.		
1.	I shall love.	We shall love.
2.	You will love.	You will love.
3.	He will love.	They will love.

PRESENT PERFECT.

	Singular.	*Plural.*
PERSON.		
1.	I have loved.	We have loved.
2.	You have loved.	You have loved.
3.	He has loved.	They have loved.

PAST PERFECT.

	Singular.	*Plural.*
PERSON.		
1.	I had loved.	We had loved.
2.	You had loved.	You had loved.
3.	He had loved.	They had loved.

FUTURE PERFECT.

	Singular.	*Plural.*
PERSON.		
1.	I shall have loved.	We shall have loved.
2.	You will have loved.	You will have loved.
3.	He will have loved.	They will have loved.

PASSIVE VOICE.

PRESENT TENSE.

PERSON.
Singular.
1. I am loved.
2. You are loved.
3. He is loved.

Plural.
We are loved.
You are loved.
They are loved.

PAST TENSE.

PERSON.
Singular.
1. I was loved.
2. You were loved.
3. He was loved.

Plural.
We were loved.
You were loved.
They were loved.

FUTURE TENSE.

PERSON.
Singular.
1. I shall be loved.
2. You will be loved.
3. He will be loved.

Plural.
We shall be loved.
You will be loved.
They will be loved

PRESENT PERFECT.

PERSON.
Singular.
1. I have been loved.
2. You have been loved.
3. He has been loved.

Plural.
We have been loved.
You have been loved.
They have been loved.

PAST PERFECT.

PERSON.
Singular.
1. I had been loved.
2. You had been loved.
3. He had been loved.

Plural.
We had been loved.
You had been loved.
They had been loved.

FUTURE PERFECT.

PERSON.
Singular.
1. I shall have been loved.
2. You will have been loved.
3. He will have been loved.

Plural.
We shall have been loved.
You will have been loved.
They will have been loved.

160. Progressive Passive Forms.—The passive voice may also be inflected in the progressive forms:

PRESENT TENSE.

PERSON.
Singular.	Plural.
1. I am being loved.	We are being loved.
2. You are being loved.	You are being loved.
3. He is being loved.	They are being loved, etc.

161. Voice and Transitivity.—Since a verb in the passive voice has for its subject a noun or pronoun which is the object of the verb when it is in the active voice, it naturally follows that only transitive verbs can be used in the passive voice, since transitive verbs are the only ones which have objects. Thus the active transitive verb in *The woodman felled the tree to the ground*, may be changed to the passive construction, *The tree was felled to the ground by the woodman;* but the intransitive active verb in *The tree fell to the ground* has no equivalent passive form.

162. The Retained Object.—Although the passive voice of the verb is never followed by a real object as the active transitive verb is, yet certain verbs of giving, naming, choosing, etc. (see **55**), which in the active voice take two objects, retain one of these objects in the passive, the other object becoming regularly the subject of the passive verb. The object which is kept in the passive is called the **Retained Object.**

EXAMPLES:

(1) He gave me a book. I was given *a book* by him.
(2) They elected him president. He was elected *president* by them.
(3) They allowed him a free hand. He was allowed *a free hand* by them, *or* A free hand was allowed *him* by them.

(4) She named her dog Carlo.   Her dog was named *Carlo* by her.
(5) The Speaker appointed Mr. Blair chairman of the committee.   Mr. Blair was appointed *chairman* of the committee by the Speaker.

163. General Statement in the Passive.—A transitive verb is frequently used in the passive voice without the noun or pronoun which forms the subject when the verb is used actively. This form of statement is convenient when one wishes to make a general statement without specifying the source of the action of the verb.

EXAMPLES:

(1) Poor Rip *was reduced* almost to despair.
(2) The world *was not made* in a day.
(3) The natives *were driven* to starvation.
(4) The dismantled ship *was set* adrift.

EXERCISES.

In the following sentences determine which verbs are passive and which are active, and wherever it is possible, change the passive verbs to the active voice and the active verbs to the passive voice.

(1) In due time, the mansion was finished.
(2) Tom is encouraged by a remark or two of the guard's, and besides is getting tired of not talking.
(3) They passed several more parties of boys.
(4) The guard had just finished an account of a desperate fight.
(5) Hardly anybody had been permitted to see the interior of this palace, but it was reported to be far more gorgeous than the outside.
(6) While the boy was still gazing up the valley, and fancying, as he always did, that the Great Stone Face returned his gaze and looked kindly at him, the rumbling of wheels was heard.

(7) He was generally seen trooping like a colt at his mother's heels.

(8) Whenever he went dodging about the village, he was surrounded by a troop of them.

(9) Rip's sole domestic adherent was his dog Wolf, who was as much henpecked as his master.

(10) Then I asked for a threepenny loaf and was told that they had none such.

(11) A report like that of a cannon interrupted his exclamation, and something resembling a white cloud was seen drifting before the wind from the head of the ship, till it was driven into the gloom far to leeward.

(12) The heat of the day and the continued trembling of the air lulled me into a sort of doze, when I was suddenly aroused by a cry from the soldier and the stopping of the coach.

(13) But half of our heavy task was done
When the clock struck the hour for retiring;
And we heard the distant and random gun
That the foe was sullenly firing.

Slowly and sadly we laid him down,
From the field of his fame fresh and gory;
We carved not a line, we raised not a stone,
But we left him alone with his glory.
—WOLFE, *The Burial of Sir John Moore.*

(14) "Come back! Come back!" he cried in grief,
"Across this stormy water;
And I'll forgive your Highland chief,
My daughter, oh, my daughter!"

'Twas vain. The loud waves lashed the shore,
Return or aid preventing:
The waters wild went o'er his child,
And he was left lamenting.
—CAMPBELL, *Lord Ullin's Daughter.*

164. Verbals.—The forms of the verb which we have been considering heretofore have this in common, that they are used together with a subject, and in the case of the transitive verbs, also with an object, to form the main structural element of the sentence or the clause. Whatever the voice, person, tense, or number of the verb, it always expresses action or state of being on the part of the verb with respect to some subject. In a way the verb is thus the most independent of all the parts of speech. We speak of the noun or pronoun as the subject or object of a verb, and of the adjective, adverb, and prepositional phrase as modifiers of the noun, pronoun, and verb. But the verb itself is regarded as the key and centre of the sentence or clause, around which the other words group themselves.

There are, however, a number of words which have largely the nature of verbs in that they express action, but which differ from them in two ways: first, in that they do not take subjects and cannot thus constitute the main structural element of the sentence; and second, in that they combine in themselves the function both of the verb and another part of speech, the noun, the adjective, or the adverb. Words of this kind are called **Verbals,** and consist of **Infinitives** and **Participles.**

DEFINITION: **Verbals** are words closely related in their use to verbs, but incapable of taking a subject, which combine in themselves the functions of a verb and a noun, adjective, or adverb. They are of two kinds, infinitives and participles.

165. Infinitives as Nouns.—Observe the construction of the italicized words in the following sentences:

(1) *To yield* is no disgrace.
(2) *To lead his party* was his highest ambition.
(3) He tried *to walk* slowly.
(4) They intended *to visit the museum.*

In these four sentences we have four infinitives, *to yield, to lead, to walk,* and *to visit.* Each of these infinitives expresses the idea of action, but not as proceeding from any particular person or thing. No one of them has a subject. That they have strong assertive function, however, is evident from the fact that they may govern nouns in the objective case, as, for example, *party* in the second sentence and *museum* in the fourth sentence, and by the fact that they may be modified by adverbs, as, for example, *slowly* in the third sentence. On the other hand, it is clear that the infinitives also have the value of nouns. *To yield* is plainly the subject of the sentence in *To yield is no disgrace; to lead* is the simple subject of its sentence, and *to walk* and *to visit* are the objects respectively of *tried* and *intended.* The infinitive, therefore, may be used as a noun,

(a) as the subject of a sentence:
EXAMPLES: *To succeed* is not the main end of existence.
To lead a life of ease weakens the spirit.

(b) as a predicate nominative:
EXAMPLES: His habit is *to pass* here daily.
Our work is *to guard* the exit.
The intention was *to discover* the source.

(c) as the object of the verb:
EXAMPLES: He wants *to come.*
They attempted *to reach* the shore.
The officer threatened *to expose* him.
They commanded him *to go* home.

(d) as the retained object in the passive voice:
EXAMPLES: He was commanded *to go* home.
He was asked *to deliver* the message by the secretary.
The plaintiff was advised *to drop* the case.
(e) as the object of a preposition:
EXAMPLES: He was willing to do anything *except to apologize*.
There was nothing to do *but to go* home.
They were *about to turn* back.

166. Sign of the Infinitive.—The infinitive is usually preceded by the preposition *to*, which is then inseparably united to it. This word is called the **Sign of the Infinitive.** The rules determining the use of the sign of the infinitive have to be learned largely by habit; in some instances the sign may be used or omitted as the speaker or writer pleases, in others it must be omitted, and in still others it must be expressed. Thus we may say either *There was nothing to do but to go home* or *There was nothing to do but go home.* In a sentence like *I saw him run*, however, the sign may not be used with the infinitive *run*, although when the sentence is turned into the passive form and the infinitive stands as the retained object, it must then have the sign—*He was seen to run.*

167. Split Infinitive.—It was stated in the last section that the sign of the infinitive, when it is used, is inseparably united to the infinitive. This is the general rule, and good usage requires that nothing shall stand between the infinitive and its sign. Occasionally, however, an adverb appears between the infinitive and its sign, and although this construction, known as the **Split Infinitive,** is usually condemned by the rhetoricians and grammarians as bad

English, examples of it are found in good writers and are heard in good speakers. It sometimes has the advantage of placing the adverb in just the position in which it is wanted. On the other hand, it will usually be found that another position of the adverb will answer as well, or often better, and the safe rule is never to place anything between the infinitive and its sign.

EXAMPLES:

(1) We shall have to indefinitely postpone our trip,
or, better,
We shall have to postpone our trip indefinitely.
(2) They shall be authorized to immediately begin this work,
or, better,
They shall be authorized to begin this work immediately.
(3) They are not yet strong enough to seriously affect the result, *or, better,*
They are not yet strong enough seriously to affect the result.
(4) Their purpose is to so arouse public opinion that the government will have to yield,
or, better,
Their purpose is so to arouse public opinion that the government will have to yield.

168. The Infinitive as Adjective.—The infinitive may also modify nouns by limiting or defining the idea expressed by the noun. In such constructions the infinitive partakes of the function of the adjective. Note the use of the infinitive in the following sentences:

Without Infinitive.	*With Adjective Infinitive.*
(1) His ability is unquestioned.	His ability to rule is unquestioned.
(2) His haste was his ruin.	His haste to become rich was his ruin.

(3) I like his readiness.   I like his readiness to help those in need.

In the first group of sentences we have the unmodified noun ideas represented by the nouns *ability, haste,* and *readiness;* in the second group these nouns are limited by the infinitives and their dependencies. Thus, in the first sentence, *to rule* shows what kind of ability is meant; in the second sentence *to become rich* does the same for *haste,* and in the third *to help those in need* defines more specifically the meaning of *readiness.* Since the infinitives are thus used to modify the meanings of nouns, they must be regarded as combining the function of the adjective with that of the verb. An infinitive adjective phrase like *to help those in need* is, of course, capable of further analysis, *those* being the object of *to help,* and *in need* a prepositional adjective phrase modifying *those.*

169. The Infinitive as Adverb.—The infinitive may also modify a verb or adverb. Observe the value of the infinitives in the following sentences:

(1) We came *to see* the game.
(2) Tom raised his hand *to guard* his face.
(3) They waited *to find out* what would come of it.

The verbal function of these infinitives is plain, since *to see* governs *the game* as object, *to guard* governs *his face,* and *to find out* has for its object the relative clause *what would come of it.* At the same time *to see* modifies *came, to guard* modifies *raised,* and *to find out* modifies *waited,* in each case by indicating the purpose of the action. On this side of their use the infinitives are therefore to be regarded as adverbs limiting the verbs of the sentences.

170. Infinitives Modifying Adjectives.—Another use of the infinitive is that according to which it limits the meaning of an adjective. As such it performs the function of an adverbial modifier of the adjective.

EXAMPLES:

(1) A man *able to work* hard is needed.
(2) He was *ready to try.*
(3) I am *glad to see* you.
(4) Is it *good to eat?*
(5) That is *easy to do.*

In these sentences the infinitives modify respectively the adjectives *able, ready, glad, good,* and *easy.* On its verbal side the infinitive *to work* is modified by the adverb *hard,* and the infinitive *to see* takes an object, *you.* They have, therefore, the double value of verbs and of adverbial modifiers of adjectives.

171. Infinitives in -ing.—The infinitive as noun has two forms. It appears as the simple form of the verb with its sign *to,* and in the second form with the ending *-ing.* Compare the following two groups of sentences:

(1) To carry wood is hard work.   Carrying wood is hard work.
(2) To eat hurriedly is a bad habit.   Eating hurriedly is a bad habit.
(3) To see is to believe.   Seeing is believing.

It will be seen from this comparison that the words *carrying, eating,* and *seeing* have exactly the same function as *to carry, to eat,* and *to see.* The word *carrying* has an object, *wood*; *eating* is modified by an adverb, *hurriedly,* and in all three sentences both the infinitives with *to* and in *-ing* are governed as nouns. Like the infinitive with *to,* the infinitive in *-ing* may be,

(a) the subject of a verb:
   (1) Hunting bear is a dangerous sport.
   (2) Playing tennis strengthens the muscles.
(b) the predicate nominative after a copulative verb:
   (1) Our work is guarding the exits.
   (2) His chief pastime was riding the bicycle.
(c) the object of a verb:
   (1) He likes climbing mountains.
   (2) A cat avoids wetting its feet.
   (3) We suggested dropping the case.
(d) the object of a preposition:
   (1) He disliked all sports except climbing mountains.
   (2) We were about abandoning the search when we found it.

It is sometimes difficult to tell whether a word in *-ing* is to be classed as an infinitive or as a pure noun. When the word is followed by an object or is modified by an adverb, there is no question that it is to be classed as an infinitive, since its strong verb function is indicated by its use. But sometimes when the word stands alone the noun function is much the more prominent, and then it is best to class the word as a noun. The *-ing* words in the following sentences are best regarded as nouns:

   (1) Singing is a difficult art to acquire.
   (2) I dislike hunting very much.
   (3) Reading makes a full man.
   (4) He is deeply interested in canoeing.

Concerning the possibility of confusion between the infinitive in *-ing* and the present participle, see **182**. Some grammars call the infinitive in *-ing* a gerund.

172. Tenses of the Infinitive.—The infinitive has two tenses, the present and the perfect. The present infinitive is the form used for present time or when the infinitive is used in a general sense without specific allusion to time.

EXAMPLES:

(1) *To love* is *to obey.*
(2) He wanted *to come.*
(3) He asked *to see* you.

The perfect infinitive is used to assert an action thought of as completed at present time.

EXAMPLES:

(1) *To have lived* is not enough.
(2) He expected *to have finished* his book before this.
(3) I am glad *to have seen* you.

The infinitive in *-ing* may also be in the perfect tense.

EXAMPLES:

(1) He was pleased at *having finished* his task.
(2) My *having seen* you saved us some inconvenience.
(3) The *having done* the thing was in itself sufficient glory.
(4) He was not conscious of *having defrauded* you.

NOTE.—A perfect or past perfect tense in the main verb is never followed by a perfect infinitive, but always by the present infinitive. The sentence *He had intended to have gone* must be *He had intended to go,* and *I should have liked to have seen him* must be *I should have liked to see him.*

173. Voice of the Infinitive.—Like the other forms of the verb, the infinitive has two voices, the active and the passive.

EXAMPLES:

Active Present.	*Passive Present.*
to see.	to be seen.
to do.	to be done.
to sing.	to be sung.
Active Perfect.	*Passive Perfect.*
to have seen.	to have been seen.
to have done.	to have been done.
to have sung.	to have been sung.

174. Infinitive as Object Complement.—Certain verbs take two objects, one of which is a noun infinitive. This infinitive object is an object complement, and the construction is parallel to that in which the verb is followed by two noun or pronoun objects (see **55**).

EXAMPLES:

(1) We made *him walk*.
(2) He asked *them to step* inside.
(3) I saw *him go*.
(4) The guard told *them to leave* the building.
(5) We heard a large *fish break* the water.
(6) She tried to make the *dog beg*, but he was unruly.

NOTE.—In such constructions as these just exemplified, the noun or pronoun object of the verb is by some grammarians said to be in the objective case as subject of the infinitive, similar to the Latin construction of accusative subject of the infinitive. This classification, however, does not sufficiently take into account the close relation existing between the main verb and the noun or pronoun object, nor is the relation of the noun or pronoun object to the infinitive object the same as that of the Latin accusative to its infinitive.

For the infinitive as retained object, see **165** (d).

In sentences which contain an anticipatory *it* (see **77**), the real subject of the sentence sometimes consists of a prepositional phrase made up of a preposition followed by a noun or pronoun object, which in turn is followed by a complementing infinitive object.

EXAMPLES:

(1) It is not good for a *man to dwell* alone.
(2) It will be well for *him to look* to his laurels.
(3) It will not be advisable for the *house to adjourn*.

175. Case of Pronouns after *to be*. — When the infinitive *to be* is the object complement of a sentence and is followed by a pronoun, the pronoun following the infinitive is in the objective case. This is in accordance with the rule that the case of a word following the forms of the copulative verb *to be* is the same as the case of the word preceding it (see **133**).

EXAMPLES:

(1) We knew the woman to be *her*.
(2) He supposed me to be *him*.
(3) We did not believe the strangers to be *them*.

176. Infinitives in Verb-Phrases.—The infinitive is used in order to form certain tenses, and with certain verbs in verb-phrases (see **141**). Thus the future tense is formed by prefixing the forms of the verbs *shall* and *will* to the infinitive of the verb, the whole forming an inseparable verb-phrase. The infinitive is also united to the auxiliaries *may, can, must, might, could, would,* and *should* to form verb-phrases, the special uses of which will be considered later (**193-194**).

EXERCISE.

Point out the infinitives in the following sentences, and indicate just what functions each has in its construction.

(1) I like to read poetry aloud.
(2) The way to be original is to be healthy.
(3) The sentinel warns them not to approach too **closely**.
(4) There is none so poor to do him reverence.
(5) We took him to be a sort of magician.
(6) It was death for a man to leave his house.
(7) We were looking for water to drink.
(8) House to let.
(9) Fools who came to scoff, remained to **pray**.
(10) I am glad to learn that you are better.

(11) We think of trying a journey on horseback.
(12) Rowing is a better exercise than playing football.
(13) That was a day to remember.
(14) He had not heard of his having passed the examination.
(15) The next morning the workmen were surprised at missing the stones, which were found in our wharf.
(16) However, living near the water, I was much in and about it, learned early to swim well, and to manage boats; and when in a boat or canoe with other boys, I was commonly allowed to govern, especially in any case of difficulty.
(17) Early to bed and early to rise makes a man healthy, wealthy, and wise.
(18) It is easier to build two chimneys than to keep one in repair.
(19) The pilot shook his head as he replied: "There is no more tacking to be done to-night. We have barely room to pass out of the shoals on this course; and if we can pass the Devil's Grip, we clear their outermost point."
(20) Such songs have power to quiet
The restless pulse of care,
And come like the benediction
That follows after prayer.
(21) I come not, friends, to steal away your hearts:
I am no orator, as Brutus is;
But, as you know me all, a plain, blunt man,
That love my friend; and that they know full well
That gave me public leave to speak of him.
For I have neither wit, nor words, nor worth,
Action nor utterance, nor the power of speech
To stir men's blood: I only speak right on;
I tell you that which you yourselves do know;
Show you sweet Cæsar's wounds, poor, poor dumb mouths,
And bid them speak for me: but, were I Brutus,
And Brutus Antony, there were an Antony
Would ruffle up your spirits, and put a tongue
In every wound of Cæsar that should move
The stones of Rome to rise and mutiny.
—*Julius Cæsar.*

177. Participles.—The participles resemble the infinitives in that they are incapable of asserting action with respect to a subject, and in that they have a double function. They combine in themselves both the function of a verb and of an adjective or adverb, but never of a noun. In the following sentences the participles are italicized:

(1) The sails, *flapping* idly in the wind, were quite empty.
(2) The collie, *gathering* the sheep one by one, soon had the flock all together.
(3) The deer, *having been driven* to his last retreat, stood at bay.
(4) This money, *contributed* by popular subscription, was in the hands of a committee.
(5) He came *staggering* down the street.
(6) This water is *boiling* hot.

In the first of these sentences, it will be observed that the participle *flapping*, on its verb side is limited by the adverb of manner *idly*, and at the same time on its adjective side it limits the noun *sails*. In the second sentence *gathering* takes an object *sheep* and at the same time limits *collie* as an adjective. The participles *having been driven* and *contributed* likewise combine the functions of the adjective and verb. In the fifth sentence, *He came staggering down the street*, the participle *staggering* is an adverb of manner modifying *came*, and in turn it is modified by the adverbial phrase *down the street*. In the last sentence, *boiling* is an adverb of degree modifying the adjective *hot*.

178. As with the infinitive, the adverbial or adjectival value of the participle as contrasted with its value as verb varies a great deal in prominence. When used as an adjective of quality, the participle is purely adjectival in value, as in the sentence, *A rushing noise was heard,* or *A surprised bear is an ugly opponent.* In such uses it is to be parsed simply as an adjective.

179. Dangling Participles.—When the participle is used with adjective value, care should be taken that the noun which the participle modifies is expressed, and that the participle be properly placed so as to modify the noun. If this is not done, the participle is left hanging loose, or dangling. In the sentence, *Standing on the hill, the whole valley was visible,* the participle *standing* has no word to modify, since it was not the valley which was standing on the hill. The sentence should read, *Standing on the hill, we could see the whole valley.* Ridiculous blunders are often made by neglecting to follow this rule. The following sentences contain examples of dangling participles which should be corrected:

(1) *Born* at Boston, a great deal of his youth was spent in that city.
(2) *Being stolen,* the bank refused to honor the note.
(3) *Looking* out for a theme, several crossed his mind.
(4) *Sitting* in the window, a squirrel was perceived.
(5) *Walking* down the street, an automobile rushed by.
(6) *Doubling* the point and *running* along the shore of the little peninsula, the scene changes.

180. The Absolute Participle.—In a few instances, however, participles and participial phrases are used without a specific noun or pronoun to which they refer, standing thus independent of the rest of the sentence. Such a participle is called an **Absolute Participle,** and the word or phrase is to be classed with the group of **Independent Elements,** to be considered later (see **230**).

EXAMPLES:

(1) *Including* to-morrow, it is two weeks to your birthday.
(2) *Considering* his abilities, he should have done better.
(3) *Awaiting* the result, the court was closed.
(4) These prayers are to be said *kneeling*.
(5) *Speaking* without prejudice, that is really the best piece of work I have seen.

It is not well, however, to use this construction freely, and, to be on the safe side, it is advisable always to use the participle as modifying some specific word.

181. Tense and Voice of Participles.—Participles have three tenses, present, past, and perfect, and, when transitive, the two voices, active and passive. The following are the forms:

Active Voice.	Passive Voice.
Present Tense.	
seeing.	being seen.
writing.	being written.
hearing.	being heard.
singing.	being sung.
appearing (Intransitive).	————
seeming (Intransitive).	————
Past Tense.	
seen.	seen.
written.	written.
heard.	heard.
sung.	sung.
appeared.	————
seemed.	————
Perfect Tense.	
having seen.	having been seen.
having written.	having been written.
having heard.	having been heard.
having sung.	having been sung.
having appeared.	————
having seemed.	————

182. Present Participle and the Infinitive in -ing.—Care should be taken not to confuse the present participle, which always ends in *-ing*, with the infinitive in *-ing*. This mistake will be avoided if it is remembered that the present participle always has, besides its verb function, the function of an adjective or adverb, whereas the infinitive in *-ing* combines in itself the functions of a verb and a noun.

EXAMPLES:

INFINITIVE IN *-ing*.	PRESENT PARTICIPLE.
(1) *Walking* the deck is tedious exercise.	*Walking* the deck, the captain has the whole ship under his eye.
(2) He has the bad habit of *reading* fiction.	The man *reading* the newspaper is a distinguished author.
(3) His *going* or not *going* does not affect me.	*Going* to the shelf, he took down a book.

183. Participles in Verb-Phrases.—It has already been pointed out that the participles, present and past, as well as the infinitive, are used in the formation of certain phrasal forms of the verb (see **143, 147**). But the participles in these verb-phrases are no longer felt to have separate existence and are to be parsed merely as parts of the verbs, the whole phrase being treated as having a single function.

EXERCISES.

1. Point out the participles in the following sentences, giving the tense, voice, and construction of each one.

(1) We saw him earnestly searching the ground.
(2) Deserted by his friends and family, the old man was living in abject poverty.
(3) The message, having been delivered in due time, was immediately acted upon.
(4) A man bearing a basket on his arm came walking down the road.
(5) Having waited in vain for an hour, we were compelled to give up the journey.
(6) We saw the deer headed in our direction.
(7) Truth crushed to earth shall rise again.
(8) Having walked to the village I was ready to sit down and rest.
(9) The stones came hurtling through the air.
(10) The mountain seen in the distance was covered by a deep blue haze.
(11) Then I went up Market Street as far as Fourth Street, passing by the door of Mr. Read, my future wife's father.
(12) Sleep, soldiers! still in honored rest
　　Your truth and valor wearing;
　The bravest are the tenderest,—
　　The loving are the daring.
　　　　—Bayard Taylor, *The Song of the Camp.*

2. Pick out all the verbals in the following passage, and show how they are used:

Major and the Geese.

The upland geese are excellent eating, and it was our custom to make an early breakfast off a cold goose, or of any remnants left in the larder. Cold boiled goose and coffee, often with no bread—it sounds strange, but never shall I forget those delicious early Patagonian breakfasts.

Now the geese, although abundant at that season, were excessively wary and hard to kill; and as no other person went after them, although all grumbled loudly when there was no goose for breakfast,

I was always very glad to get a shot at them when out with the gun. One day I saw a great flock congregated on a low mud bank in one of the lagoons, and immediately began to manœuvre to get within shooting distance without disturbing them. Fortunately they were in a great state of excitement, keeping up a loud incessant clamor, as if something very important to the upland geese was being discussed, and in the general agitation they neglected their safety. More geese in small flocks were continually arriving from various directions, increasing the noise and excitement; and by dint of much going on hands and knees and crawling over rough ground, I managed to get within seventy yards of them, and fired into the middle of the flock. The birds rose up with a great rush of wings and noise of screams, leaving five of their number floundering about in the shallow water. Major was quickly after them, but two of the five were not badly wounded, and soon swam away beyond his reach; to the others he was guided by the tremendous flapping they made in the water in their death struggles; and one by one he conveyed them, not to his expectant master, but to a small island about one hundred and twenty yards from the shore. No sooner had he got them all together than, to my unspeakable astonishment and dismay, he began worrying them, growling all the time with a playful affectation of anger, and pulling out mouthfuls of feathers which he scattered in clouds over his head. To my shouts he responded by wagging his tail and barking a merry crisp little bark, then flying at the dead birds again. He seemed to be telling me, plainly as if he had used words, that he found it very amusing playing with the geese, and intended to enjoy himself to his heart's content.

—HUDSON, *Idle Days in Patagonia*, Chapter V.

184. Mood.—By mood is meant the way in which a verb makes an assertion. We distinguish three moods of the verb, the **Subjunctive**, the **Imperative,** and the **Indicative.** These distinctions of mood are indicated by accompanying differences of form only in rare instances, and the question of mood is of importance only in those few occurrences of the subjunctive in which a separate form is used to indicate the subjunctive.

> NOTE.—This comparatively rare use of the subjunctive mood is a development of modern English. In earlier times, in the Middle English and the Anglo-Saxon periods, the use of the subjunctive was much more general. Nowadays the subjunctive is more used in poetic and elevated style, which is always conservative and highly traditional, than it is in daily speech and writing. The regular tendency has been to make the indicati·e take the place of the subjunctive, with the result that the subjunctive has almost completely disappeared from normal spoken and written modern English usage.

185. Forms of the Subjunctive Mood.—In the verb *to be*, the subjunctive mood has distinctive forms for the present tense, singular, and plural, and for the past tense, first and third person singular. The following are the forms of the verb *to be* in the subjunctive; the word *if* is prefixed not as part of the inflection of the verb, but because it is in clauses beginning with *if* that the subjunctive is usually found.

To be.
SUBJUNCTIVE MOOD.
PRESENT TENSE.

PERSON.	*Singular.*	*Plural.*
1.	If I be.	If we be.
2.	If you be.	If you be.
3.	If he be.	If they be.

PAST TENSE.

PERSON.	*Singular.*	*Plural.*
1.	If I were.	If we were.
2.	If you were.	If you were.
3.	If he were.	If they were.

186. In all other verbs the only distinctive form for the subjunctive is the third person singular of the present tense, which omits its inflectional *-s* and thus remains the same as the first and second person singular.

> EXAMPLES: If he do, If he have, If he sing, If he write, If he go, etc.

Verbs in the passive voice have naturally all the forms of the subjunctive which the verb *to be* has.

EXAMPLES: If I be elected, If you be elected, If he be elected, etc.

187. Imperative Mood.—The verb in the imperative sentence, that is, in the sentence expressing a command, wish, or entreaty, is in the **Imperative Mood.**

EXAMPLES:

(1) *Give* me the book.
(2) God *grant* you prosperity.
(3) *Lend* me a hand, will you?
(4) *May* you never *regret* this.
(5) So *be* it.
(6) *Let* us not *forget* that we owe a duty to our country.

188. Indicative Mood.—This is the mood of the verb in by far the greatest number of sentences. In general, all verbs in the principal clauses of interrogative and declarative sentences are in the indicative mood, and all verbs in subordinate clauses, except those in which the specific subjunctive form is used. The verbs in the following sentences are all in the indicative mood:

(1) Grant was commander of the army.
(2) Who was commander of the army?
(3) I do not know who the commander was.
(4) If Grant had been commander of the army, the battle would not have been lost.

The general rule is that all verbs which are not in imperative sentences and which have not one of the few distinctive forms of the subjunctive mood are in the indicative mood.

189. Uses of the Subjunctive Mood.—The subjunctive is the mood of the verb in certain kinds of subordinate clauses, the main uses being the following:

(a) The subjunctive is used in subordinate clauses to express **Uncertain Condition.** In sentences of this sort the subjunctive may usually be replaced by the indicative, always, however, with a slight difference in the shade of meaning conveyed. The subjunctive expresses a degree more of doubt and uncertainty with respect to the assertion of the verb of the subordinate clause than the indicative would.

EXAMPLES:
(1) If I *be* not mistaken, you are the man I am looking for.
(2) If it *prove* as difficult as it appears, we shall have a hard time of it.
(3) If it *turn* out as we hope, we shall have much to be grateful for.
(4) If he *keep* a stiff upper lip, never *show* the white feather, and *be* always fair, no one need ask any more of him.
(5) If the water *hold* out one day longer, we shall be saved.

(b) The subjunctive is used in subordinate clauses to express a **Condition Contrary to Fact.** In sentences of this kind the statement of the subordinate clause is contrary to what is the actual state of affairs. The indicative is used in subordinate clauses of somewhat similar meaning, but there is a real, though subtle, difference between the subjunctive and indicative, which should be carefully studied.

EXAMPLES:
(1) If he *were* not so indifferent, he could accomplish more.
(2) If I *were* you, I should be very cautious.
(3) I wish it *were* in my power to help you.
(4) I feel as though I *were being borne* bodily through the air.

These sentences with the subjunctive should be compared with sentences like the following, with the indicative:

(1) If he *was* there, I did not see him.
(2) If you *are* right, I am wrong.
(3) If I *was* unjust to you, I apologize for it.

In the first group of sentences the subordinate clause in each instance implies that the actual state of affairs is contrary to the statement which is made; in the second group, the subordinate clauses carry with them no such implication, but leave the question of the truth of the statement of the subordinate clause open.

In subordinate clauses containing a condition contrary to fact, the conjunction *if* may be omitted, in which case the verb is placed before the subject, as in the following sentences:

(1) *Were* I to tell all I know, it would fill volumes.
(2) I should not do it, *were* I in your place.
(3) He would take any risk, *were* he not *dissuaded*.

(c) The subjunctive is used in subordinate clauses which express a concession. Such clauses are called **Concessive Clauses,** and are usually introduced by the conjunctions *though, although, even though,* etc. The verb in the subjunctive in the concessive clause does not imply that the statement is a fact, but that it may or may not be a fact.

EXAMPLES:

(1) Though your sins *be* as scarlet, they shall be as white as snow.
(2) He will not be able to carry the point, even though he *do* as you tell him.
(3) Criminal though he *be*, there are still rights which he can claim.

When the verb in the concessive clause is in the indicative, it implies that the statement of the clause is not doubtful, but is a fact. For example, the third sentence above might be paraphrased to read, *Criminal though he may be, there are still rights which he can claim;* but when the verb is indicative, as in *Criminal though he is, there are still rights which he can claim,* the sentence does not allow any doubt that the person spoken of is a criminal.

Like the condition contrary to fact, the concessive clause may also omit the conjunction, placing the verb in the subject at the head of the clause.

EXAMPLES:

(1) *Be* he never so wise, a man will sometimes err (=Though he be never so wise, a man will sometimes err).
(2) I will have it, *cost* what it may (=I will have it, though it cost what it may).
(3) *Think* what he may, I shall still insist (=I shall still insist, though he think what he may).

(d) In official and parliamentary language, the subjunctive is often used in noun clauses after verbs of requesting, moving, voting, etc., in the main clause.

EXAMPLES:

(1) It was moved that the bill *be placed* on the table.
(2) The chairman requested that the committee *meet* him in the anteroom.
(3) It is deemed advisable that the house *remain* in session some time longer.

In spoken and informal language, however, this subjunctive is replaced by a verb-phrase with *should*, as in the sentence, *The chairman requested that the committee should meet him in the anteroom.*

190. Conjugation of the Verb.—Having discussed the various forms of the verb, we may give now the complete conjugation of a typical verb of each class.

(a) **Conjugation of the Regular Verb " to love."**

ACTIVE VOICE.

INDICATIVE MOOD.	SUBJUNCTIVE MOOD. [1]
PRESENT TENSE.	PRESENT TENSE.
Singular.	*Singular.*
PERSON.	
1. I love.	
2. You love.	
3. He loves.	If he love.
Plural.	*Plural.*
PERSON.	
1. We love.	
2. You love.	
3. They love.	
PAST TENSE.	PAST TENSE.
Singular.	*Singular.*
PERSON.	
1. I loved.	
2. You loved.	
3. He loved.	
Plural.	*Plural.*
PERSON.	
1. We loved.	
2. You loved.	
3. They loved.	
FUTURE TENSE.	FUTURE TENSE.
Singular.	*Singular.*
PERSON.	
1. I shall love.	
2. You will love.	
3. He will love.	

[1] Forms are given for the subjunctive only when they are distinctive for that mood.

PERSON. *Plural.*   *Plural.*
1. We shall love.
2. You will love.
3. They will love.

PRESENT PERFECT TENSE.   **PRESENT PERFECT TENSE.**

PERSON. *Singular.*   *Singular.*
1. I have loved.
2. You have loved.
3. He has loved.   If he have loved.

PERSON. *Plural.*   *Plural.*
1. We have loved.
2. You have loved.
3. They have loved.

PAST PERFECT TENSE.   **PAST PERFECT TENSE.**

PERSON. *Singular.*   *Singular.*
1. I had loved.
2. You had loved.
3. He had loved.

PERSON. *Plural.*   *Plural.*
1. We had loved.
2. You had loved.
3. They had loved.

FUTURE PERFECT TENSE.   **FUTURE PERFECT TENSE.**

PERSON. *Singular.*   *Singular.*
1. I shall have loved.
2. You will have loved.
3. He will have loved.

PERSON. *Plural.*   *Plural.*
1. We shall have loved.
2. You will have loved.
3. They will have loved.

THE PARTS OF SPEECH.

IMPERATIVE MOOD.
2d and 3d Person, Singular and Plural.
Love.

PRESENT PARTICIPLE.
Loving.

PAST PARTICIPLE.
Loved, *or* Having loved.

INFINITIVE.
PRESENT. Love, *or* To love.
PAST.   To have loved.

PASSIVE VOICE.

INDICATIVE MOOD.	SUBJUNCTIVE MOOD.
PRESENT TENSE.	PRESENT TENSE.
Singular.	*Singular.*
PERSON.	
1. I am loved.	If I be loved.
2. You are loved.	If you be loved.
3. He is loved.	If he be loved.
Plural.	*Plural.*
PERSON.	
1. We are loved.	If we be loved.
2. You are loved.	If you be loved.
3. They are loved.	If they be loved.
PAST TENSE.	PAST TENSE.
Singular.	*Singular.*
PERSON.	
1. I was loved.	If I were loved.
2. You were loved.	
3. He was loved.	If he were loved.
Plural.	*Plural.*
PERSON.	
1. We were loved.	
2. You were loved.	
3. They were loved.	

FUTURE TENSE.

PERSON. *Singular.*
1. I shall be loved.
2. You will be loved.
3. He will be loved.

PERSON. *Plural.*
1. We shall be loved.
2. You will be loved.
3. They will be loved.

FUTURE TENSE.

Singular.

Plural.

PRESENT PERFECT TENSE

PERSON. *Singular.*
1. I have been loved.
2. You have been loved.
3. He has been loved.

PERSON. *Plural.*
1. We have been loved.
2. You have been loved.
3. They have been loved.

PRESENT PERFECT TENSE.

Singular.

If he have been loved.

Plural.

PAST PERFECT TENSE.

PERSON. *Singular.*
1. I had been loved.
2. You had been loved.
3. He had been loved.

PERSON. *Plural.*
1. We had been loved.
2. You had been loved.
3. They had been loved.

PAST PERFECT TENSE.

Singular.

Plural.

FUTURE PERFECT TENSE.

PERSON. *Singular.*
1. I shall have been loved.
2. You will have been loved.
3. He will have been loved.

FUTURE PERFECT TENSE.

Singular.

THE PARTS OF SPEECH.

PERSON.   *Plural.*   *Plural.*
1. We shall have been loved.
2. You will have been loved.
3. They will have been loved.

IMPERATIVE MOOD.
2d and 3d Person, Singular and Plural.
Be loved.

PRESENT PARTICIPLE.
Being loved.

PAST PARTICIPLE.
Loved, *or* Having been loved.

INFINITIVE.
PRESENT.   To be loved.
PAST.   To have been loved.

(b) Conjugation of the Irregular Verb "to break."

ACTIVE VOICE.

INDICATIVE MOOD.   SUBJUNCTIVE MOOD.
PRESENT TENSE.   PRESENT TENSE.

PERSON. *Singular.*   *Singular.*
1. I break.
2. You break.
3. He breaks.   If he break.

PERSON. *Plural.*   *Plural.*
1. We break.
2. You break.
3. They break.

    PAST TENSE.   PAST TENSE.
PERSON. *Singular*   *Singular.*
1. I broke.
2. You broke.
3. He broke.

Plural.   *Plural.*

PERSON.
1. We broke.
2. You broke.
3. They broke.

     FUTURE TENSE.   FUTURE TENSE.
       Singular.   *Singular.*

PERSON.
1. I shall break.
2. You will break.
3. He will break.

       Plural.   *Plural.*

PERSON.
1. We shall break.
2. You will break.
3. They will break.

  PRESENT PERFECT TENSE.   PRESENT PERFECT TENSE.
       Singular.   *Singular.*

PERSON.
1. I have broken.
2. You have broken.
3. He has broken.   If he have broken.

       Plural.   *Plural.*

PERSON.
1. We have broken.
2. You have broken.
3. They have broken.

   PAST PERFECT TENSE.   PAST PERFECT TENSE.
       Singular.   *Singular.*

PERSON.
1. I had broken.
2. You had broken.
3. He had broken.

       Plural.   *Plural.*

PERSON.
1. We had broken.
2. You had broken.
3. They had broken.

THE PARTS OF SPEECH.

FUTURE PERFECT TENSE. FUTURE PERFECT TENSE.

Singular.   *Singular.*

PERSON.
1. I shall have broken.
2. You will have broken.
3. He will have broken.

Plural.   *Plural.*

PERSON.
1. We shall have broken.
2. You will have broken.
3. They will have broken.

IMPERATIVE MOOD.

2d and 3d Person, Singular and Plural.

Break.

PRESENT PARTICIPLE.

Breaking.

PAST PARTICIPLE.

Broken, *or* Having Broken.

INFINITIVE.

PRESENT. Break, *or* To break.
PAST. To have broken.

PASSIVE VOICE.

INDICATIVE MOOD. SUBJUNCTIVE MOOD.

PRESENT TENSE. PRESENT TENSE.

Singular.   *Singular.*

PERSON.
1. I am broken.   If I be broken.
2. You are broken.   If you be broken.
3. He is broken.   If he be broken.

Plural.   *Plural.*

PERSON.
1. We are broken.   If we be broken.
2. You are broken.   If you be broken.
3. They are broken.   If they be broken.

PAST TENSE.   PAST TENSE.
Singular.   *Singular.*
PERSON.
1. I was broken.   If I were broken.
2. You were broken.
3. He was broken.   If he were broken.

Plural.   *Plural.*
PERSON.
1. We were broken.
2. You were broken.
3. They were broken.

FUTURE TENSE.   FUTURE TENSE.
Singular.   *Singular.*
PERSON.
1. I shall be broken.
2. You will be broken.
3. He will be broken.

Plural.   *Plural.*
PERSON.
1. We shall be broken.
2. You will be broken.
3. They will be broken.

PRESENT PERFECT TENSE.   PRESENT PERFECT TENSE.
Singular.   *Singular.*
PERSON.
1. I have been broken.
2. You have been broken.
3. He has been broken.

Plural.   *Plural.*
PERSON.
1. We have been broken.
2. You have been broken.
3. They have been broken.

PAST PERFECT TENSE.   PAST PERFECT TENSE.
Singular.   *Singular.*
PERSON.
1. I had been broken.
2. You had been broken.
3. He had been broken.

Plural.   *Plural.*

PERSON.
1. We had been broken.
2. You had been broken.
3. They had been broken.

FUTURE PERFECT TENSE.   FUTURE PERFECT TENSE.
Singular.   *Singular.*

PERSON.
1. I shall have been broken.
2. You will have been broken.
3. He will have been broken.

Plural.   *Plural.*

PERSON.
1. We shall have been broken.
2. You will have been broken.
3. They will have been broken.

IMPERATIVE MOOD.

2d and 3d Person, Singular and Plural.

Be broken.

PRESENT PARTICIPLE.

Being broken.

PAST PARTICIPLE.

Broken, *or* Having been broken.

INFINITIVE.

PRESENT.   To be broken.
PAST.   To have been broken.

191. Anomalous or Unclassified Verbs.—Besides those verbs which fall into the classes of regular and irregular verbs, there are in English some few verbs which are best grouped alone because of their marked individual peculiarities. These verbs we call **Anomalous** or **Unclassified Verbs.** Some of them have already been considered, the verbs *to be, to have,* and *to do,* and the auxiliaries *shall* and *will*. Others to be placed here are *may, can, must, need, dare, ought*. All of these verbs may be used as auxiliary verbs in forming verb-phrases, though some, like *be, have, do, need,* and *dare*, are also used alone. Thus in *He needs another pen* and in *He dares anything,* the verbs are used alone and their forms are the same as those of other regular verbs. But in the sentences, *He need pay no attention to it* and *I dare say you will find it,* the verbs *need* and *dare* are auxiliaries in the verb-phrases *need pay* and *dare say*. For examples of anomalous verb-phrases, see **193**.

192. Inflection of Anomalous Verbs.—The inflections of the anomalous verbs are in some respects peculiar. In the third person singular of the present indicative, they all, with the exception of *be, have, do,* and *dare*, take the same form as the first person, that is, they do not have the ending *-s*. The verb *dare*, as auxiliary, has two forms in the third person, *dare* by analogy to the other anomalous verbs, and *dares* by analogy to the regular verbs. The inflection, therefore, of these verbs in the present tense is as follows:

Singular Number.

PERSON.
1. I may, can, might, must, ought, need, dare, etc.
2. You may, can, might, must, ought, need, dare, etc.
3. He may, can, might, must, ought, need, dare, *or* dares, etc.

Plural Number.

PERSON.
1. We may, can, must, ought, need, dare, etc.
2. You may, can, must, ought, need, dare, etc.
3. They may, can, must, ought, need, dare, etc.

In the formation of their principal parts these **anomalous** auxiliary verbs have other peculiar features. The following are the principal parts of the most important:

Present.	Past.	Past Participle.
am	was	been
have	had	had
do	did	done
can	could	——
may	——	——
might	——	——
must	——	——
ought	——	——
will	would	——
shall	should	——
need	needed	needed
dare	durst, dared	dared

Of these *may, might, must,* and *ought,* are used only in the present tense, and these verbs, together with *can, will,* and *shall,* have no past participles. Verbs like *may, can, must,* etc., which are lacking in one or more of their principal parts are called **Defective Verbs.** Verbs which, like *dare,* have two forms for one or more of the principal parts are called **Redundant Verbs;** for numerous examples, see the lists in **157.**

193. Anomalous Verb-Phrases.—The chief use of the anomalous verbs is to form verb-phrases. Of these we have already described the future tense, formed with *shall* and *will,* and such verb-phrases as the progressive forms of the verb, formed with *am, is,* etc., and the emphatic forms, made by the help of *do, does,* etc. Verb-phrases formed by the aid of *may, can, must, might, could, would,* and *should* are also very numerous. They are, however, often very subtle and idiomatic in their meanings, and only some of the more obvious uses can be noted here. In many instances they are used in sentences which, in earlier stages of the language, would have used the subjunctive mood. They are not to be regarded, however, as subjunctives, although they have become, in a way, subjunctive equivalents. In these, as in many other instances, the language has developed a phrase for the expression of ideas which were once expressed by inflections, and the new phrasal forms of expression are not to be grouped under the heads of the old classification. The following are some of the more important uses of the anomalous verb-phrases:

(a) Verb-phrases with *may*. The verb *may* followed by an infinitive is used to form verb-phrases expressing:
- (1) permission, as in *You may come when you are ready*, or *You may have another piece*.
- (2) possibility, as in *I may come if the weather is good*, or *I may go and I may not*.
- (3) a wish, as in *I hope you may have a good time*, or *May you live long and prosper*.

(b) Verb-phrases with *can*. With the infinitive, *can* forms verb-phrases expressing:
- (1) ability, as in *I can read it if I have time enough*, or *I can lift one hundred pounds*.
- (2) possibility, as in *You can take a ten o'clock train*, or *He can see us here if he climbs that rock*.

(c) Verb-phrases with *must*. With the infinitive, *must* forms a verb-phrase expressing:
- (1) necessity, as in *You must do as you are bidden*, or *He must suffer the consequences*.
- (2) obligation or duty, as in *Every man must do his best*, or *You must not think that I do this willingly*.

(3) probable inference, as in *You must be a good deal troubled about it*, or *He must know more than anybody else about the affair.*

(d) Verb-phrases with *ought*. Verb-phrases formed with *ought* express duty or obligation. as in *We ought to be grateful for what we have.*

(e) Verb-phrases with *might*. Combined with *might*, originally the past tense of *may*, the infinitive forms certain verb-phrases expressing:
  (1) permission, as in *He said that you might come.*
  (2) possibility, as in *We might go if nothing arose to prevent us.*
  (3) wish or desire, as in *We prayed that he might be delivered from his great affliction.*

(f) Verb-phrases with *could*. Combined with *could*, the past tense of *can*, the infinitive forms verb-phrases expressing:
  (1) a possibility conditional on some other fact, as in *I could go if my father were here.*
  (2) a condition contrary to possibility, as in *If he could see me now, I should be happy.* In complex sentences of this kind the main clause is often omitted, as in *If we could only get word to him!*

(g) Verb-phrases with *would*. Combined with *would*, the past tense of *will*, the infinitive forms verb-phrases expressing:
  (1) readiness or willingness in contingent clauses (*i. e.*, in clauses in which one action depends upon another), when the verb is in the second or third person, as in *He would gladly do it if he had time*, or *You would certainly go if you knew how fine it is.*
  (2) determination, as in *He would have his own way.*
  (3) habitual action, as in *They would take their prisoners and immure them alive.*
  (4) future time in a subordinate clause, as in *The doctor said that he would return in two hours.*

(h) Verb-phrases with *should*. Combined with *should*, the past tense of *shall*, the infinitive forms verb-phrases expressing:

(1) duty or obligation, as in *You should not speak so of absent friends*, or *He should pay closer attention.*
(2) readiness or willingness in contingent clauses (*i. e.*, in clauses in which one action depends upon another), when the verb is in the first person, as in *I should be glad to do it, if I have time,* or *If they ask me, I should not think of mentioning it.* See above, (g), (1), for similar uses in the second and third persons.
(3) future time in a subordinate clause when the verb is in the first person, as in *I said that I should be glad to go,* or *We agreed that I should keep the book.* The form *should* is retained sometimes when the verb is in the third person, provided in direct discourse the verb would be in the first person, as in *He said that he should be ready in ten minutes,* which in direct discourse would read, *He said "I shall be ready in ten minutes."* But the more usual form here is *would, should* in the second and third persons, usually indicating duty or obligation (see above,(1)).

(i) Verb-phrases with *had*.
  (1) Besides its use to form the past perfect tense, *had* is used to form certain idiomatic verb-phrases with *rather* and *better* followed by the infinitive. In this construction *had rather* and *had better* are interchangeable in use with *would rather* and *would better.*

EXAMPLES:
1. *I had rather be right than president.*
2. *I had rather not go,* or *I would rather not go.*
3. *He had better not come at all than come too late,* or *He would better not come at all than come too late.*

  (2) Followed by an infinitive with the sign *to, had* is used to form verb-phrases expressing necessity, as in *We had to dress in five minutes.*

194. Tense of Anomalous Verb-Phrases.—It should be observed that verb-phrases formed with *might, could,* *would, should,* and *had,* followed by the infinitive, express only present or future time, although the verbs themselves are past tense in form. When past time is to be expressed, the verbs must be placed in the form of the perfect tense.

EXAMPLES:

Present or Future Tense.	*Past Tense.*
(1) You should remember to bring your books.	You should have remembered to bring your books.
(2) He might look into this closet.	He might have looked into this closet.
(3) I would rather go.	I would rather have gone.

195. Parsing the Verb and Verbal.—In parsing the verb, state:

    (1) whether it is a simple verb or a verb-phrase;
    (2) whether it is transitive, intransitive, or copulative;
    (3) whether it is active or passive voice;
    (4) whether it is a regular, irregular, or an anomalous verb, giving its principal parts;
    (5) its tense, person, number, and mood;
    (6) its construction, pointing out its subject and, if it has one, its object.

In parsing the verbal, state:

    (1) whether it is an infinitive or a participle;
    (2) its voice;
    (3) its tense;
    (4) its construction.

The verbs and verbals in the sentence, *We walked along the shores of the stream, following it in all its windings to its source in a little spring, where Tom stopped to drink,* are parsed as follows:

    Walked is a simple, intransitive, active, regular verb; its principal parts are *walk, walked, walked;* it is in the past tense, first person, plural number, and indicative mood. It is the verb in the principal clause of the sentence, and its subject is *we*.

Following is a participle, active voice and present tense. It is used as an adjective modifying *we* and also as a verb governing its object *it*.

Stopped is a simple, intransitive, active, regular verb; its principal parts are *stop, stopped, stopped;* it is in the past tense, third person, singular number, and indicative mood. It is the verb in the subordinate clause *where Tom stopped to drink,* and its subject is *Tom*.

To drink is an infinitive, active voice and present tense. It is used as an adverb of purpose, modifying the verb *stopped*.

In the sentence, *If I had another opportunity, I should do this differently,* the verbs are parsed as follows:

Had is a simple, transitive, active, irregular verb; its principal parts are *have, had, had*. It is in the past tense, first person, singular number, and indicative mood. It is the verb in the subordinate clause *If I had another opportunity,* and its subject is *I* and its object *opportunity*.

Should do is an anomalous phrasal verb, transitive, active voice, present or future tense, first person, singular number, indicative mood. It is the verb in the principal clause of the sentence, its subject being *I* and its object *this*.

EXERCISE.

Parse all the verbs and verbals in the following two passages:

THE MONEY DIGGERS.

"This will be a rough night for the money diggers," said mine host, as a gust of wind howled round the house and rattled at the windows.

"What! are they at their works again?" said an English half-pay captain, with one eye, who was a very frequent attendant at the inn.

"Ay are they," said the landlord, "and well may they be. They've had luck of late. They say a great pot of money has been dug up in the fields just behind Stuyvesant's orchard. Folks think it must have been buried there in old times by Peter Stuyvesant, the Dutch governor."

"Fudge!" said the one-eyed man of war, as he added a small portion of water to a bottom of brandy.

"Well, you may believe it or not, as you please," said mine host, somewhat nettled, "but everybody knows that the old governor buried a great deal of his money at the time of the Dutch troubles, when the English redcoats seized on the province. They say, too, the old gentleman walks, ay, and in the very same dress that he wears in the picture that hangs up in the family house."

"Fudge!" said the half-pay officer.

"Fudge, if you please! But didn't Corney Van Zandt see him at midnight, stalking about in the meadow with his wooden leg, and a drawn sword in his hand, that flashed like fire? And what can he be walking for but because people have been troubling the place where he buried his money in old times?"

—IRVING, *Tales of a Traveller.*

TO A BUTTERFLY.

I've watched you now a full half-hour,
Self-poised upon that yellow flower;
And, little Butterfly, indeed
I know not if you sleep or feed.
How motionless! Not frozen seas
More motionless! And then
What joy awaits you when the breeze
Hath found you out among the trees
And calls you forth again!

This plot of orchard-ground is ours;
My trees they are, my sister's flowers.
Here rest your wings when they are weary,
Here lodge as in a sanctuary!
Come often to us, fear no wrong,
Sit near us on the bough.

> We'll talk of sunshine and of song,
> And summer days, when we were young,
> Sweet childish days, that were as long
> As twenty days are now.
> —WORDSWORTH.

SUMMARY OF DEFINITIONS: THE VERB.

127. A **Verb** is a word, or, in the case of the verb-phrase, a word group, which asserts action or state of being with respect to some noun or pronoun.

129. A **Transitive Verb** is one in which the assertion of the verb passes over from one person or thing, the grammatical subject, from which or whom the action proceeds, to another person or thing, the grammatical object, which is directly affected by the action of the verb.

130. An **Intransitive Verb** is one in which the action of the verb does not pass over from the subject causing the action to an object immediately affected by the action, but in which the action is completely expressed by the subject and predicate.

133. A **Copulative Verb** is one which asserts state of being with respect to a subject. When followed by a predicate nominative, it couples or joins the subject and the predicate nominative by asserting the identity of the two.

135. A verb which asserts action or being in present time is in the **Present Tense.**

A verb which asserts action or being in past time is in the **Past Tense.**

A verb which asserts action or being in time to come is in the **Future Tense.**

141. Auxiliary Verbs are verbs which are used to help form verb-phrases.

142. The **Present Perfect Tense** indicates an action which is completed just at the time of speaking.

The **Past Perfect Tense** indicates an action completed at some past time before some other action took place.

The **Future Perfect Tense** indicates an action that will be completed at some future time.

154. Regular Verbs form their past tenses by adding *-d* or *-ed* to the uninflected form of the present.

Irregular Verbs form their past tenses by changing the root-vowel of the present.

155. The first person singular of the present tense, of the past tense, and the past participle of a verb are together called its **Principal Parts**.

158. A verb which asserts the action of a subject upon an object is in the **Active Voice**. All verbs in the active voice are transitive verbs.

A verb which expresses the subject as receiving the action of the verb is in the **Passive Voice**. All verbs in the passive voice are verb-phrases. An intransitive verb cannot be in the passive voice.

164. Verbals are words closely related in their use to verbs, but incapable of taking a subject, which combine in themselves the functions of a verb and a noun, adjective, or adverb. They are of two kinds, infinitives and participles.

165. Infinitives are verbals which combine in themselves the functions of a verb and a noun, an adjective or an adverb. The infinitive as noun has two forms, consisting of the simple form of the infinitive, or with the sign *to*, and of the infinitive in *-ing*.

177. Participles are verbals which combine in themselves the functions of a verb and an adjective, or an adverb. The present participle always ends in *-ing*.

187. The verb in the imperative sentence, that is, in the sentence expressing a command, wish, or entreaty, is in the **Imperative Mood.**

188. All verbs in the principal clauses of interrogative and declaratory sentences are in the **Indicative Mood,** and all verbs in subordinate clauses are also indicative, except those in which the subjunctive form is used.

189. The **Subjunctive Mood** is the use of the verb in subordinate clauses mainly to express uncertain condition, condition contrary to fact, and concession. It is always indicated by special inflectional forms.

QUESTIONS AND SUGGESTIONS FOR REVIEW.

1. Why is the verb an important word structurally in the sentence? 2. Give the definition of the verb. 3. Define transitive, intransitive, and copulative verbs, and select from some book five illustrations of each class. 4. What is meant by transitivity in the verb? 5. Give illustrations by means of sentences to show that the same verb may be either transitive or intransitive. 6. Tell what the function of the copulative verb is in the sentence. 7. Give five sentences illustrating the use of the copulative verb. 8. Define predicate adjective and give **three** sentences as illustrations. 9. Name the various

tenses of the verb and show how they are used. 10. What is meant by the person of the verb? the number? 11. Conjugate the verbs *to be* and *to do* through the present and past tenses. 12. What are auxiliary verbs? Give illustrations of the way in which they are used. 13. Give the principal rules for the use of *shall* and *will* in order to express futurity. 14. Give some of the other uses of *shall* and *will*. 15. Take a passage in dialogue in some standard book and gather together the illustrations of the use of *shall* and *will*. 16. What are progressive verb-phrases? Give illustrations. 17. Give the proper contracted forms of the verbs *have, do,* and *be,* when combined with *not*. 18. Define and illustrate regular and irregular verbs. 19. Name the principal parts of the verb. 20. When is a verb in the active voice? 21. When is a verb in the passive voice? 22. Collect ten sentences containing verbs in the active and ten in the passive voice. 23. Name the verbals. 24. Show by the analysis of an example how the verbal combines in itself two functions. 25. Give five illustrations of infinitives as verbals, and show the double function in each. 26. What are the two forms of the infinitive as verbal noun? 27. Give three sentences illustrating the use of the infinitive in *-ing*. 28. How can we distinguish the infinitive in *-ing* from the pure noun? 29. Give three illustrations of the infinitive as object complement. 30. Give five sentences illustrating the use of participles as verbals, and show how in each example the participle has double function. 31. What is meant by dangling participle? 32. How can we distinguish the present participle from the infinitive in *-ing?* 33. When is a verb in the imperative mood? in the indicative mood?

in the subjunctive mood? 34. For what purposes is the subjunctive used? Give illustrations. 35. Give the complete conjugation of the verb *talk* and of the verb *sing*. 36. Name the chief anomalous verbs. 37. In a passage of dialogue in some standard book, pick out the anomalous verb-phrases and tell the value of each one. 38. What characteristics are given in parsing the verb?

The Adverb.

196. The Adverb.—Compare the following two groups of sentences:

(1) The horse ran.	The horse ran swiftly.
(2) The birds were flying.	The birds were flying low.
(3) The Indian made his way	The Indian made his way silently through the forest.
(4) The ball fell.	The ball fell to the ground.

It will be observed that the words *swiftly, low, silently,* and the prepositional phrases *through the forest* and *to the ground,* in the second group of sentences are closely related to the verbs *ran, were flying, made,* with its object *his way,* and *fell.* They all limit or modify the meaning of the verbs by giving some attendant circumstance of the action indicated by the verbs. Words which perform this function are called **Adverbs**.

197. Adverbs Modifying Adjectives.—But compare also the following groups of sentences:

(1) It was a costly experiment.	It was an extremely costly experiment.
(2) He was a generous giver.	He was a prudently generous giver.
(3) I am hungry.	I am very hungry.

In the first group of sentences, *costly, generous,* and *hungry* are plainly adjectives, because they give qualifying details concerning the nouns *experiment* and *giver,* and the pronoun *I.* In the second group, *extremely, prudently,* and *very* are closely united to the adjectives *costly, generous,* and *hungry,* to which they add modifying details. Words which thus limit or define the meaning of adjectives are also adverbs.

In sentences like the following it should be noted that we have two or more adjectives all modifying the same noun, not adverbs modifying adjectives:

(1) It was a warm, sunny day.
(2) He gave me a shiny, red Astrakhan apple.
(3) A confused, rumbling, far away sound was heard.

198. Adverbs Modifying Other Adverbs.—Adverbs modify not only verbs and adjectives; they perform still another function in modifying other adverbs. Observe the following sentences:

(1) The Indian walked lightly.   The Indian walked very lightly.
(2) It was well done.   It was surprisingly well done.
(3) He consented readily.   He consented quite readily.

In the first group *lightly, well,* and *readily* are all adverbs modifying the verbs *walked, was done,* and *consented.* In the second group these same adverbs are themselves modified in turn by the adverbs *very, extremely,* and *quite.*

199. Phrases and Clauses as Adverbs.—An adverbial modifier may consist of a single word, of a phrase, or of a clause. The three kinds of modifiers are illustrated by the following three sentences:

He left { early.
by the nine o'clock train.
when he had finished his lessons.

Exercise.

In the following sentences, pick out the adverbs, the adverbial phrases, and the adverbial clauses, and state what word each modifies.

(1) He lives in the corner house.
(2) Come early, if you can.
(3) The boat drifted swiftly towards the open water.
(4) He died as he had lived, peacefully and kindly disposed towards all.
(5) When you have seen him, you will think differently.
(6) The sun sets exactly at six o'clock now.
(7) We expect a visitor to-morrow.
(8) He came to see our new house.
(9) The train was delayed by an accident.
(10) The snow fell silently and swiftly, covering the earth with a dazzlingly white mantle.
(11) We made a path by laying down the planks.
(12) In our time it was not customary for young men to behave so.

200. Classification of the Adverb.—It is convenient to classify adverbs and adverbial phrases and clauses as to their meaning, according to the way in which they modify verbs, adjectives, and adverbs. We have thus four classes: (a) **Adverbs of Place,** (b) **Adverbs of Time,** (c) **Adverbs of Manner,** (d) **Adverbs of Degree.**

(a) **Adverbs of Place** usually modify verbs by indicating the place at which the action of the verb occurs or the direction which it takes. Some of the more frequent are *here, there, in, out, before, behind, around,* etc.

Examples:

(1) He lives *here.*
(2) The ball went *over the fence.*
(3) You go by the direct road and they will go *around.*
(4) I find it *there by the roadside.*

(b) **Adverbs of Time** indicate when or how often an action takes place or how long it lasts. Some of the more frequent are *soon, early, then, before, afterwards, yesterday,* etc.

EXAMPLES.

(1) He came *yesterday*.
(2) We landed just *at the break* of day.
(3) I have seen you *before*.
(4) I knew him *when he was a little boy*.
(5) He fell *three times*.
(6) We walked *two hours* without stopping.

(c) **Adverbs of Manner** modify verbs, adjectives, and other adverbs by showing how or in what way an action is committed, or an adjective or adverb is limited or defined in its meaning.

(1) Adverbs of manner modifying verbs:
(1) The mistake was *skilfully* covered.
(2) The battle raged *fiercely*.
(3) *Merrily* sang the monks at Ely.
(4) He ran *fast*.
(5) We shouted *with all our might*.
(2) Adverbs of manner modifying adjectives:
(1) He was *astonishingly* clever.
(2) They were *proudly* reckless.
(3) Adverbs of manner modifying other adverbs:
(1) He came *unexpectedly* near.
(2) My brother works *unnecessarily* hard.

(d) **Adverbs of Degree** modify verbs, adjectives, and other adverbs by showing the extent to which the action indicated by the verbs, or the qualification indicated by the adjective and the adverb apply.

(1) Adverbs of degree modifying verbs:
(1) The owner was *greatly* disturbed.

(2) He *little* knew what was in store.
(3) I was *much* relieved.

(2) Adverbs of degree modifying adjectives:
(1) He was *completely* ignorant of the matter.
(2) The work was *very* easy.
(3) It was not *so* easy.
(4) The mark was *hardly* visible.
(5) He spent *over* five dollars.

(3) Adverbs of degree modifying other adverbs:
(1) They walked *very* rapidly.
(2) It is not *so* easily done.
(3) He spoke *quite* respectfully.

A convenient way of telling the class to which an adverb belongs is the following: Adverbs of place answer the question "Where"? Adverbs of time answer the question "When"? Adverbs of manner answer the question "How"? and Adverbs of degree answer the question "How much"? "To what extent"?

201. Negative Adverbs.—The negative adverb *not* modifies verbs, adjectives, and adverbs.

EXAMPLES:
(1) He did *not* speak.
(2) They are *not* beautiful.
(3) It is *not* very far.

The words *Yes* and *No*, used in answering questions, are sometimes classed as adverbs; they are better regarded, however, as abbreviated sentences, the single words being equivalent to whole sentences (see **230-231**).

202. Interrogative Adverbs.—Interrogative adverbs are used in asking questions. The most common are *how, why, when, where, whence,* etc. They are used in both direct and indirect questions.

EXAMPLES:

(1) *Why* have you done this?
(2) *How* can you think of such a thing?
(3) I don't see *how* you can think of such a thing.
(4) *Where* are you going?

203. Compound Adverbs.—Certain adverbs are combined with *-ever* so as to form compound adverbs, as, for example, *however, wherever, whenever*, etc. Other compounds are words like *always, henceforth, hereafter, indeed, whereby, thereby, sometimes,* and others. Often, also, phrases are used the elements of which are not written together as one word, but which are used with the value of a single word, and are to be so construed. The following are a few of the many examples: *at once, again and again, all right, as yet, at all, at least, at most, until then, by and by, for good, in short, in truth* (cf. *indeed*), *in vain, of course, of late, of old, one by one, day by day,* etc.

EXAMPLES:

(1) He will come *by and by*.
(2) They have tried *of late* to inaugurate a new system.
(3) The animals entered *one by one*.
(4) The fish rose to the surface *again and again*.

204. Comparison of Adverbs.—Many adverbs admit of comparison to indicate differences of degree, the manner of comparison being similar to that of the adjective.

Positive.	*Comparative.*	*Superlative.*
The report came *soon*.	The report came *sooner* than I had expected.	His report came *soonest*.
He walked *quickly* down the road.	He walked *more quickly* after that.	He walked *most quickly* of all.

205. Anticipatory "there."—Like the pronoun *it* (see **77**), the adverb *there* is used in anticipation of a subject which follows later in the sentence. For example, the sentence, *There were two men in the house* is equivalent to *Two men were in the house.* In the following sentences remove the anticipatory *there* and place in its stead the word or words which it anticipates:

(1) There are two sides to the question.
(2) There is little choice between the two.
(3) I don't believe that there are more than twenty men present.
(4) There is not sufficient time to take up the matter.
(5) There was a sound of revelry by night.
(6) There is nothing so certain as taxes.
(7) Is there nothing to be done?
(8) Let there be light.
(9) May there never come to you a less happy day.
(10) Was there no other time to do this?

206. Some Special Uses of the Adverb.—Some special uses of the adverb require separate treatment.

(1) **The Adverb " the " in Comparison.**—In sentences like *I like him the better for it*, or *It is none the worse for that*, the comparative adverb *better* and the comparative adjective *worse* are modified by the adverb *the*. In the second sentence the adjective *worse* is also modified by the adverb *none*. Other examples are the following:

(1) *The sooner* you do this, *the better* it will be for you.
(2) You will get along *all the more readily* for this long preparation.
(3) A man usually accomplishes less, *the less* he has to do.

NOTE.—In its origins the adverbial use of *the* is due to the fact that it was in Anglo-Saxon a special inflected case of the definite article, known as the instrumental case. It was equivalent in value to the prepositional phrase *by this* or *by that*. The sentence, *The sooner he comes, the better it will be*, is therefore equivalent to *by what he comes sooner, by that it will be better*. But the feeling for the case has long since become lost, and the construction persists only in this one example as an idiomatic survival.

(2) **Extent of Time, Space, and Amount.**—Nouns and noun-phrases are used without a governing word in expressions denoting extent of time, space, and amount with the value of adverbs.

EXAMPLES:
(1) He walked *a mile*.
(2) I usually study *two hours* in the evening.
(3) He can jump *eight feet*.
(4) This train makes *fifty miles an hour*.
(5) This book cost *two dollars*.
(6) I helped him *many times*.
(7) He doesn't care *a farthing* for such things.

(3) **Locative Adverb.**—Similar to the use of the adverb in expressing extent of time, space, and amount, is the use to express place. This is restricted now to the word *home*, in sentences like *I am going home*.

NOTE.—Adverbs expressing extent of time, space, amount, and the locative adverb are sometimes called adverbial objectives, because in the earlier stages of the language they were inflected for the objective case. They are not felt now, however, to have any case value and should be parsed as pure adverbs.

(4) **Adverbs which Look Like Adjectives.**—Words which are adjectives in form and are ordinarily used as adjectives, are sometimes adverbs, the part of speech being determined here, as always, not by the forms of the words, but by their use.

EXAMPLES:
(1) Do not speak so *loud*.
(2) Go *slow* and you will arrive the quicker.
(3) He ran very *fast*.

(5) **Sentence-Modifying Adverb.**—Sometimes adverbs are used without specific relation to any one word in the sentence, but rather as limiting the thought of the sentence as a whole. They are to be regarded then as sentence-modifying adverbs.

EXAMPLES:

(1) *Truly* this is an unfortunate state of affairs.
(2) That is an excellent plan *indeed*.
(3) *Unfortunately* he had to stand up and thus overtaxed his strength.

Perhaps the sentence equivalents *yes* and *no* (see **201**) should be classed under this head also, since they may be regarded as modifying a whole sentence which is unexpressed. Thus the question *Have you finished?* may be answered simply by *Yes*, which is equivalent to *Yes, I have finished*. Similar elliptical sentence-modifying adverbs are *Certainly, To be sure, Of course,* etc. See **231**.

(6) **The Adverbs " as " and " so."**—The word *as* has various uses which should be carefully distinguished. In the sentence, *He is as old as I am*, the first *as* is an adverb of degree modifying the adjective *old;* the second *as* is an adverbial conjunction. In the sentence *As I was coming home this morning, I found a purse, As* is an adverbial conjunction (see **216, (2)**, b), equivalent in meaning to *when*, or *while*. For the use of *as* as relative pronoun, see **89**.

The adverb *so* is used as an adverb of degree, as in *He is not so well this morning*, and also as a conjunctive adverb of manner, as in *As ye sow, so shall ye reap*.

(7) **Position of the Adverb.**—Care should be taken to place the adverb in such position in the sentence that it shall modify the word which it is meant to modify. The adverb *only* often gives a wrong meaning because it is not placed in its proper position. The various correct uses of *only* are exemplified in the following sentences:

(1) Only John came to see me (meaning John and no one else came to see me).

(2) John came to see me only (meaning John came to see me and no one else).
(3) John came only to see me (meaning that John came for no other purpose than to see me).
(4) This hat cost only two dollars (implying that two dollars was a small amount to pay for a hat).

207. Parsing the Adverb.—In parsing the adverb state (1) its kind, (2) the word which it modifies, and (3), if it is compared, the degree of its comparison. The interrogative adverb and the sentence-modifying adverb do not modify single words, and in parsing them it is necessary to state only that they introduce a question or modify the sentence as a whole. In parsing the relative adverb and the conjunctive adverb, state merely what clauses they join. The adverbs in the sentence *When the president heard this, he immediately signed the bill, although before he had hesitated many days in great uncertainty*, are parsed as follows:

> *When* is an adverbial conjunction of time, joining the subordinate clause *When the president heard this*, to the main clause which follows it.
> *Immediately* is an adverb of time, modifying the verb *signed*.
> *Before* is an adverb of time, modifying the verb *had spent*.
> *Many days* is an adverbial phrase expressing extent of time, modifying the verb *had hesitated*.
> *In great uncertainty* is an adverbial prepositional phrase of manner, modifying the verb *had hesitated*.

EXERCISE.

Parse the adverbs in the following sentences:
(1) Let us go quickly.
(2) They came soon after breakfast.
(3) The wind blew fresh.
(4) She was going away.

(5) He had heard of this once or twice before.
(6) We did not like to ask her why she was so sad.
(7) In those few weeks he had frightfully dissipated his capital.
(8) Never have I seen such strength so easily exerted.
(9) The gardener has only apples to sell this morning.
(10) We lived in that house ten years and then it was torn down to make room for this new one.
(11) You had better go home now; you have been working too hard to-day.
(12) We shall have time for that at least, though we may be too late if we stay until the end.
(13) He lived beside the church, whither he had gone every morning for twenty years to attend the early service.
(14) We held fast as long as we could, but we felt our strength slowly ebbing away.
(15) The past sends no messages back to tell what it has discovered.
(16) If he had desired merely to succeed, he might well have called his life successful; but he had hoped for more than this, he had expected also to be happy.

(17) I was walking a mile,
More than a mile from the shore,
The sun look'd out with a smile
Betwixt the cloud and the moor,
And riding at set of day
Over the dark moorland,
Rapidly riding far away,
She waved to me with her hand.
There were two at her side,
Something flashed in the sun,
Down by the hill I saw them ride,
In a moment they were gone:
Like a sudden spark
Struck vainly in the night,
Then returns the dark
With no more hope of light.
—TENNYSON, *Maud*.

SUMMARY OF DEFINITIONS: THE ADVERB.

196-198. An **Adverb** is a word used to modify a verb, adjective, or another adverb.

200. Adverbs are classified as **Adverbs of Place, Time, Manner,** and **Degree.**

202. Interrogative adverbs are used in asking questions.

206. (2) Nouns and noun-phrases are used without a governing word in expressions denoting extent of time, space, and amount, with the value of adverbs.

QUESTIONS AND SUGGESTIONS FOR REVIEW.

1. Pick out from some standard author five sentences containing adverbs modifying verbs, the same number of adverbs modifying adjectives, and of adverbs modifying other adverbs.   2. Give three sentences containing adverbial phrases and three containing adverbial clauses.   3. Name the four main classes of adverbs and give illustrations.   4. What is meant by negative adverbs?   5. Interrogative adverbs?   6. Compound adverbs?   7. How is the adverb compared?   8. Explain the use of anticipatory "there."   9. Explain the use of the adverb *the* in comparison.   10. Give illustrations of adverbs which in form look like adjectives.   11. What is meant by a sentence-modifying adverb? Give an illustration.   12. Give sentences illustrating the proper use of the adverb *only*.

The Preposition.

208. Prepositions.—The prepositions are link-words, and are used to point out the relation existing between other words. Their use is illustrated by the italicized words of the following sentences:

(1) The fall *of* rain was very great.
(2) He brought a book *for* you.
(3) They left *at* noon.
(4) He stood *at* the end *of* the line.
(5) I left *on* the ten o'clock train.
(6) The horse took the hurdle *with* ease.

In the first of these sentences, the preposition *of* serves to connect the noun *rain* with *fall* by showing what kind of fall is meant. In the same way, in the second sentence, the preposition *for* connects the noun *book* and the pronoun *you*. In the third sentence, the preposition *at* shows the relation existing between the verb *left* and the noun *noon*, the adverbial prepositional phrase *at noon* indicating the time at which the action of the verb took place. The fourth sentence contains two prepositions and two prepositional phrases, *At the end* being an adverbial prepositional phrase modifying *stood*, and *of the line* an adjective prepositional phrase modifying *end*. In the fifth and sixth sentences *on the ten o'clock train* is an adverbial prepositional phrase modifying *left*, and *with ease* is an adverbial prepositional phrase modifying *took*.

209. The Object of the Preposition.—The preposition is always followed by a noun, pronoun, or noun clause, which it unites to some other noun, pronoun, adjective, or verb, thus forming an adjective or adverbial prepositional phrase. The noun or pronoun or noun clause which follows the preposition is called its object.

EXAMPLES:

(a) Noun and pronoun objects of prepositions:
(1) They live in a brick *house*.

(2) It was not intended for *him*.
(3) The boys were punished for *leaving* school.

(b) Noun clauses as objects of prepositions:
(1) He sold it for *what it was worth*.
(2) We did not know with *whom we had spoken*.

The preposition may have a compound object, just as a verb may have a compound object (see **17**).

EXAMPLES:

(1) He is fond *of bugs and flies*.
(2) It was intended *for neither you nor me*.
(3) They are very expert *with bow and arrows*.

210. Compound Prepositions.—In some instances two prepositions have united so closely that they are written together as a single word, as, *e. g.*, *into, within, without, beside, because, before*, etc. Others have not developed quite so far and are still written apart, although functionally they are used as single words and should be so parsed. The following are a few of the more common instances: *out of, out in, next to, aside from, according to, in spite of, because of, up to, on to, on top* (written together as *atop*), etc.

EXAMPLES:

(1) He came *up to* me with a smile.
(2) He fell *out of* the boat into the water.
(3) They left him *out in* the cold.
(4) The boat lay *alongside of* the dock.

211. Prepositional Adverbs.—Prepositions are sometimes used without objects with the value of adverbs. These adverbs, however, do not readily fall under the classes of adverbs of time, place, manner, and degree, and it is better to speak of them as prepositional adverbs.

The difference between the pure preposition and the prepositional adverb is illustrated by the following two sentences:

> He ran up the stairs.
> He ran up a bill.

In the first sentence *stairs* is the object of *up*, and the whole phrase *up the stairs* is an adverbial prepositional phrase modifying the verb *ran*. In the second sentence *bill* is not the object of *up*, nor is *up a bill* a prepositional phrase modifying the verb. It is best to regard *up* as an adverb modifying *ran* and *bill* as the noun object of *ran*.

EXAMPLES:

(1) The men fell *to* and ate silently but heartily.
(2) The boat came *about* quickly.
(3) We hailed them as we passed *by*.
(4) They haven't much to live *on*.
(5) Night came *on* suddenly.

NOTE.—It will be observed that adverbial prepositions of this sort are very closely joined in meaning to the verbs, and they may therefore be regarded as parts of compound verbs which are not written together as compounds. In earlier stages of the language they would actually have been written together, the prepositions serving as prefixes in compound verbs, as is still done in words like *undergo, overtax, inclose, infix,* etc.

212. Prepositions in Relative Clauses.—The regular order of words in relative clauses containing a relative pronoun which is the object of a preposition is to place the relative pronoun immediately after the preposition, as in *I know the house in which he lives*. But the preposition may also stand at the end of the relative clause, as *I know the house which he lives in;* or the relative may be omitted altogether and the preposition be retained at the end of the clause without an object, as in *I know the house he lives in*. The retained preposition in sentences of this kind is to be regarded as a prepositional adverb. The compounds *wherein, whereby, whereat*, etc., which are equivalent in meaning to *in which, by which, at which*, are used as substitutes for a preposition followed by a relative pronoun object, as in *That is the point wherein he has fallen short*, equivalent to *That is the point in which he has fallen short.*

213. Some Special Uses of Prepositions.—Among the special uses of the preposition the following should be noted:

(1) **Adjective Prepositions.**—These are words like *near, nearer, nearest, next; like, more like, most like*, which in their origin are adjectives, and which retain the adjective characteristic of comparison, but which are used with the function of prepositions in sentences like the following, and should be therefore parsed as prepositions:

(1) He was sitting *near the door.*
(2) The building *next the postoffice* is the high school.
(3) He looks *like his father.*
(4) He looks *more like his father* than his brother does.

(2) **Conjunctive Prepositions.**—A few words like *but, except, save, notwithstanding*, which are generally used as conjunctions, sometimes have the value of prepositions. The following sentences illustrate this use:

(1) He saw no one *but me*, or He saw no one *save*, or *except me.*
(2) *Notwithstanding his promise*, he left school before the hour of dismissal.

(3) **"Than" as Preposition.**—The adverbial conjunction *than* following an adjective in the comparative degree has a strong tendency to be used as a preposition and is then followed by the objective case. This is the

rule when *than* is followed by the relative pronoun *whom*, as in the sentence *The winner of the prize was a student than whom none was more deserving.* One frequently hears, also, in colloquial speech, such sentences as *He is older than me.* It is better, however, to say *He is older than I*, since the sentence is an elliptical form of *He is older than I am old*, and structurally is exactly parallel to the sentence in which the adjective is in the positive degree, as in *He is as old as I (am old).*

(4) **The Partitive Preposition.**—After words denoting a part of an object or group of objects, the preposition *of* is used, followed by the noun or pronoun denoting the whole. This is called the **Partitive** use of the preposition *of*, and corresponds to the Latin and Greek partitive genitive:

EXAMPLES:
(1) *Ten of the men* were discovered.
(2) *Many of us* heard his speech.
(3) *Most of the building* was consumed by the fire.

Even when both nouns connected by the preposition name the whole, the construction remains the same, as in *All of the speakers were interesting.*

(5) **"As" as Preposition.**—The word *as* is sometimes used in the sense of *like, for, in the manner of*, with the value of a preposition, as in the sentence, *We used the building as a depot*, in which *as a depot* is an adverbial prepositional phrase modifying *used*.

EXAMPLES:
(1) We took our blankets *as* protection against the cold.
(2) He served *as* president for three years.
(3) The officers regarded this expedient *as* a makeshift.
(4) We went *as* guests of the owner.

214. Parsing the Preposition.—In parsing the preposition state:

(1) Whether it is a simple or compound preposition;
(2) what its object is;
(3) what word the prepositional phrase modifies, and whether it modifies it as an adjective or adverbial modifier or has some more special characteristic.

The prepositions in the sentence, *We all of us complain of the shortness of time and yet have much more than we know what to do with*, are parsed as follows:

Of is a simple partitive preposition, its object is *us*, and it unites the phrase *of us* to the word *all*.

Of in *of the shortness* is a simple preposition, its object is *shortness*, and it unites the phrase *of the shortness* as an adverbial modifier to the verb *complain*.

Of in *of time* is a simple preposition, its object is *time*, and it unites the phrase *of time* as an adjective modifier to the noun *shortness*.

With is an adverbial preposition, it has no object, and it modifies the infinitive *to do*.

Exercise.

Parse all the words of prepositional function in the following sentences:

(1) He built a cottage on the bank of the river.
(2) Nowhere in this country are such care and industry to be seen.
(3) It exploded with a report that was heard for miles around.
(4) He came in spite of all his protestations to the contrary.
(5) He lost all his property but a single house in the suburbs.
(6) He declares that he has nothing to live for.
(7) We spent two hours looking for the little cove in which we had landed.
(8) Time and tide wait for no man.

(9) The boat refused to answer to the helm, and we were in danger of drifting on the rocks.
(10) You must use a fine quality of white, porous paper.
(11) I have often wished for this book, and am grateful to you for sending it to me.
(12) He hurried through his lessons with a rapidity that was in about equal proportion to the inadequacy of his preparation.
(13) The boat, which we had spent two weeks waiting for, struck a submerged rock on its first trip and had to be sent back for repairs.
(14) It is strange that such a simple thing as matches should ever be imported from a country so far away as Sweden.
(15) Out of the parts of three old ones, he managed to put together a clock that would go.
(16) Luckily he came in just as we were about to leave for home.
(17) He ran up an account with amazing rapidity.

Summary of Definitions: the Preposition.

208. The **Prepositions** are link-words and are used to point out the relation existing between other words.

209. The noun, pronoun, or noun clause which follows the preposition and which is united to some other word is called the object of the preposition.

Questions and Suggestions for Review.

1. What is meant by calling the preposition a "link-word"? 2. Do prepositions when standing alone express ideas as clearly as nouns, pronouns, adjectives, and adverbs, when standing alone? 3. What is the object of the preposition? 4. Give three sentences each containing a prepositional adjective phrase. 5. Give three, each containing a prepositional adverbial phrase. 6. Give three

sentences in which the object of the preposition is a clause. 7. What are compound prepositions? 8. Explain the use of prepositions in relative clauses. 9. When may the preposition stand at the end of the sentence? 10. Comment on the use of *than* as a preposition.

The Conjunction.

215. Conjunctions.—Besides the prepositions, there is one other class of link-words, the chief function of which is to connect words or groups of words. These are the **Conjunctions.** Observe the way in which the italicized forms, all of which are conjunctions, are used in the following sentences:

(1) The dog *and* his master were both injured.
(2) The dog *or* his master will be injured.
(3) The dog was injured *but* his master was not.
(4) The gun burst *and* both the dog *and* his master were injured.
(5) He would be injured *if* the gun should burst.
(6) The gun burst *because* it was not clean.
(7) He was surprised, *for* he had not expected it.

It will be noted that conjunctions may connect two nouns, as, for example, *and* and *or* in the first and second sentences and the second *and* in the fourth; or they may connect two complete sentences, like *but* in the third sentence, the first *and* in the fourth, *if* in the fifth, *because* in the sixth, and *for* in the seventh sentences. But note that these conjunctions connect words and sentences in a different way from prepositions. The object of a preposition combines with the preposition to form an adjective or an adverbial phrase. The conjunction, however, differs from the preposition in that it does not have an object and in that it is not used to form adjective or adverbial modifying phrases or clauses. Its function is merely to connect a word or group of words with another.

216. Coördinating and Subordinating Conjunctions.—Conjunctions fall into two principal classes, coördinating and subordinating conjunctions.

(1) **Coördinating Conjunctions,** the chief of which are *and, or, nor,* and *but,* are used to connect two words (nouns, adjectives, pronouns, verbs, or adverbs), two phrases, or the parts of a compound sentence. They are called coördinating because they unite two elements of like grammatical kind and rank. The following sentences illustrate their use:

> (1) The house *and* the barn were built last summer.
> (2) I left it on the table *or* writing-desk, I forget which.
> (3) We did not see the doctor *but* we saw his assistant.
> (4) He *and* I came first.
> (5) I like either a sweet *or* a sour apple.
> (6) Stealthily *and* silently he crept upstairs.
> (7) I have not read *or* written a line to-day.

(2) **Subordinating Conjunctions,** which are numerous, are those which connect a dependent or subordinate statement to a main statement or to a preceding subordinate statement. Subordinating conjunctions connect only clauses or equivalents of clauses. The relations which the subordinating conjunction indicates between the subordinate and the main clauses are as follows:

> (a) The subordinate conjunction *that* is used to introduce a subordinate noun clause.
>
> EXAMPLES:
>
> (1) I told him *that* I should come.
> (2) We believed *that* he was the first man to enter that valley.

The conjunction *that* is frequently omitted, as in the sentence, *I told him I should come.*

(b) Time is expressed by such subordinating conjunctions as *before, until, after, when, whenever, since, as, as soon as, as long as, while.*

EXAMPLES:

(1) He came *before* he was expected.
(2) *While* we were waiting, the postman drove up.
(3) The train came in *as* we were turning the corner.

(c) Place, expressed by the conjunction *where.*

EXAMPLE:

(1) We found him *where* we had expected to do so.

(d) Cause or reason, expressed by the conjunctions *because, for, since, as, inasmuch as, whereas, why.*

EXAMPLES:

(1) I like him *because* he is so frank and open.
(2) We couldn't go to see him, *for* we were just then busy with our examinations.
(3) *Inasmuch as* you have broken your word, you will have to abide strictly by the rules hereafter.
(4) I don't know *why* you have come.

(e) Condition, expressed by the conjunctions *if, except, unless, provided, without, supposing, once.*

EXAMPLES:

(1) I shall go *if* the weather is fair.
(2) We can't go *unless* we hear from our trunks.
(3) The project will fail *except* this condition be agreed upon.
(4) *Once* he accepted an acquaintance, his manner was very gracious.

(f) Concession, expressed by the conjunctions *though, although, albeit, notwithstanding.*

EXAMPLES:

(1) We found the book, *though* it had been much injured by the rain.
(2) He accepted this position, *notwithstanding* he had been receiving higher pay.

(g) Purpose, expressed by the conjunctions *that, in order that, so that, lest.*

EXAMPLES:

(1) We did this *that* he might know who we were.
(2) We did this *lest* he should know who we were.

(h) Manner, expressed by the conjunctions *as, as if, as though.*

EXAMPLES:

(1) We did it *as* we best knew how.
(2) It looks *as though* it would rain.
(3) They pretended *as if* they hadn't seen us.

The preposition *like* is often improperly used as a conjunction of manner, as in the sentence, *It looks like it would rain,* or *John doesn't work like he does,* which should read *It looks as though it would rain,* or *It looks like it,* and *John doesn't work as he does* or *John doesn't work like him.*

(i) The adversative relation, expressed by the conjunctions *yet, and yet.*

EXAMPLES:

(1) He was not invited to come, *yet* here he is.
(2) We do not like this state of affairs *and yet* we permit it to continue.

(j) Result, expressed by the conjunction, *that, so that.*

EXAMPLES:

(1) He fell in such a way *that* his head did not strike the ground.
(2) He trembled *so that* he could hardly stand up.

217. Correlative Conjunctions.—A more emphatic way of uniting two words or clauses than by the use of the simple conjunction is that of the correlative conjunction, which is a double conjunction, each of the parts joined being provided with a conjunctive element. The most common of the correlative conjunctions are *either . . . or, neither . . . nor, not only . . . but also, not only . . .but as well, both . . . and, when . . . then, whether . . . or.*

EXAMPLES:

(1) *Either* the horse *or* the pony will do.
(2) *Neither* the horse *nor* the pony will do.
(3) We saw *not only* John *but also* his sister, *or* We saw *not only* John *but* his sister *also*.
(4) *Both* father *and* son perished in the flames.
(5) *When* you reach home, *then* you can change your clothes.

218. Appositive Coördination.—Sometimes the coördinate conjunctions *and* and *or* are used to unite two words which do not name different objects but the same object looked at from two points of view. In such uses the second noun is equivalent in meaning to an appositive noun, and the conjunction may be regarded as an appositive coördinating conjunction.

EXAMPLES:

(1) The bison *or* buffalo is an almost extinct animal.
(2) Mr. Worth, sheriff *and* postmaster of the village, presided.

In a similar way the conjunction *that* is used to introduce a noun clause which is in apposition to a preceding word, the meaning of which it states more explicitly:

EXAMPLES:

(1) The superstition *that Friday is an unlucky day* is a widespread one.
(2) We heard a report *that you had gone home.*

219. Conjunctions in Comparison.—In the positive degree the second term in a comparison is introduced by the conjunction *as*, as in the sentence, *The task was not so difficult as we thought it would be;* in the comparative degree it is introduced by the conjunction *than*, as in *They put a heavier load on the wagon than it would stand.*

220. Expletive Conjunctions.—Sometimes a sentence begins with a conjunction, or a conjunction is inserted in the body of a sentence, without being used to connect any two parts of the sentence, but to serve as a general introduction to, or modification of, the sentence as a whole. This is called the expletive use of the conjunction. See **230**.

EXAMPLES:

(1) *Nevertheless*, we have decided to continue as we have begun.
(2) *Indeed*, I didn't know you were in town at all.
(3) You can't tell, *though*, until you make the experiment.

221. Parsing the Conjunction.—In parsing the conjunction, point out what kind of conjunction it is and what elements of the sentence it serves to unite. In the following sentence the conjunctions are parsed as examples:

The general belief among country people that the jay hoards up nuts for winter use has probably some foundation in fact, though one is at a loss to know where he could place his stores so that they would not be pilfered by the mice and squirrels.

That is a conjunction introducing the appositive clause *that the jay hoards up nuts for winter use*, which is appositive to the noun *belief*.

Though is a subordinating conjunction, introducing the concessive clause *though one is at a loss to know where he could place his stores,* etc., which it unites to the main clause *The general belief . . . that the jay hoards up nuts . . . has probably some foundation in fact.*

Where is a subordinating conjunction, introducing the noun clause *where he could place his stores,* which it unites as object of the verb *to know* to the preceding clause. As an adverbial conjunction *where* has a double function; as conjunction it unites the two clauses, and as adverb it modifies the verb *could place* in the subordinate clause.

So that is a subordinating conjunction, introducing the result clause *so that they would not be pilfered by the mice and squirrels,* which it unites to the preceding subordinate clause.

EXERCISE.

Parse the conjunctions in the following passage by stating their kinds and by showing what parts of their respective sentences they unite:

THE ATTACK.

While the ship was hauling round to the south end of a small island, which the lieutenant had named Portland from its very great resemblance to Portland in the British Channel, she suddenly fell into shoal water and broken ground. The soundings were never twice the same, jumping at once from seven fathom to eleven. However, they were always seven fathom or more, and in a short time the *Endeavor* got clear of danger, and again sailed in deep water. While the ship was in apparent distress, the inhabitants of the island, who in vast numbers sat on its white cliffs and could not avoid perceiving some appearance of confusion on board and some irregularity in the working of the vessel, were desirous of taking advantage of her critical situation. Accordingly five canoes, full of men and well armed, were put off with the utmost expedition; and they came so near and showed so hostile a disposition by shouting, brandishing their lances, and using threatening gestures, that the lieutenant was in pain for his small boat, which was still engaged in sounding. By a musket which he ordered to be fired over them they were rather provoked than intimidated. The firing of a four-pounder loaded with grape-shot, though purposely discharged wide of them, produced a better effect. Upon the report of the piece the Indians all rose up and shouted; but instead of continuing the chase, they collected themselves together, and, after a short consultation, went quietly away.

Captain Cook's *Voyages Round the World*, Vol. I, p. 59.

Summary of Definitions: the Conjunction.

215. Conjunctions are words which are used to connect words or groups of words.

216. (1) **Coördinating Conjunctions** are used to connect words, phrases, or clauses of the same grammatical function. They are called co rdinating conjunctions because they unite two elements of like kind and equal rank.

(2) **Subordinating Conjunctions** are used to connect subordinate clauses to the clauses on which they depend.

217. Correlative Conjunctions are double conjunctions, each of the parts of the sentence joined being provided with one of the conjunctive elements.

Questions and Suggestions for Review.

1. Show the difference between the preposition and the conjunction as link-words in the sentence. 2. Give five sentences containing coördinating conjunctions and the same number containing subordinating conjunctions. 3. Name some of the relations which are indicated by the subordinating conjunctions. 4. What is meant by conjunctive adverb? 5. What are correlative conjunctions? Give illustrations. 6. What is meant by appositive coördination? 7. State the use of the conjunction in comparison. 8. What are expletive conjunctions?

The Interjection.

222. Interjections.—Like the expletive conjunctions, interjections do not have close connection with any specific word or words in the sentence. They neither name objects, like nouns, nor assert actions, like verbs, nor give qualifying details concerning nouns and verbs, like adjectives and adverbs; nor, on the other hand, are they link-words, like prepositions and conjunctions, uniting one word or group of words to another. They stand outside the fabric of the sentence and express a general emotion with respect to the whole idea of the sentence. Since they have no further grammatical function, all that grammar need note with respect to them is their classification as interjections. It should be observed that the number of interjections in the spoken language is much greater than it is in the written and printed language, and also that the spelling is often an imperfect and conventional representation of the real spoken form of the interjection. The following is a list of a few of the more commonly used written and printed interjections:

Oh, Ah, Alas, Pshaw, Lo, Fie, Hello, Hurrah, Hem, Humph, Hush, Hist, etc.

The interjection is usually followed by an exclamation point.

223. Weakened Interjections.—Often, in colloquial speech, a sentence begins with an interjection expressing a mild degree of feeling or emotion. Thus a sentence may begin with *Why,* as in *Why, how did you get here?* or, with *Well,* as in *Well, if he must, let him come,* or even *Oh* may be used thus, as in *Oh, don't trouble yourself* *about it*. Words of this sort are to be regarded as weak forms of the interjections. The frequent use of them should be discouraged, as it tends to develop into a bad habit of beginning almost every sentence with *Why*, or *Well*, or *Say*, or some similar unnecessary word.

224. Interjectional Phrases or Clauses.—A phrase like *Good heavens!*, *Heaven and earth!*, *Mercy on us!*, or a clause like *What a day it was!*, *If I could only see him!*, may be used with the value of an interjection. For the close relation between the interjection and the exclamatory sentence, see **7-8**.

Numerals.

225. Numerals.—Numerals, as the name indicates (from Latin *numerus*, "number") are words which express ideas of number. They differ from words of indefinite quantity or number, like *much, many, great*, etc., in that they indicate number exactly, as in *ten men, the tenth man, a million dollars*. According to their function, numerals are adjectives, nouns, or adverbs.

EXAMPLES:

Numerals as adjectives:
  (1) We found *two* large planks on the beach.
  (2) *Twenty-five* years we have been waiting for this day.
  (3) The *third* trial was successful.
  (4) We were given a *double* allowance that day.
  (5) There is talk of a *triple* alliance.

Numerals as nouns:
  (1) *Two* of the candidates were disqualified.
  (2) We can take only *ten* with us.
  (3) *Five* and *seven* make *twelve*.

Numerals as adverbs:
(1) He tried *twice* to reach the float.
(2) The cock crew *thrice*.
(3) Try it *once* and you will try it often.

226. Classification of Numerals.—Numerals are classified as (a) **Cardinals** and (b) **Ordinals**.

(a) Cardinal numerals give the number of persons or things spoken about.

EXAMPLES:
(1) There are *twenty* boys in the class.
(2) *Five* houses on this street are empty.
(3) *One* day will not be long enough.

(b) Ordinal numerals indicate the place or position of a person or thing in a series.

EXAMPLES:
(1) Ask the *third* boy from the end.
(2) This is the *twentieth* day of January.
(3) They are on the *fourth* lap.

227. Both cardinals and ordinals may be used as nouns, as in the following examples:

(1) There are *twenty* in the class.
(2) *One* will not be enough.
(3) Ask the *third* from the end.
(4) This is the *twentieth* of January.

In these instances, however, the numerals combine in themselves the characteristics of the pronoun, in that they indicate persons or objects without naming them, and of the adjective, in that they limit in some degree the person or object implied by the numeral.

Cardinal numerals when used merely as the name of a number are pure nouns. As such they are also capable of receiving a plural form.

EXAMPLES:

(1) *Ten* comes after *nine*.
(2) A *billion* is an inconceivable number.
(3) Nine *tens* make *ninety*.
(4) The strikers gathered by *twos* and *threes*.

228. Distributive Numerals.—The correlative numerals *one . . . another, the one . . . the other* are used with distributive value, as in the sentences, *Some went in one direction, some in another; I shall take neither the one nor the other.*

229. Form of the Numerals.—Cardinal numerals are represented either by words written out, as *one, two, three*, etc., or the Arabic numerals 1, 2, 3, etc., or Roman numerals, I, II, III, etc.

Ordinal numerals are either written out *first, second, third*, etc., or are represented by the Arabic symbols with abbreviation, 1st, 2nd, 3rd, etc., or less frequently by the Roman symbols, Ist, IInd, IIIrd, etc.

Whether written out or represented by symbols the function of the numeral in its relation to other words remains the same.

CHAPTER IV.—INDEPENDENT AND ELLIPTICAL ELEMENTS.

230. Independent and Parenthetical Sentence Elements.—Although in general every word in the sentence has close and immediate connection with some other word in the sentence, and the fabric of the sentence is thus a closely knit and interdependent whole, there are nevertheless a number of instances in which words and phrases are introduced into the structure of the sentence in a loose and independent way, modifying the thought of the sentence as a whole rather than any specific part of it. We have already spoken of sentence-modifying adverbs **(206 (5))** and expletive conjunctions **(220)** from this point of view. There are, besides, several other ways in which independent elements may be introduced into the body of the sentence, the most important of which are the following:

(1) **The Parenthesis.**—When the progress of a thought in the sentence is interrupted for a moment in order to introduce a related, but somewhat remote, thought, the interrupting part of the sentence is often enclosed within parentheses, as in the following example:

Such of my readers as may not be familiar with Scottish history (though the manner in which it has of late been woven with captivating fiction has made it a universal study), may be curious to learn something of the subsequent history of James.

A parenthetical sentence or phrase, as in the above example, may usually be set off from the rest of the sentence merely by commas, but the parentheses serve to separate it more sharply and distinctly from the main body of the sentence. The extent to which the parenthetical sentence is used varies greatly in different writers, being used so frequently by some as to constitute a distinct mannerism of style. In the following examples the italicized words are parenthetical in thought, but are separated from the body of the sentence only by commas:

(1) This house, *as I have heard*, was the first bank established in the city.
(2) The bill, *thanks to the minority leader*, was easily passed.
(3) Dissatisfaction with the present state of affairs, *it seems*, had been growing for a long time.

In general one should avoid a too frequent use of parentheses.

(2) **The Independent Infinitive Phrase.**—An infinitive phrase may be inserted into the body of the sentence, modifying thus the thought of the sentence as a whole.

EXAMPLES:
(1) We didn't know, *to tell the truth*, whether you were coming or not.
(2) This, *to repeat*, is the most serious cause of discontent.

(3) **The Independent Participial Phrase.**—Similar to the independent infinitive phrase is the independent participial phrase, used in the same way and with the same value.

EXAMPLE:
Speaking of investigations, there is no reason to suppose that this one will result differently from the rest.

Both the independent infinitive and the participial phrase are equivalent in thought to subordinate sentences; they are used, however, without the close connection with the rest of the sentence that the subordinate sentence has.

(4) **Words of Address.**—In speaking and in writing, the name of the person addressed is often inserted into the body of the sentence, either to arouse the attention of the person spoken to, or, in more familiar conversation, to serve as a mild indication of interest or affection on the part of the speaker towards the person spoken to.

EXAMPLES:

(1) *Mr. Williams*, will you take the part of Iago?
(2) I don't know, *Tom*, if I shall have time for that or not.

In poetry and elevated discourse persons and inanimate objects are often addressed directly for the purpose of calling the ideas they express more vividly before the mind.

EXAMPLES:

(1) Stars, hide your fires,
Let not night see my dark and deep desires!
(2) O my Country, what a wound did you then receive!

(5) **Independent Prepositional Phrases.**—Closely related to the sentence-modifying adverbs are the independent prepositional phrases, as in the following examples:

(1) *Between you and me*, I don't believe he has told the whole story.
(2) You will know the result, *of course*, by Saturday.
(3) Do you know, *by the way*, that we haven't yet called on our new neighbor?

231. Elliptical Sentences and Clauses.—Ellipsis is the omission from the expression of an idea of certain parts of the thought which may easily be supplied from the context. The chief purpose of ellipsis is economy and brevity of expression. Elliptical sentences and clauses should be analyzed and parsed as they stand, being classified simply as elliptical sentences or clauses; the unexpressed parts should not be supplied for the purposes of parsing, inasmuch as they are not necessary for the expression of the thought and are not silently understood in the mind of the speaker or writer who uses the elliptical construction. Such sentences are often perfectly natural and proper, although they do not contain all the elements necessary to a complete grammatical analysis of them. The following are the chief kinds of elliptical sentences:

(a) Ellipsis of the verb in a subordinate clause:
  (1) You are not as tall as he=You are not as tall as he is tall.
  (2) Your news is important if true=Your news is important if it is true.
  (3) Lawsuits are not so common here as in the city=Lawsuits are not so common here as they are in the city.
  (4) The tallest man takes the right end, the shortest the left=The tallest man takes the right end, the shortest man takes the left end.
  (5) I don't want to go but John does=I don't want to go but John does want to go.
  (6) There is no country more liberal than this=There is no country more liberal than this country is liberal.
  (7) We talked it over while walking down the street=We talked it over while we were walking down the street.

(b) The noun which an adjective modifies is omitted:
  (1) Washington's birthday is on the twenty-second of February=Washington's birthday is on the twenty-second day of February.

(2) I shall be eighteen on the first of May=I shall be eighteen years old on the first day of May.

(3) The oldest man in the town is also the richest=The oldest man in the town is also the richest man in the town.

(c) A relative pronoun is omitted:
(1) You are the man I mean=You are the man whom I mean.
(2) That is the prize you want to try for=That is the prize which you want to try for.
(3) He doesn't realize the trouble he is making=He doesn't realize the trouble which he is making.

(d) The infinitive verb is omitted after its sign *to*.[1]
(1) You need not go unless you want to=You need not go unless you want to go.
(2) If you have to, stay over until to-morrow=If you have to stay, stay over until to-morrow.

(e) A number of examples may be grouped under the head of incomplete sentences. In a way they are sentences, since they are capable of expressing a thought. They are exceptional, however, in that they do not follow the ordinary structure of a regularly expressed sentence.

(1) Such sentence equivalents as *Yes, No, To be sure, Certainly*, etc., may be regarded as a kind of short-cut sentence. They have no grammatical structure and are incapable of analysis.

(2) Exclamatory sentences like *Water!*, meaning *Give me some water;* or *More!*, meaning *I want more;* incomplete wishes like *If I only knew where to look for it!*, meaning *I should be glad if I only knew where to look for it*, or *Oh, to be in England now that April's there!*, to be completed in the same way; phrases like *Six months at sea!*, meaning *Think of being six months at sea!*, or *You a lawyer!*, meaning *Do you mean to say that you are a lawyer?*—

---

[1] This use, though permissible in colloquial, everyday speech, is hardly good literary style.

all these are to be classed simply as incomplete sentences incapable of grammatical analysis.

(3) Certain sentences intentionally omit their conclusion for the sake of emphasis, as in *Well, if that's the best you can do*——; or *You had better drop that or*——, in which cases the reader or listener is expected to fill out the thought for himself.

CHAPTER V.—ANALYSIS AND DIAGRAM.

232. Analysis of Sentences.—In analyzing sentences we separate them into the various parts of which they are composed, so as to indicate the relation of the parts to each other.

In analyzing the simple sentence state:

(1) the kind of sentence it is;
(2) the simple subject, then the complete subject, stating how the parts of the complete subject modify the simple subject;
(3) the simple predicate, then the complete predicate, stating how the parts of the complete predicate modify the simple predicate;
(4) the simple object, if there is one, then the complete object, stating how the parts of the complete object modify the simple object. Or if the predicate is a copulative verb, state then the predicate nominative in the same way as the object.

In analyzing the complex sentence, state:

(1) the kind of sentence it is and the clauses of which it is composed;
(2) the analysis of the principal sentence, as in the simple sentence;
(3) the subordinate clause or clauses, stating how each is dependent on the rest of the sentence;
(4) then the analysis of the subordinate clause or clauses as in the simple sentence.

In analyzing the compound sentence, state:
(1) the kind of sentence it is;
(2) the members of which the compound sentence is composed, naming the conjunctions by which they are joined;
(3) then the analysis of each member of the compound sentence as in the simple sentence.

EXAMPLES:

The early bird catches the worm is a simple declarative sentence. The simple subject is *bird*, the complete subject is *The early bird*, and *bird* is modified by the adjectives *the* and *early*. The simple predicate is *catches*. The simple object is *worm*, the complete object is *the worm*, and *worm* is modified by the adjective *the*.

This is the book which belongs here is a complex declarative sentence, composed of the two clauses *This is the book* and *which belongs here*. The principal subject of the principal sentence is *This*. The simple predicate is the copula *is*. The simple predicate nominative is *book*, which is modified by the adjective *the* and also by the subordinate clause. The subordinate clause *which belongs here* is a relative adjective clause modifying *book*. The simple subject of the subordinate clause is *which*, the simple predicate is *belongs*, which is modified by the adverb *here*.

Will you come or will you stay at home? is a compound interrogative sentence. It is composed of the two members *Will you come* and *will you stay at home*, connected by the conjunction *or*. The simple subject of the first member is *you*, the simple predicate is *will come*. The simple subject of the second member is *you*, the simple predicate is *will stay*, which is modified by the adverbial prepositional phrase *at home*.

233. Diagram.—In order to make the analysis of the sentence easily visible, it may be represented in diagram as follows, beginning with the simple sentence:

Time flies.

| Time | flies |

ANALYSIS AND DIAGRAM. 233

Cæsar conquered Gaul.

| Cæsar | conquered | Gaul |

The early bird catches the worm.

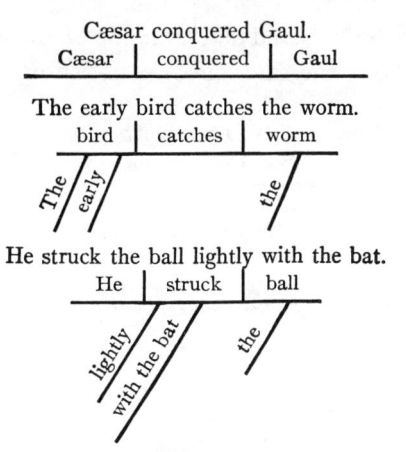

| bird | catches | worm |

The / *early* \ \ *the*

He struck the ball lightly with the bat.

| He | struck | ball |

lightly / *with the bat* \ *the*

234. When the verb of the sentence is a copulative verb, a slightly different arrangement is necessary:

This house was Washington's headquarters.

house | was | headquarters

This \ *Washington's*

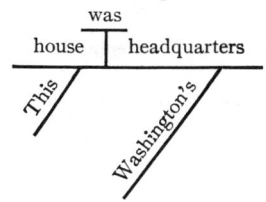

The relation of an adverb to the copulative verb is indicated as follows:

This house was Washington's headquarters for a short time.

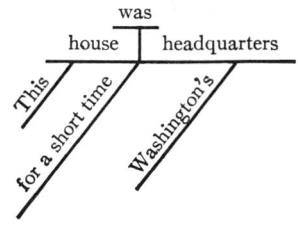

house | was | headquarters

This \ *a short time* \ *Washington's*
for

235. The analysis and diagramming of the interrogative sentence follows the same method as the declarative sentence:

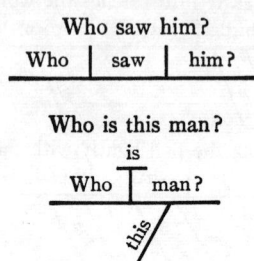

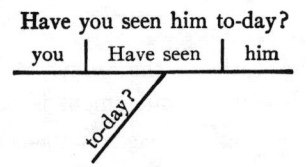

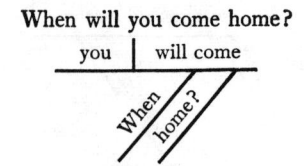

Who saw him?

| Who | saw | him? |

Who is this man?

Who | is | man?
 \ this

Have you seen him to-day?

you | Have seen | him
 \ to-day?

When will you come home?

you | will come
 \ When \ home?

How many men were found in the house?

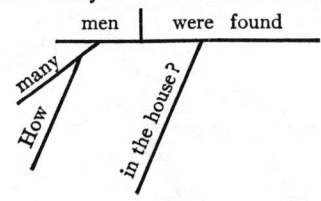

men | were found
 \ many \ in the house?
 \ How

Whom shall we send?

| we | shall send? | Whom |

236. Imperative sentences by their nature are frequently not capable of analysis. An imperative sentence of a single word, like *Listen*, is complete in itself. It may be limited, however, by an adverb, an adverbial phrase, or an adverbial clause, as:

>Listen closely.
>Listen with all your attention.
>Listen while I repeat the lines.

Sentences expressing a wish, however, are usually capable of analysis:

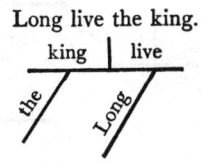

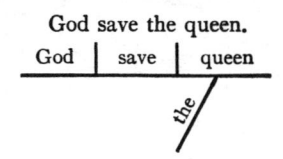

Long live the king.

God save the queen.

Exclamatory sentences are analyzed as follows:

How pleasant are the memories of childhood!

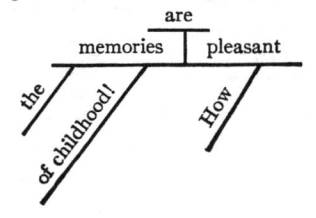

237. Compound subject, predicate, and object are analyzed and diagrammed as follows:

The house and barn were burned.

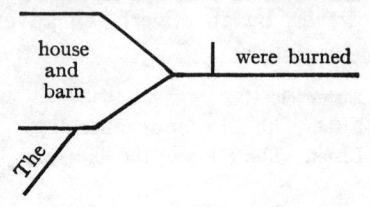

```
    house      |
    and        |  were burned
    barn       |
       \
       The
```

The horse stumbled and fell.

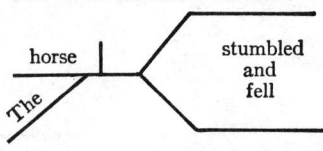

```
            |   stumbled
    horse   |   and
            |   fell
      \
      The
```

They destroyed their ammunition and supplies.

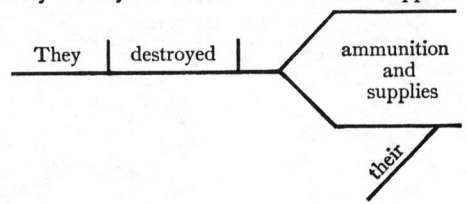

```
                              ammunition
    They | destroyed |        and
                              supplies
                                 \
                                 their
```

He was my guide, philosopher, and friend.

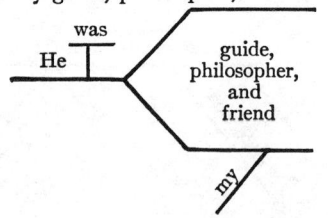

```
         was
    He  —|—        guide,
                   philosopher,
                   and
                   friend
                      \
                      my
```

ANALYSIS AND DIAGRAM.

238. Apposition is indicated as follows:

Mr. Smith, the well-known lawyer, argued the case.

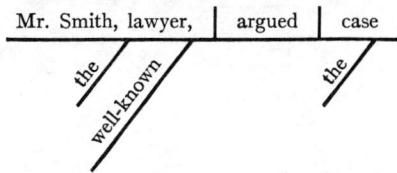

[Diagram: Mr. Smith, lawyer, | argued | case — with modifiers "the", "well-known" under "Mr. Smith, lawyer," and "the" under "case"]

We discovered the host, a foolish, weak man, asleep on a barrel.

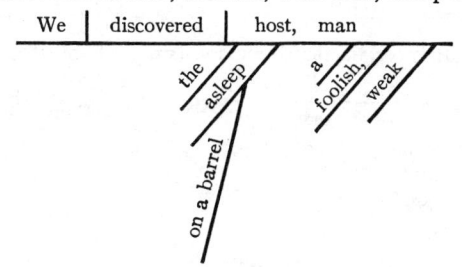

[Diagram: We | discovered | host, man — with "the" and "asleep" under "host"; "a", "foolish", "weak" under "man"; and "on a barrel" under "asleep"]

The buffalo, or bison, is now almost extinct.

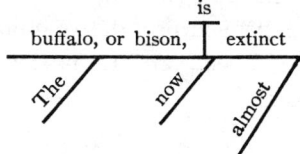

[Diagram: buffalo, or bison, | is | extinct — with "The" under the subject, "now" under "is", and "almost" under "extinct"]

239. Sentences in which the anticipatory *it* or *there* takes the place of a logical subject which follows later in the sentence, are diagrammed as follows:

It is not always the kindest charity to give gifts of money.

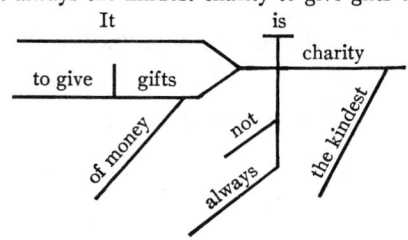

[Diagram: It | is | charity — with "to give | gifts" on a stem replacing "It"; "of money" under "gifts"; "not", "always" under "is"; "the kindest" under "charity"]

There were two hundred people in the house.

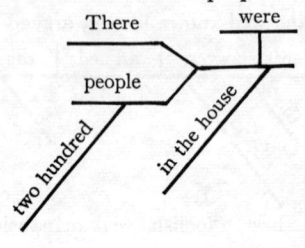

It is certain that the moon is not inhabited.

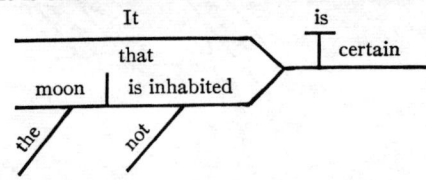

240. Verbs which take two objects, that is, an object and an object complement or a dative object, or an object and an infinitive object, are to be analyzed and diagrammed as follows:

They elected him chairman.

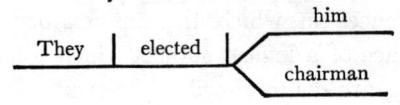

He sold us two apples.

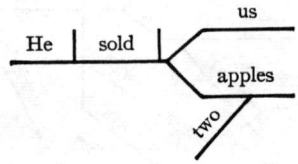

ANALYSIS AND DIAGRAM.

I gave him permission to go home.

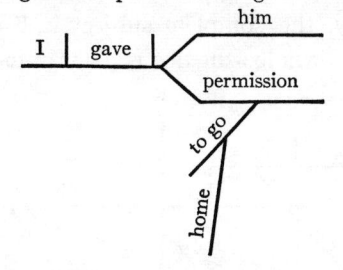

```
       |        | him
   I   | gave  /
       |      /_____
              \  permission
               \
                \ to go
                 \
                  | home
```

We saw him fall.

```
       |       | him
  We   | saw  /
       |      \
               \ fall
```

They begged him to turn back.

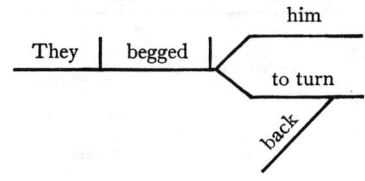

```
        |          | him
  They  | begged  /
        |         \
                   \ to turn
                    \
                     \ back
```

The retained object is expressed as follows:

He was elected president of his class.

```
  He | was elected | president
     |             \
                    \ of his class
```

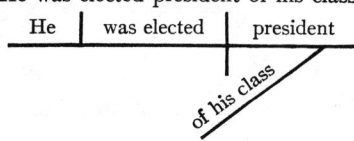

241. Sometimes a whole phrase which itself is capable of further analysis is used as the subject or object of a simple sentence, or as a modifier. For example, in the sentence, *To give gifts of money is not always the kindest charity*, the complete subject is *To give gifts of money*, and the whole sentence is diagrammed as follows:

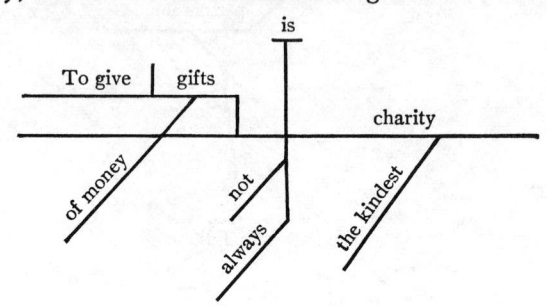

I expected to find him here.

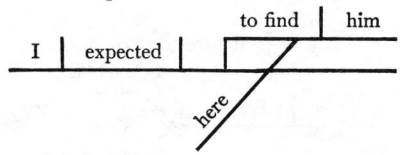

He came to visit his brother.

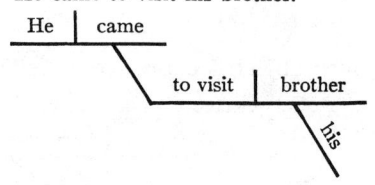

You have time to finish your dinner.

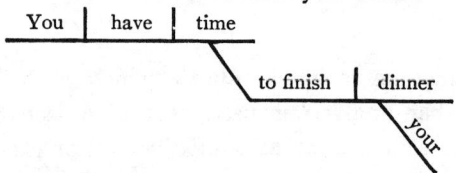

Watching him closely we detected his disguise.

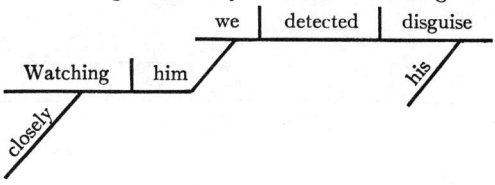

242. Compound sentences are diagrammed as follows:

We left our unfinished work and went to the fire.

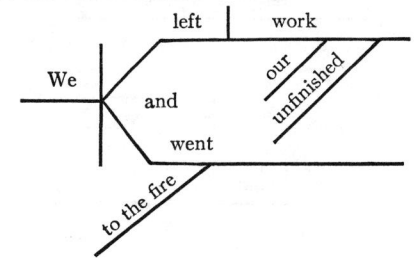

The house was not finished but we moved into it.

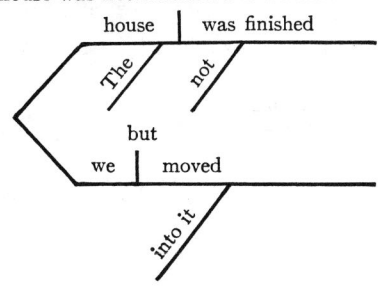

Either Tom has forgotten what I said, or he has met with some accident.

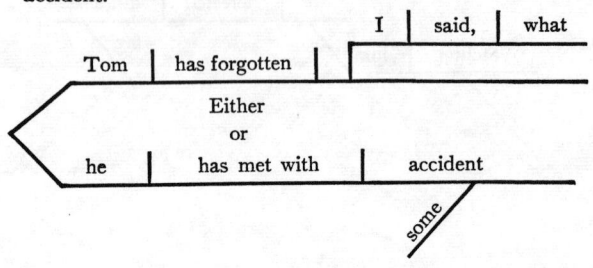

The house we have bought is new, but it already looks old.

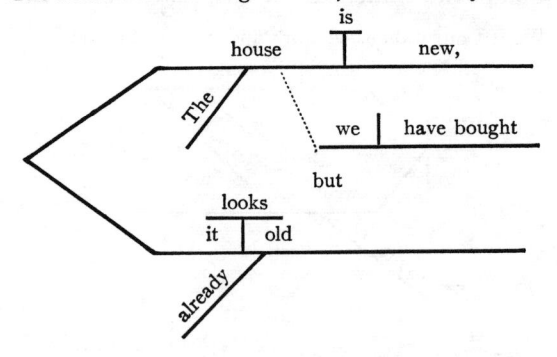

243. Complex sentences assume a great variety of forms, some of the more important of which, beginning with relative subordinate clauses, are analyzed as follows:

This is the book which belongs here.

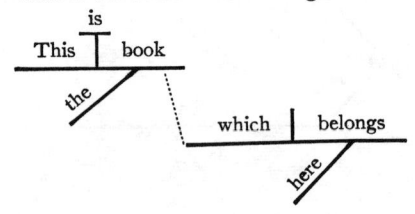

ANALYSIS AND DIAGRAM.

You know the man whom I mean.

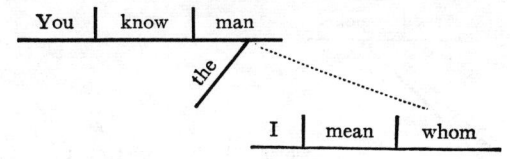

This is the house in which I was born.

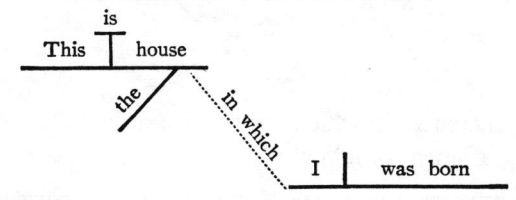

I don't know the hour at which he came.

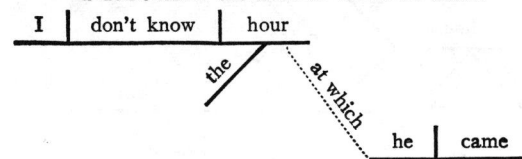

I know whose hat this is.

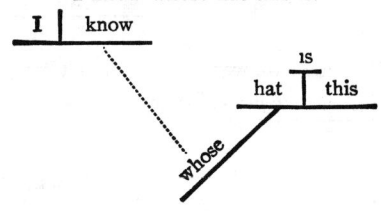

He spoke from a platform which had been built in the courtyard.

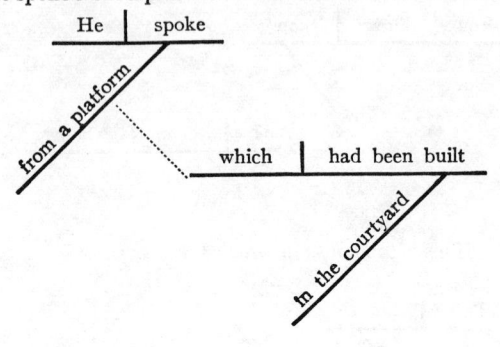

244. Sentences in which the relative pronoun is omitted are diagrammed as follows:

The house we live in is very old and has a very interesting history.

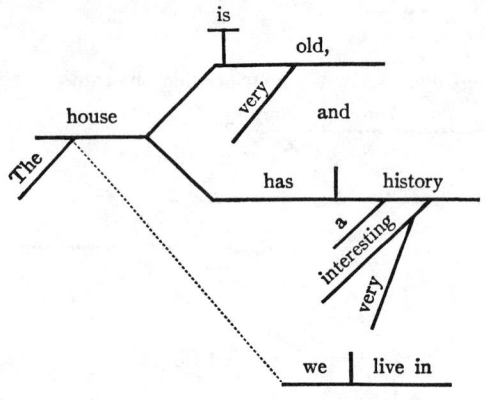

The man we wanted we couldn't get.

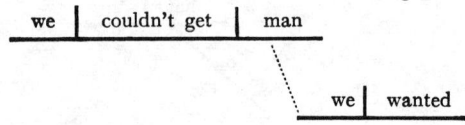

This is the book you were looking for.

```
        is
This  |  book
──────┼──────────────────────
   the \
         \   you | were looking for¹
```

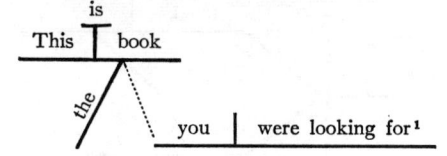

245. Other examples of complex sentences are the following:

There is no man but would give ten years of his life to write such a book.

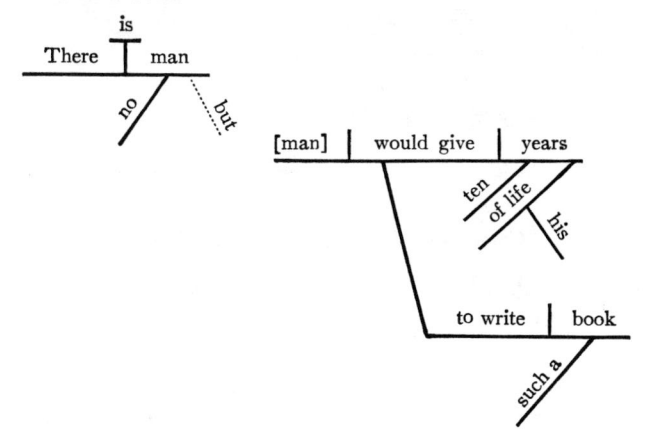

```
         is
There  |  man
──────┼──────
   no \   \ but
          [man] | would give | years
                       ten / / of life  \ his
                   
                   to write | book
                             \ such a
```

¹ It should be remembered that elliptical sentences which omit the relative and which in the full form of the sentence govern the relative as object of a preposition, e. g., *The house we live in is very old*=*The house in which we live is very old*, or *The house which we live in is very old*; *This is the book you were looking for*=*This is the book for which you were looking*, or *This is the book which you were looking for*, retain the preposition in the elliptical form of the sentence without an object. The preposition may then be regarded as an integral part of the verb, or it may be treated as an adverbial modifier of the verb.

Whoever breaks this law shall suffer for it.

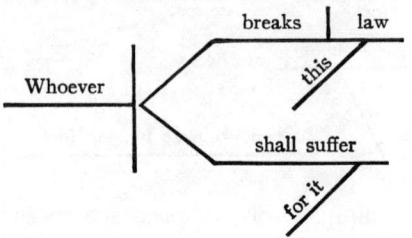

This is the hour when he is expected.

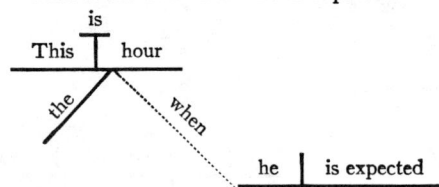

Come to me if you can't find the place.

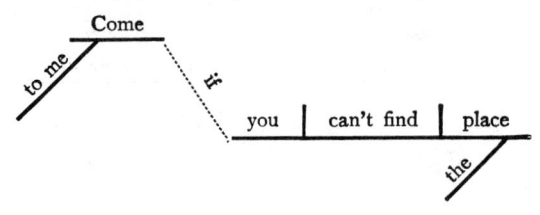

He is happy because he is busy.

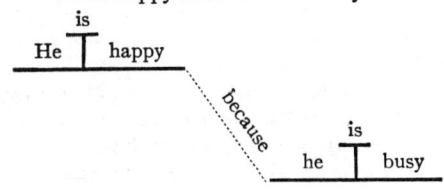

I had no difficulty in finding the place, although I had never been there before.

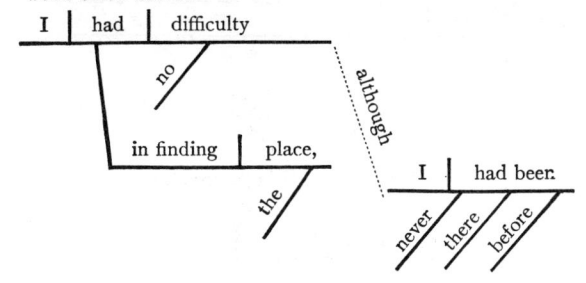

Whenever I see him I am reminded of my old uncle who also was a soldier.

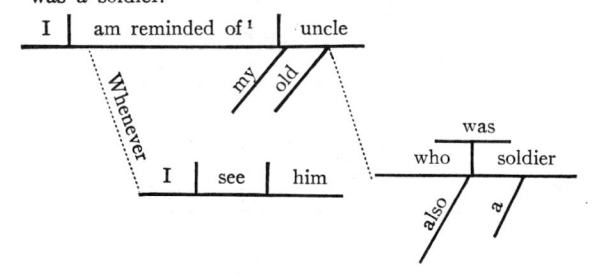

246. Indirect questions and noun clauses are diagrammed as follows:

He knew what the trouble was.

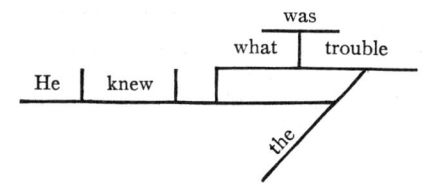

[1] Or *of my old uncle* may be taken as an adverbial prepositional phrase, modifying *am reminded*.

I ate what was set before me.

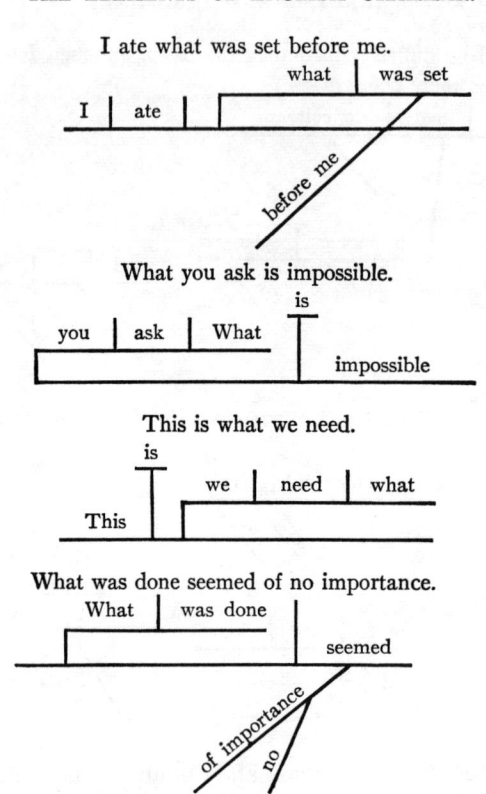

What you ask is impossible.

This is what we need.

What was done seemed of no importance.

I forget what day was appointed for the final examination.

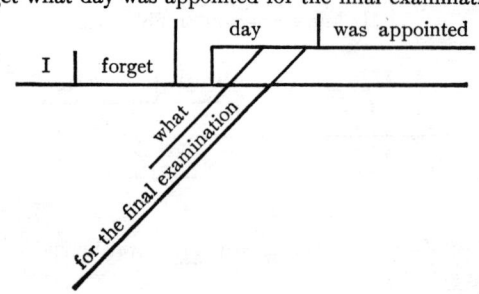

He doesn't know which way we ought to take.

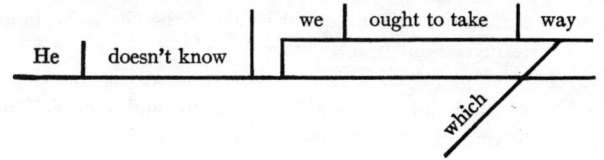

EXERCISES.

Analyze and diagram the following sentences:[1]
(1) The cockswain cast a cool glance at the crests of foam.
(2) In far antiquity, beneath a darksome shadow of venerable boughs, a spring bubbled out of the leaf-strewn earth.
(3) The sun rolls blazing through the sky and cannot find a cloud to cool his face with.
(4) The light boat skimmed along the water like a duck.
(5) He laughed, turned himself away from the tempting sight, and tried not to think of it.
(6) This thirsty dog, with his red tongue lolling out, does not scorn my hospitality, but stands on his hind legs and laps eagerly out of the trough.
(7) How enviable is the consciousness of being usefully employed!
(8) The foolish and the dead alone never change their opinions.
(9) Has Mr. Green brought back our wheelbarrow?
(10) The snow lay deep upon the housetops, but was rapidly dissolving into millions of waterdrops, which sparkled downward through the sunshine with the noise of a summer shower.
(11) Downward the figure came with a stately and martial tread, and reaching the lowest stair, was observed to be a tall man, booted and wrapped in a military cloak.
(12) Our stateroom was large and commodious, the captain, although a thoroughly sea-bred man, polite and attentive, the table not bad, and the travelling company agreeable.

[1] After each colon, semicolon, or period, begin a new analysis and diagram.

(13) Although we live on the outskirts of the city, we find nevertheless that the noise and bustle of the city is beginning to invade our peaceful region.

(14) I never permitted myself to skip a word the meaning of which I did not clearly understand, and I never failed to consult the dictionary in every doubtful case.

(15) And thus spake on that ancient man,
   The bright-eyed mariner.

(16) Here on this beach a hundred years ago,
   Three children of three houses, Annie Lee,
   The prettiest little damsel in the port,
   And Philip Ray, the miller's only son,
   And Enoch Arden, a rough sailor's lad,
   Made orphan by a winter shipwreck, played
   Among the waste and lumber of the shore.
             —TENNYSON, *Enoch Arden.*

(17) Not a drum was heard, not a funeral note,
      As his corpse to the rampart we hurried;
   Not a soldier discharged his farewell shot
      O'er the grave where our hero we buried.

   We buried him darkly at dead of night,
      The sods with our bayonets turning,
   By the struggling moonbeam's misty light
      And the lantern dimly burning.

   No useless coffin enclosed his breast,
      Not in sheet or in shroud we wound him;
   But he lay like a warrior taking his rest,
      With his martial cloak around him.
       —WOLFE, *The Burial of Sir John Moore at Corunna.*

(18) Analyze each sentence of the following paragraphs:
   (a) The sun shone out of a cloudless sky. Close at the zenith rode the belated moon, still clearly visible, and, along one margin, even bright. The wind blew a gale from the north; the trees roared; the corn and the deep grass

in the valley fled in whitening surges; the dust towered into the air along the road and dispersed like the smoke of battle. It was clear in our teeth from the first, and, for all the windings of the road, it managed to keep clear in our teeth until the end. For some two miles we rattled through the valley, skirting the eastern foothills. Then we struck off to the right, through haughland, and presently, crossing a dry watercourse, entered the Toll road, or, to be more local, entered on "the grade." . . . Vineyards and deep meadows, islanded and framed with thicket, gave place more and more as we ascended to woods of oak and madrona, dotted with enormous pines. It was these pines, as they shot above the lower wood, that produced that pencilling of single trees I had so often remarked from the valley. Thence, looking up and however far, each fir stands separate against the sky no bigger than an eyelash, and all together lend a quaint fringed aspect to the hills. The oak is no baby; even the madrona, upon these spurs of Mount Saint Helena, comes to a fine bulk and ranks with forest trees; but the pines look down upon the rest for underwood. As Mount Saint Helena among her foothills, so these dark giants out-top their fellow-vegetables. Alas! if they had left the redwoods, the pines, in turn, would have been dwarfed. But the redwoods, fallen from their high estate, are serving as family bedsteads, or yet more humbly as field fences along all Napa valley.

—ROBERT LOUIS STEVENSON, from a description of Mount Saint Helena in *Silverado Squatters*.

(b) It was ten o'clock before the ships arrived at the quay. The whole population was there to welcome them. A screen made of casks filled with earth was hastily thrown up to protect the landing-place from the batteries on the other side of the river; and the work of unloading began. First were rolled on shore barrels containing six thousand bushels of meal. Then came great cheeses, casks of beef, flitches of bacon, kegs of butter, sacks of pease, ankers of brandy. Not many hours before, half a pound of tallow and three-quarters of a pound of salted hide had been weighed out with niggardly care to every fighting man. The ration which each now received was three pounds of flour, two pounds of beef, and a pint of pease. It is easy to imagine with what tears grace was said over the suppers of that evening. There was little sleep on either side of the wall. The bonfires shone bright along the whole circuit of the ramparts. The Irish guns continued to roar all night, and all night the bells of the rescued city made answer to the Irish guns with a peal of joyous defiance. Through the three following days, the batteries of the enemy continued to play. But, on the third night, flames were seen arising from the camp; and when the first of August dawned, a line of smoking ruins marked the site lately occupied by the huts of the besiegers; and the citizens saw far off the long column of spikes and standards, retreating up the left bank of the Foyle towards Strabane.

So ended this great siege, the most memorable in the annals of the British Isles. It had lasted a hundred and five days. The garrison had been reduced from about seven thousand effective men to about three thousand. The loss of the besiegers cannot be precisely ascertained. . . . It was a contest not between engineers, but between nations; and the victory remained with the nation which, though inferior in numbers, was superior in civilization, in capacity for self-government, and in stubbornness of resolution.

—MACAULAY'S *History of England*, Chapter XII.,
"The Relief of Londonderry."

APPENDIX I.

Historical Sketch of the English Language.

THE English language has had a long and an honorable history. Beginning in a small section of the kingdom of England at the middle of the fifth cen-
Growth in the Use of English. tury, it has not only become the standard speech of the whole of England, but as England has grown, it has become the speech of the British empire, and by the separation of the United States from the mother country in 1776, also the speech of a second great nation. English is to-day the most widely used speech in the western world, and it bids fair to become even more widely used in the near future. It is spoken by nearly twice as many people as any other language of modern Europe. It is estimated that in the year 1900, English was spoken by about 120 millions of people, German and Russian each by about 80 millions, French and Spanish by less than 50 millions each, and Italian by about 40 millions.

Of all the languages of Europe, either ancient or modern, English stands the best chance of becoming a world-
English as the World-Language. language. By this it is not meant that other nations will give up their own native speech in daily intercourse for English, for there is not the least likelihood of this ever happening.

It is probable, however, that English will become more and more, as it is already to a large extent, the language of international communication, the language of travel, of commerce, and of diplomacy. In this sense English may already be called a world-language, and it is likely to deserve this name more and more as time passes.

But the history of English is not merely one of its geographical and numerical expansion as a spoken language. It has been the language of a great literature which extends in an unbroken line from the seventh century to the present day. No other national literature of modern Europe goes so far back or presents such a complete picture of the changing life of the nation as does the literature of the English people. This heritage of language and literature is the common inheritance of all English-speaking peoples of the world to-day; and as it is one of the most venerable of the possessions of the English race, it need not be said that it should be diligently studied and cherished by all.

English as a Literary Language.

The beginnings of the English language in England go back to the middle of the fifth century. For English was not the original native speech of England. When first we hear about England, or Britain as it was then called, it was occupied by a Celtic people who spoke the Celtic language. From the earliest historical times down to the present day, Celtic has always been spoken in certain parts of England, and the modern Welsh language spoken in Wales and the Gaelic of the Scotch High-

The Celts in Britain.

lands are survivals of the original Celtic speech of ancient Britain.

In the first century of the Christian era, Britain was visited by the Romans, who were then the most powerful nation in Europe. The Romans straightway set about the conquest of Britain, and they soon made of it a Roman military colony, such as they had established in various other parts of the world. The native Celts were made slaves or were driven back into the mountainous parts of the island. Finally, however, the Roman empire began to go to pieces. Rome itself was invaded by the barbarous Germanic tribes from the north of Europe, and the distant Roman colonies could be no longer defended. The Roman legions were consequently withdrawn from Britain, the last one leaving in the year 411, and the country was left to the mercy of its enemies.

The Romans in Britain.

Now the most important of these enemies were naturally the subjugated Celts, who had been driven out of the fertile lands back into the hills and mountainous regions. As soon as the Roman legions left England, the Celts swarmed out of their retreats and began to attack the undefended Roman cities. The Romans of the cities, who were unaccustomed to warfare because they had always left the fighting to the Roman legions, were hard pressed, and in their extremity they turned to certain warlike Germanic tribes on the Continent, remote kinsmen of the very people who had conquered Rome, and invited them to come over to Britain and help them subdue the Celts. In answer to this invitation, in the year 449, two Saxon chiefs, Hengest

The Coming of the Anglo-Saxons.

and Horsa, came over to Britain with their followers. At first they did fight against the Celts, but observing how rich the country was and how weak the Romans were, they sent back word to their friends and kinsmen in north Germany to come over that they might possess the country in common. And so more and more tribes came over, and fought not only against the Celts but against the Romans too, and in a short time they had gained possession of the whole country.

The Germanic warriors who thus conquered Britain came from three tribes which were settled in the northwest part of Germany, the Jutes, the Angles, and the Saxons. The two most important of these tribes were the Angles and the Saxons, and so we speak of the nation which they established as the Anglo-Saxon nation, and of their language as Anglo-Saxon. The country itself came to be called *Engla-land*, literally "land of the Angles," from which comes our name England. The language was also called *Englisc*, a word also derived from the name of the Angles, from which we get our "English." Nowadays we usually speak of the early period of English, before the Norman Conquest, as Anglo-Saxon or Old English; of the period from the Conquest to 1500 as Middle English; and of the period from 1500 to the present as Modern English.

The Name of the Anglo-Saxons.

The language which the Anglo-Saxons brought over to England was their own native tongue, and this was of course a Germanic or Teutonic language. It was closely related to the language from which modern German has sprung, and this accounts for the fact that many words in English to-

English and German.

day are like modern German words. Thus the German word *hund,* "dog," is plainly the same as our word *hound.* German *kalt* is English *cold,* *bald* is English *bold,* *halt(en)* is English *hold,* *falt(en)* is English *fold,* *find(en)* and *sing(en)* are English *find* and *sing;* and so with a great many other words in the two languages. But words in the two languages which are really closely related are often very dissimilar in form, as, for example, German *ritz(en)* and English *write,* because each language has developed in its own peculiar way. We must not think therefore of English as having borrowed its words from German or German from English. They have words in common because they are sister languages and both go back to the same Teutonic original.

After they had conquered the native inhabitants of England, the Anglo-Saxons soon settled down into a peaceful agricultural life. They raised cattle and sheep, tilled the soil, and to some extent worked the mines of the country. In religion they were worshippers of Thor and Woden and other heathen gods. But in 596 the Roman missionary Augustine came to England, sent by Pope Gregory, and in a comparatively short time the country was converted to Christianity. Schools were established at various places, a literature both in prose and verse began to flourish, and altogether the country developed a fairly high civilization. English scholars were famous on the Continent, and when the Emperor Charlemagne wished to establish a school at his court, he sent to York in England for the scholar Alcuin to organize and conduct this school.

The peaceful development of this civilization was soon

interrupted, however, by the invasions of the Danes. These were also Germanic peoples, who came from regions further north in Europe than those from which the Anglo-Saxons had originally come. From about the year 750 they began to appear in England in ever increasing numbers; and just as several centuries before the Anglo-Saxons had wrested the country out of the hands of the Celts and Romans, so now the Danes and Northmen endeavored to take it away from the Anglo-Saxons. The warfare was a bitter one and was waged with varying success. In the end, however, the Danes were victorious, and the Danish king Cnut in the year 1017 became king of all England, being at the same time king of both Denmark and England. The Danes, however, accepted the Anglo-Saxon language, which indeed closely resembled their own. It is for this reason that the language of the country did not become Danish, although Danish exercised some influence over Anglo-Saxon, chiefly in the introduction of Danish words.

The Danish Conquest.

Once again and for the last time England was conquered by a foreign enemy when in the year 1066 it yielded to the forces of William the Conqueror. William was the duke of Normandy, a province of France, and he, of course, spoke the French language. As a result of the Conquest the English were brought into intimate relations with the French, and though the English language maintained its existence in spite of the Norman Conquest, just as it had in spite of the Danish Conquest, it nevertheless came to be very much influenced by French.

The Norman Conquest.

Many words were borrowed from French, a great many more than had been borrowed from Danish. To name only a few examples, such words as *courage, chivalry, courtesy, charity, crown, false, faith,* etc., were taken over from the French. Indeed so many words were taken into the language from the French that the language was practically made over. Instead of remaining a pure Germanic language as it had been at the end of the Anglo-Saxon period, with practically all of its words derived from Germanic originals, it now became a mixed language, made up of Germanic and French elements.

Now French is merely a late and derived form of the Latin language, being a development of the Latin which the Roman colonists of ancient Gaul spoke. English having thus acquired the habit of borrowing words from French, readily extended this habit to Latin words. From the Middle English period to the present time, English has borrowed freely from Latin, especially words of a learned character. Some words, like *animal, exit,* and others, have exactly the same form in English as they have in the original Latin. Other Latin borrowings are words like *attempt, accord, human, domestic, mental, familiar, visual, different, consequent, construct,* etc. The number of words of French and Latin origin now in general use in English is very large; and the words have become so much a part of the language that no one ever notices whether they are of native Germanic origin or of French or Latin origin.

Latin Words in English.

The development of the English language since the Middle English period has been on the whole a peaceful one. As the people grew in culture and in experience, the language became fuller and richer. Great poets like Spenser, Shakespeare, Milton, and Dryden arose to dignify the language by writing their works in it.

Modern English.

When the English people began to emigrate from the little kingdom of England, they carried their English speech and traditions with them. They settled North America, which thus became an English-speaking country; and in later times they settled Australia, India, South Africa, and other parts of the world. Wherever they may be, however, whether in Australia, Africa, or America, the English-speaking peoples of the world go back to the little Anglo-Saxon kingdom in England for the origins of their language. The whole line of tradition in language and literature from Hengest and Horsa in 449 through Chaucer, Spenser, Shakespeare, and Milton, down to the present day, is as much the possession of every English-speaking person as it would be if the English language were still confined within the narrow limits of the island of Britain.

In the course of its long development, the English language has naturally undergone a great many changes. The growth of its vocabulary by the addition of French and Latin words has already been mentioned. The sounds of the language have also undergone many changes, the sounds of the Anglo-Saxon period being for the most part so different from those of Modern English that it is often difficult to recognize the Anglo-Saxon original of a Modern English word when the two are placed side by side. The changes of sounds, however, have followed regular laws, and with a little study the relations of modern words to

Sound Changes in English.

their earlier originals can be readily determined. Thus Anglo-Saxon long *a* has changed regularly to Modern English long *o*, and so Anglo-Saxon *ban* = Modern English *bone, stan=stone, cald=cold, rap=rope, bat=boat*, etc.

The language has also changed a great deal in its structure. Anglo-Saxon was much more an inflectional language than Modern English is. In its inflectional uses, the earlier periods of English seem nearer akin to modern German, or to Latin, than they do to Modern English. Thus the phrase *of all good old wise men* would be expressed in Anglo-Saxon as follows: *ealra godra ealdra wisra monna*. These words are all in what is called in Anglo-Saxon the genitive case, the syllable *-ra* being the inflection for the genitive plural in the adjective and *-a* the inflection for the genitive plural in the noun *monna*. The genitive inflection expresses the idea which Modern English expresses by the preposition *of*. It should be noted also that all adjectives are inflected for number and case in Anglo-Saxon to agree with the nouns which they modify, just as they are in Latin. The phrase *to all good old wise men* would also be expressed in Anglo-Saxon by inflectional forms, in this instance by the forms of the dative case, as follows: *eallum godum ealdum wisum monnum*. It will be seen therefore that Modern English, by inflectional change and loss, has freed itself from many unnecessary inflectional forms and rules of concord, especially between the adjective and its noun. By these changes the grammar of Modern English has in many ways become simpler than that of the earlier periods of the English language.

Inflectional Change in English.

As always happens when a language is spoken over a wide extent of territory, local differences have grown up in the use of the English language. Thus the English which is spoken in England to-day differs to some extent from that which is spoken in America. Englishmen, for example, call an elevator a "lift"; they speak of baggage as "luggage," and they call candy "sweets." In pronunciation also there are more or less striking differences. To distinguish the various kinds of English, it is convenient to give each a name; and so we speak of British English, of American English, of Canadian English, etc., meaning the English spoken respectively in England, the United States, Canada, etc. But even in the separate countries there grow up differences of speech that are often very striking. Thus in the United States we can often distinguish a New Englander or a man from the South or from the West, each by his individual way of speaking. When these local differences are sufficiently marked, they constitute what is called a local dialect.

Dialects of English.

The fact that we speak of dialects supposes the existence of a general or universal form of the language of which the dialects are a special development. This general form of the language is known as standard English. It is that use of the language least marked by local or other special peculiarities, which is regarded as regular and customary use wherever the language is spoken. Standard English is the English of literature and of careful speech, and it is made the basis of all systematic grammatical or rhetorical study of the language.

Standard English.

In spoken English it should be noted that there are several different planes on which our speech may rest. We may distinguish Formal, Colloquial, and Vulgar English. By Formal English is meant a very careful and deliberate manner of speaking, such, for example, as a public speaker would use in addressing an audience. Formal English is, of course, appropriate only when some formality and dignity of expression are required. Colloquial English, on the other hand, is the English of everyday natural conversation. It differs considerably, both in vocabulary and pronunciation, from literary and formal English, and rightly so. For it is not necessary that our ordinary daily conversation should be as stately and as deliberate as our most formal expression. A person who always speaks "like a book," or tries to, rightly makes himself ridiculous. Examples of colloquial English are the contractions *I'll, I sha'n't, I'm, we'll,* etc. The extent to which colloquial English may be allowed to differ from formal English is a matter of opinion that must be left to the discretion of each individual speaker. The third kind of spoken English, Vulgar English, is the manner of speech which immediately marks the person who uses it as illiterate. The breaking of the ordinary rules of grammar are examples of vulgar English, such as the use of *done* for *did* in *He done me a great injustice,* or *them* for *these,* and *ain't* for *aren't* in *Them trees ain't well planted.* It is hardly necessary to warn any one against the use of vulgar English, since no one probably uses it voluntarily, but only through ignorance.

APPENDIX II.

Punctuation and Capitalization.

The purpose of punctuation in printing and writing is to mark off words into the groups which they naturally form. In speaking, this division of words into groups is indicated by pauses or by the tones of the voice, and most of the marks of punctuation are merely mechanical devices for making these characteristics of oral speech visible to the eye in printed or written speech. The common marks of punctuation are the period (.), the interrogation point (?), the exclamation point (!), the colon (:), the semicolon (;), the comma (,), the apostrophe ('), quotation marks (" "), parentheses (( )), brackets ([ ]), and the hyphen (-).

The Period.—The period is used to mark the end of declarative and imperative sentences.

EXAMPLES:

(1) For nearly three months there was no rain to wet the ground. Large forest trees withered and cast their leaves. In spots, the mountain looked as if it had been scorched by fire.

(2) Please shut the door.

The period is also used after all abbreviations.

EXAMPLE:

J. G. Whittier was born in Haverhill, Mass., on Dec. **17, 1807**.

The Interrogation Point.—The interrogation point is used at the end of the interrogative sentence.

EXAMPLE:

Who does not suffer in his spirit in a drought and feel restless and dissatisfied?

The Exclamation Point.—The exclamation point is used after interjections and at the end of exclamatory sentences.

EXAMPLES:
(1) Oh, the terrible drought!
(2) Alas! he had long since ceased to remember her.
(3) How we had longed for this day!

The Colon.—The use of the colon is comparatively infrequent. Its purpose is to indicate a pause within the sentence in expectation of something which follows. The principal uses are exemplified in the following sentences:

(1) After he had called the family together, the lawyer read from a paper as follows: Whereas in due process of time it has seemed fit, etc.

(2) We had many things to tell each other: where we had been the past five years, what sights we had seen and what feats we had accomplished, and, above all, what news we had to tell of those old friends of our youth.

The Semicolon.—The semicolon is used in the body of the sentence to indicate a shorter pause than the colon. Its chief uses are as follows:

(1) to separate a group of independent sentences in a paragraph which are so closely related that periods would make too great a pause between them, as:

In advance of the storm, you may often see the clouds grow; the condensation of the moisture into vapor is a visible process; slender, spiculæ-like clouds expand, deepen, and lengthen; in the rear of the low pressure, the reverse process, or the wasting of the clouds, may be witnessed.

(2) to separate a group of co-ordinate clauses, as:

When the sky becomes tarnished and opaque with dust and smoke; when the shingles on the houses curl up, the clapboards warp, the paint blisters, the joints open; when the cattle rove disconsolate and the hive-bee comes home empty; when the earth gapes and all nature looks widowed, and deserted, and heart-broken,—in such a time, what thing that has life does not sympathize and suffer with the general distress?

The Comma.—The comma is used within the body of the sentence to indicate a still briefer pause than the semicolon. The principal occurrences are as follows:

(1) to separate a series of words having the same grammatical function, as:

1. He was a wild, troublesome, cruel sort of boy.

or

He was a wild, troublesome, and cruel sort of boy.

Some writers do not insert the comma between *troublesome* and *and*.

2. Sink or swim, live or die, survive or perish,
I give my hand and my heart to this vote.

(2) to separate the elements of a compound sentence, as:

1. We hunted long for him, but we found nothing.
2. We walked about a mile, or perhaps it may have been more.
3. He stopped at the corner, dismounted, and examined the ground carefully.

(3) to separate the elements of a complex sentence, as:[1]

1. If you have time to come, we shall be glad to see you.
2. They arrived first, although they had taken the longer way.
3. This tree, which had long withstood the summer's storms, was recently struck by lightning.

[1] For the punctuation of restrictive and non-restrictive **relative clauses**, see **84.**

(4) to separate a word or phrase in apposition to another from the main word, as:

> Tennyson, England's poet-laureate, lived to a good old age.

(5) to mark off participial modifying clauses and independent or parenthetic elements in the sentence:
   1. The boat, turning a point suddenly, ran into a sunken log.
   2. This story, strange to say, made no impression upon me.
   3. This house, it should be remembered, has not been occupied for many years.

(6) to separate the quoted part from the descriptive part in passages of dialogue, as:
   1. "It may not be too late," says Esmond.
   2. "I shall open to no one," says the man, shutting the glass window, as Frank drew a pistol.

(7) Prepositional phrases are sometimes set off in the sentences by commas, sometimes not, depending on the closeness of their relation to the rest of the sentence, as:
   1. William ordered his right wing, under the command of Meinhart Schomberg, one of the Duke's sons, to march to the bridge of Slane.
   2. The nuts lay under the boughs in the greatest profusion.

It is extremely difficult to reduce the use of the comma to a set of rules, and students are advised to learn the correct use by studying the punctuation of good and careful modern writers, as exemplified in the better class of magazines and newspapers. The custom in punctuation has changed a great deal, and often the practice of the older books is not a very good guide to follow.

The Apostrophe.—The apostrophe has three uses:

(1) to indicate the possessive case, as:
   1. A primrose by the river's brim.
   2. The horses' tails were all docked.

(2) to indicate the omission of one or more letters in a contracted word, as:
1. He doesn't have to answer your letter.
2. We'll meet you at the corner.
3. He's not so well to-day.

(3) to indicate the plurals of figures and letters:
1. He makes his p's and his q's alike.
2. All the 8's on this page are larger than the other figures.

Quotation Marks.—Quotation marks are used to separate words of direct quotation from a context of indirect quotation. For this purpose the marks used are double quotations (" "). A quotation within a quotation is indicated by the single quotation (' '). For illustrations, see above, **pp. 13, 78, 188.**

Parentheses.—Parentheses are used to separate from the rest of the sentence a group of words which are inserted as a sort of general comment or explanation more or less independently of the rest of the sentence, as:

(1) I will translate the whole, or nearly the whole, of the idyll (it is not long) in which the poem occurs.
(2) We found Fido (alas for his curly locks!) all daubed and plastered with mud.

The extent to which writers use the parenthesis varies greatly; in general it should be sparingly used, since a frequent use of it tends to make one's style rough and broken.

Brackets.—Brackets are used to enclose explanatory insertions made in the body of a text by author, editor, or printer, as:

These petty princes [*i. e.*, of the house of Hanover] were regarded with much disfavor by the older aristocracy.

Brackets should be still more sparingly used than parentheses. The resort to brackets is usually appropriate only in scientific or technical writing, and it is usually better to make a footnote than to use brackets.

Hyphen.—The uses of the hyphen are to separate compound words, *e. g.*, Chicago Inter-Ocean; to indicate the division of a polysyllabic word at the end of a line of writing or printing, and to indicate a broken or interrupted sentence structure, as:

> Innumerable fires in forests and peat-swamps made the days and the weeks—not blue, but a dirty, yellowish white.

Hyphens are sometimes used to include an inserted phrase somewhat after the manner of parentheses, as:

> Swarms of black flies—those insect wolves—waylaid us and hung to us.

Capitalization.—The principal rules are as follows:

(1) Capitalize the first word of every sentence, no matter what the word may be. A quoted sentence within a sentence is to be treated like a new sentence and therefore begins with a capital.

(2) Capitalize all proper nouns, as Sunday, Easter, Paris, San Francisco, New York City, James Russell Lowell, Mount Shasta, Lake Erie. Capitalize also the abbreviated titles: Mr., Mrs., and Miss.

(3) Capitalize all proper adjectives, as the Caucasian Race, the Russian victory, a Parisian accent, a Boston terrier.

(4) Capitalize all names of the Deity, as God, Jehovah, the Father, the Son, the Trinity, the Holy Ghost. Capitalize Heaven when the word refers to the Christian Paradise. The names of religious denominations are capitalized, as: Baptist, Presbyterian, Episcopalian, Puritan, Nonconformist.

(5) Capitalize the pronoun I, the interjection O, **and Oh.**

(6) The use of capitals in titles of nobility, rank, and office varies a great deal and can best be learned by observation. Thus one writes King Edward, but Edward, king of England. Other illustrations are: the President of the United States; the Governor of New York; the Bishop of St. Louis; the Prince of Wales; the House of Commons; Congress; the Assembly; the Chamber of Commerce.

(7) In the titles of books, articles, essays, etc., capitalize only the nouns and adjectives, but not the article, except when it is the first word in the title, e. g., The Prince of the House of David.

(8) In the names of streets, capitalize both the name and the word street, etc., as Dolphin Street, St. Charles Street, Forty-first Street, Riverside Drive, Lake Boulevard.

Spacing and Indentation.—Between two sentences a short space is left blank in order to indicate the division of the sentences. The first line of a piece of writing or printing begins a little to the left of the place at which the other lines begin. This is called *Indentation*. Every new paragraph should begin on a new line, and the beginning of each new paragraph is also indicated by indentation of the first line. For illustrations of these rules, look at several pages of any well-printed book.

Exercise.

Write out the following passage, inserting the proper punctuation and capitalization:

solomon macey a small hale old man with an abundant crop of long white hair reaching nearly to his shoulders advanced to the indicated spot bowing reverently while he fiddled as much as to say that he respected the company though he respected the key-note more as soon as he had repeated the tune and lowered his fiddle he bowed again to the squire and the rector and said i hope i see your honor and your reverence well and wishing you health and long life and a happy new year and wishing the same to you mr lammeter sir and to the other gentlemen and the madams and the young lasses

as solomon uttered the last words he bowed in all directions solicitously lest he should be wanting in due respect but thereupon he immediately began to prelude and fell into the tune which he knew would be taken as a special compliment by mr lammeter

thank ye solomon thank ye said mr lammeter when the fiddle paused again thats over the hills and far away that is my father used to say to me whenever we heard that tune ah lad I come from over the hills and far away theres a many tunes I dont make head or tail of but that speaks to me like the blackbirds whistle i suppose its the name theres a deal in the name of a tune

but solomon was already impatient to prelude again and presently broke with much spirit into sir roger de coverley at which there was a sound of chairs pushed back and laughing voices

ay ay solomon we know what that means said the squire rising its time to begin the dance eh lead the way then and we'll all follow you

so solomon holding his white head on one side and playing vigorously marched forward at the head of the gay procession into the white parlor where the mistletoe-bough was hung and multitudinous tallow candles made rather a brilliant effect gleaming from among the berried holly-boughs and reflected in the old-fashioned oval mirrors fastened in the panels of the white wainscot a quaint procession old solomon in his seedy clothes and long white locks seemed to be luring that decent company by the magic scream of his fiddle luring discreet matrons in turban-shaped caps nay mrs crackenthorp herself the summit of whose perpendicular feather was on a level with the squires shoulder luring fair lasses complacently conscious of very short waists and skirts blameless of front-folds luring burly fathers in large variegated waistcoats and ruddy sons for the most part shy and sheepish in short nether garments and very long coattails

INDEX

The numbers refer to pages

Absolute participle, 163.
Address, words of, 227.
Adjective, defined, 2, 38, 100; descriptive, 100; pronominal, 101; possessive, 101; nouns as adjectives and adjectives as nouns, 102; comparison of, 102–104; attributive, appositive and predicate adjectives, 104, 116; objective complement, 105; articles, 106–109.
Adjective preposition, 209.
Adverb, defined, 3, 38, 194; classification of, 196; negative and interrogative adverbs, 198; compound, 199; comparison, 199; extent of time, space, etc., 201.
Analysis of sentences, 231–232.
Anglo-Saxon, 255–256.
Anomalous or unclassified verbs, 181–183.
Antecedent of pronouns, 70–71.
Anticipatory subject, 74.
Apostrophe, use of, 267.
Apposition, 62–64.
Appositive coördination, 217.
Articles, definite and indefinite, 106–109.
As, relative pronoun, 84; adverb, 202; preposition, 210.
Auxiliary verbs, 121.

Brackets, use of, 268.
But, relative pronoun, 85.

Capitalization, rules of, 269–270.
Cardinal numerals, 223.
Case, nominative, 56; predicate nominative, 56, 116; objective, 57; object complement, 57; dative object, 58; possessive, 58–61.
Celtic Britain, 254.
Clause, defined, 25; noun clauses, 30; adjective clauses, 80; adverb clauses, 195.
Cognate object, 114.
Colon, use of, 265.
Comma, use of, 266.
Comparison, 47, 102–104.
Conjugation, 47, 119.
Conjunction, defined, 3, 39, 213; coördinating and subordinating, 214–216; correlative, 216–217; appositive, 217; expletive, 218.
Construction of words, 5, 14.
Contraction, 133.
Copulative verbs, 115–116.

Dangling participles, 163.
Danish Conquest, 258.
Dative object, 58.
Declension, 47.
Defective verbs, 183.
Demonstrative adjectives, 94.
Demonstrative pronouns, 93–94.
Diagraming of sentences, 232–252.

Elliptical sentences and clauses, 228–230.
Emphatic verb-phrases, 131.

273

English language, extent of use, 253–254; as literary language, 254; compared with German, 256–257; Latin words in, 259; Modern English, 260; sound changes, 260; inflectional changes, 261; dialects of, 262; standard English, 262; formal, colloquial, and vulgar English, 263.
Exclamation point, use of, 265.
Expletive conjunction, 218.
Extent of time, space, and amount, 201.

Gender, defined, 42; ways of indicating, 42–45.
Grammar, defined, 5.

Hyphen, use of, 269.

Impersonal subject and object, 74.
Indefinite adjective, 96.
Indefinite pronoun, 95–96.
Indentation, 270.
Independent elements, 225–228.
Infinitive, in verb-phrases, 123; as noun, 151–152; sign of, and split infinitive, 153–154; as adjective, 154–155; as adverb, 155–156; in -ing, 156–157; as object complement, 159; independent infinitive phrase, 226.
Inflection, defined, 4; ways of indicating, 46.
Interjection, defined, 4, 221; weakened interjections, 221–222.
Interrogation point, use of, 265.
Interrogative adjective, 90–91.
Interrogative pronouns, 89–90.
Interrogative verb-phrases, 131.

Negative verb-phrases, 131.
Norman Conquest, 258–259.
Noun clauses, 30.
Noun, defined, 2, 37; common and proper, 40–41; masculine, feminine, common and neuter, 42–46; singular and plural, 47–55; collective, 51.

Number, of nouns, 47; of verbs, 119.
Numerals, defined, 222; cardinals and ordinals, 223–224.

Object, defined, 15; simple and complete, 15–16; compound, 23; cognate, 114; retained in passive, 148.
Object complement, 57.
Objective complement, 105.
Order of words, 16–21.
Ordinal numerals, 223.

Parsing, defined, 64.
Participles, in verb-phrases, 123; dangling and absolute, 163–164; tense and voice of, 164; distinguished from infinitive in -ing, 165; independent participial phrase, 226.
Parts of speech, defined, 1–4; how to determine, 35.
Period, use of, 264.
Person, of pronouns, 71; of verbs, 118.
Personification, 45.
Phrase, defined, 25; prepositional, 3; adjective and verbal, 105–106; independent, 226–227.
Possessive case, 58–61.
Predicate, defined, 15; simple and complete, 15–16; compound, 23.
Predicate adjective, 104, 116–117.
Predicate nominative, 56.
Preposition, defined, 3, 38, 205–206; object of, 206–207; compound, 207; prepositional adverb, 207–208; adjective and conjunctive, 209.
Progressive verb-phrases, 130.
Pronoun, defined, 2, 37, 68; kinds of, 69–70; antecedent of, 70–71; personal, 71–73; impersonal, 74; anticipatory subject, 74; compound personal, 75; reflexive, 76; relative, 78–89; double relative, 79; restrictive and non-restrictive

Pronoun, defined—*continued*.
  relative, 80–81; relative adjectives and adverbs, 86–87; interrogative, 89–93; indirect question, 90; interrogative adjectives and adverbs, 90–91; demonstrative, 93–95; indefinite, 95–98.
Punctuation and capitalization, 264–271.

Quotation marks, use of, 268.

Redundant verbs, 183.
Reflexive pronouns, 76.
Regular and irregular verbs, 136.
Relative adjectives and adverbs, 86–87.
Relative pronouns, 78–89.
Retained object, 148.
Romans in Britain, 255.

Semicolon, use of, 265.
Sentences, how indicated, 1; defined, 8; distinguished from phrases, 8–9; of one word, 9–10; declarative, imperative, interrogative and exclamatory, 10–11; length of, 11–12; simple, complex and compound, 24–28; independent and elliptical elements, 225–230.
Shall and *will*, in future verb-phrases, 124–127; other uses of, 127–129.

So, demonstrative pronoun, 94; adverb, 202.
Spacing, 270.
Split infinitive, 153.
Subject, defined, 15; simple and complete, 15–16; compound, 23.
Subjunctive mood, 168–172.

Than, as preposition, 209–210.
That, relative pronoun and conjunction, 85.
The, as adverb, 200.
There, anticipatory, 199–200.
Transitivity, 114.

Verb, defined, 3, 38, 112; transitive and intransitive, 113–114; copulative, 115; tenses of, 117, 122; person of, 118; number of, 119; conjugation of, 119, 173–181; regular and irregular, 136–145; voice, 145–147; moods, 167–172; anomalous or unclassified, 181–187.
Verbals, 151–167, see separately under infinitives and participles.
Verb-phrases, defined, 19; separated, 20; in forming tenses, 120–122; progressive, 130–131; emphatic, interrogative, and negative, 131–132.
Voice, of verbs, 145.
What, double relative, 79; exclamatory, 92.